The Household Dimension
of the Family in India

This volume is sponsored by
The Center for South and Southeast Asia Studies
University of California, Berkeley

The Center for South and Southeast Asia Studies of the University of California is the unifying organization for faculty members and students interested in South and Southeast Asia Studies, bringing together scholars from numerous disciplines. The Center's major aims are the development and support of research and language study. As part of this program the Center sponsors a publication series of books concerned with South and Southeast Asia. Manuscripts are considered from all campuses of the University of California as well as from any other individuals and institutions doing research in these areas.

RECENT PUBLICATIONS
OF THE CENTER FOR SOUTH AND SOUTHEAST ASIA STUDIES:

Richard G. Fox
Kin, Clan, Raja, and Rule: State-Hinterland Relations in Preindustrial India

Robert N. Kearney
Trade Unions and Politics in Ceylon

Robert Lingat
The Classical Law of India
Translated by J. Duncan M. Derrett

David N. Lorenzen
The Kāpālikas and Kālāmukhas: Two Lost Śaivite Sects

Leo E. Rose
Nepal—Strategy for Survival

Prakash Tandon
Beyond Punjab: A Sequel to Punjabi Century

Elizabeth Whitcombe
Agrarian Conditions in Northern India
Volume One: The United Provinces under British Rule, 1860–1900

The Household Dimension of the Family in India

A Field Study in a Gujarat Village
and a Review of Other Studies

A. M. Shah

With a Foreword by
M. N. Srinivas

University of California Press
Berkeley Los Angeles London

University of California Press
Berkeley and Los Angeles, California

University of California Press, Ltd.
London, England

Copyright
©
1974, by
The Regents of the University of California

ISBN : 0-520-01790-0

Library of Congress Catalogue Card Number : 71-126757
Typeset in India.   Printed and bound in the United States

To
the Memory of
My Mother

Foreword

The study of the Hindu family illustrates the typical deficiencies and difficulties of sociology in India, and perhaps also in other Oriental countries. The existence of a caste of hereditary literati whose business is to record as well as interpret custom, law, and ritual has influenced, directly and indirectly, the perceptions of social reality of not only the educated laymen but also of modern lawyers and sociologists.

While it is true that in every society, including the most primitive, there are to be found concepts, and sometimes even theories ("home-made models"), about its component sections and groups and their behaviour, in civilized countries such as India there are in addition the concepts and theories of the literati. In India in particular these concepts and theories were developed over the centuries and subjected to diverse and sophisticated comment, elaboration, and interpretation. The hereditary literati had their own traditions, attitudes, biases, and interests which influenced their comment and interpretation. As if this was not sufficiently complicated, during British rule certain ideas and myths regarding Indian family organization obtained wide currency through the British law courts and judges, and the new class of lawyers. The economic and political forces released during British rule, when combined with British legal concepts and procedures, resulted in a reinterpretation of Hindu (and also Islamic) legal concepts, and the perception of Indian society has been affected in a variety of ways by this ideological amalgam.

Educated Indians do not derive their idea of the joint family entirely from what they see and experience. On the contrary, and surprising as it may seem, what they see and experience is influenced by moral norms derived from epics, folk tales, and bits and pieces of Hindu Law filtering through newspapers and litigious friends, neighbours, and relatives. According to the Mitaksara school of Hindu Law, which the majority of Hindus follow, a joint family is a coparcenary in which each agnatic member acquires a share at birth, and the right to sue for partition of the ancestral estate as soon as he reaches the legal age of majority. The joint family is also a co-residential and commensal group, and its living members periodically propitiate a body of manes. Each such family has a head manager *(karta)*, who is usually the senior male, and his rights and powers receive much attention in Hindu Law. (For instance, the rights and powers of the *karta* to incur debts in the course of the performance of his duties have been the subject of a considerable amount of litigation.) Dr. Arvind Shah points out that this type of joint family, inclusive of three generations of agnatically related males and their wives, is only an ideal type, representing "the maximum extent of the progression of the developmental process of the household." It bears little relation to the usual household which is the unit of day-to-day living. It is on the household that Dr. Shah concentrates in his study, and one of his major concerns is the delineation of the relation between the household at the existential level and the joint family as conceived by lawyers and Indologists.

It is the joint family of the Mitaksara school of Hindu Law that has been regarded as the normal living unit for Hindus in many parts of the country. And this is due to the bibliocentric bias of Indology and Hindu Law. Moreover, educated Indians — coming generally from the upper castes, and wealthier than the others — tended to live in kinship units that resembled in some respects the joint family of Hindu Law and to assume that their institutions were universal. They did not consider it necessary to find out the kind of household units in which Hindus belonging to the lower castes and the poorer sections lived. Such an attitude is perhaps not unnatural in a highly stratified and heterogeneous society, but what is a matter for astonishment is that even after a century of British rule during which officials wrote painstaking survey and settlement reports and conducted decennial censuses, the myth is still current that generally Indians live in joint families (whatever it may mean).

Dr. Shah argues that the principle of the residential unity of patrikin and their wives is stronger among the more Sanskritized, higher castes than among the lower. He also makes the point that traditional towns in Gujarat include more members of the higher castes than the villages, in which the lower castes are preponderant. From this he argues, contrary to popular belief, that it was not the village that was the stronghold of the joint family but the town. He rightly questions the validity of equating the village with traditional society especially in a country such as India where pilgrimage centres, royal capitals, and monastic and temple towns have been important centres for the dissemination of the Great Tradition of Hinduism.

The question that needs to be asked is whether, generally speaking, the upper castes are richer, better educated, and more powerful than the lower castes. In rural India, for instance, large joint households comprising more than one nuclear family, generally tend to own more land than those living in smaller households. Conversely, among the poorest section of rural society, landless labourers' households tend to be quite small even when not strictly nuclear. Dr. Shah indicates how this question of relation between wealth and household needs to be systematically investigated.

Dr. Shah's analysis of the census data on the size of households similarly yields illuminating if unorthodox conclusions. He shows that the size of the household — the only kinship unit for which we have figures for 90 years for India as a whole, and for nearly 140 years for some regions within it — has not only not decreased since 1820 but has actually increased. Admittedly, this increase may have some relation to reduced infant and maternal mortality rates, to increased longevity, and to the general rise in the age at marriage. It is also not unlikely that this indicates increased "jointness". In any case, while the rise in household size does not provide conclusive evidence of increased jointness, it certainly does not lend support to the popular view — hailed by some and bemoaned by others — that the joint family is fast disintegrating.

Even when an urban household has the nuclear form it is not unlikely that it is only a satellite of a joint household elsewhere, for with increased spatial and social mobility, the joint family seems to be acquiring a "federal", multi-centred character in place of former "unitariness" and uni-centredness. Indeed, the whole subject of inter-household relations within a joint family is an important one. Dr. Shah has dealt with it only briefly in this study. I hope, however, he will take it up later for further inquiry.

The popular belief among Indians that the joint family system is disintegrating under the pressure of modern forces demands an explanation. Its possible source is the 1911 Census Report in which the theory of the disintegration of the Indian joint family system was advanced in order to explain the fact that the average size (4.9 persons) of the Indian household was no greater than that in European countries. The Census officials seem to have had the idea that all Indians traditionally lived in huge joint families, and that as a result of the forces let loose by British rule (and in particular the "spirit of individualism") they began to show an increasing preference for the Western-type nuclear family. Why did the Census officials assume that Indians traditionally lived in joint families? A variety of factors may have contributed to such an assumption: the importance given to the joint family in Hindu Law and in the ancient scriptures, to the social prominence of the higher *varnas* such as Brahmins, Kshatriyas, and Vaishyas, and to a widespread tendency to regard the past as great and characterized by harmony and the present as poor, miserable and conflict-ridden. If they had looked at the vast bulk of the poor people instead of the privileged and articulate sections of the society, they might have reached a different conclusion.

It is necessary to make clear that while Dr. Shah disputes the existence of a sociological trend from large and complex (or joint) to small and simple households, he does not conclude that the Indian household system has remained stationary. In fact, he detects a more complex process of change than the simple, unidirectional one just mentioned. He argues that the Sanskritization of the tribes and low castes may have resulted in an increased emphasis on the residential unity of the patrikin, whereas the Westernization of the higher castes may have weakened that principle. The hypothesis needs to be tested in more than one region of India: it relates changes in household form among different sections of the Hindus to wider cultural and social processes.

It is in the context of the changes occurring in the society as a whole that Dr. Shah finds the existing formulation of the concept of the developmental cycle of the household less than satisfactory. There is no simple and unvarying movement from the nuclear to the joint and then back to the nuclear house-hold. As a matter of fact, there are several types of households from single-member units to large ones accommodating patrikin belonging to three generations and their wives, and there is no regular and invariant cycle of forms through which each house-hold passes. In other words, each type is not a point through which all households must necessarily pass. Further, the forces present in the wider society are resulting in the emergence of different forms of the household in different sections of the population.

Dr. Shah's book makes an important contribution to the sociological literature on the family in general, and to that on the Indian family in particular. His movement from the micro-study of the family system in one village to the region, his use of historical and quantitative data, and his critical evaluation of earlier writings are particularly impressive. I have no doubt whatever that Dr. Shah's study is a milestone in the sociological analysis of the Indian family, and that all students of family and kinship everywhere will find it thought-provoking.

M. N. Srinivas

Preface

From May 1955 to June 1958 I worked, with the assistance of my friend Ramesh Shroff, on a research project undertaken by the Department of Sociology of the Maharaja Sayajirao University of Baroda, under the direction of Professor M. N. Srinivas and supported by a generous grant from the Department of Anthropology of the University of Chicago. The project aimed at the study of a village for which historical data were available in some measure, and it also included the study of the Vahivancha Barots, a caste of genealogists and mythographers in Gujarat. Our data were derived from (1) field work in Radhvanaj, a village in central Gujarat, and among the Vahivancha Barots, and (2) historical records, especially the documents in the possession of the Barots and in the government record offices.

We presented the analysis of our data on the Barots in 1958 in a long paper entitled "The Vahivancha Barots of Gujarat: A Caste of Genealogists and Mythographers", with a foreword by Professor Srinivas, in *Traditional India: Structure and Change,* edited by Professor Milton Singer. How to present the voluminous data on the village was, however, a big problem. In July 1958 I took up a teaching appointment at the University of Baroda and Ramesh Shroff began work on a project of his own. This prevented me from devoting sufficient attention to the analysis of the village data. Soon after, however, I was given leave for a year to work on my project. I divided this time between the Department of Anthropology of the University of Chicago and the Center for Advanced Study in the Behavioural Sciences at Stanford. While in the United States and for a considerable time afterwards, I was stimulated to attempt a comprehensive account of the village which would include all aspects of Radhvanaj society, past as well as present.

However, some time later I felt that I was pursuing an aim I would never realise and therefore decided to present the analysis of my data in parts. My doctoral dissertation submitted to the University of Baroda grew from what was to be a chapter on the history of the village, and the present book has grown from what was to be a chapter on the family. I gave priority to the publication of the latter for the family was a basic social unit and a proper analysis of the data on other aspects of the society depended on a proper analysis of the family. Some further information about the growth of the book is given in the Introductory Notes to Parts I and II of the book.

The writing of the book was frequently interrupted by professional duties I was called upon to perform from time to time. And the publication was delayed by various mishaps with regard to printing.

I do not have adequate words to express my gratefulness to Professor Srinivas. His contribution to the book as my teacher and as director of my research project is immeasurable. He also read closely several drafts of the manuscript and made detailed and incisive comments on them. It was he who first suggested that I critically review the literature on the Indian family.

I cannot help recalling the kindness of the late Professor Robert Redfield who initiated the project and took keen interest in its progress. I am grateful to Professor Milton Singer for his constant encouragement and help in my research and for many other kindnesses.

I thank Professor I. P. Desai for his contribution to the management of the project, for constant encouragement, and for critical comments on the manuscript of the book. Ramesh Shroff's companionship in the project was only a manifestation of deeper friendship. Narayan Sheth made useful comments on an early draft of the manuscript. Pramod Mehta, a Radhvanaj boy who came to study sociology at Baroda University following the field workers, gave valuable assistance in fieldwork and analysis of data. Aneeta Ahluwalia, Veena Dua, Mohini Anjum,

Viswa Nath and Chander Mohan Bhatia helped in the pre-paration of the manuscript for the press.

The people of Radhvanaj have absorbed Ramesh Shroff and me into their village. We feel proud of belonging to it. I thank in particular Ranchhodbhai Patel, Ratibhai Mehta, Balashanker Dave, Tejabhai Rathod, Prithviraj Rathod and Fatesingh Rathod for their continuing friendship and cooperation.

The University of California Press played a special role in shaping the book. I admire their creative editing and their blend of courtesy, patience, and firmness. It is a pleasure to work with everyone at Cal Press.

Delhi, February 25, 1973.   A. M. Shah

Contents

List of Tables

The Household Dimension
of the Family in India

Part I

The Household
in a Gujarat Village

Introductory Note

The focus of this book is the household dimension of the family in India. In common English parlance the word "family" is used in several different senses: "1. The household . . . 2. The body of persons who live in one house or under one head, including parents, children, servants, etc. 3. The group consisting of parents and their children, *whether living together or not;* in a wider sense, all those who are *nearly* connected by blood *or* affinity . . . 4. Those descended or claiming descent from a common ancestor; a house, kindred, lineage . . ." (*The Shorter Oxford English Dictionary,* 3rd ed., 1959, italics mine; see also *Notes and Queries on Anthropology,* 1957, p. 70). The four social units indicated by the four meanings are usually related to each other, but they should be clearly distinguished from each other for sociological analysis.

The distinction between "household" and "family" has become common in sociology and social anthropology, particularly since the publication of *The Developmental Cycle in Domestic Groups* (Goody [ed.], 1958). To be more explicit, the household is one of the several dimensions of the family and should be viewed in relation to the other dimensions. We shall see how the term "family" refers on the one hand to genealogical models, without any definite indication of the activities or functions of the persons composing a model (as in "nuclear family" and "extended family") and on the other hand to social groups having certain activities or functions, without any definite indication of the persons composing the group (as in "family" in the sense of "household", and in "joint family" in the sense of a kind of property-holding group).

3

This book has resulted out of an endeavour to view the family system in a village in Gujarat in the perspective of the family system in India as a whole. It is almost inevitable for field studies of little communities in great civilizational areas like India to view the microcosm in the perspective of the macrocosm. This perspective necessitates the comparison of my micro-study with other micro-studies of the family in India and the integration of micro-studies with macro-studies such as those conducted by the Census of India and the Indian Statistical Institute.

To achieve these aims to some degree of satisfaction, it is necessary to have a common set of terms and concepts, if not also a common framework of analysis. In order that my micro-study could fit into the existing body of literature on the family in India, I made several trials to analyse my field data with the help of terms and concepts used in this literature. All the trials, however, failed to give satisfactory results. I was therefore compelled to devise a few new terminological tools for the analysis of my data. Not only that, I also found most of the currently used terms and concepts so confusing and certain assumptions underlying them so false that I decided to avoid these terms and concepts completely in the analysis of the village data which is presented in Part I of the book.

Among the terms most conspicuous by their absence in Part I are the "elementary or nuclear family" and the "joint or extended family." This dichotomy has been not merely a matter of verbal usage but also the foundation on which the superstructure of the entire study of the family in India has rested for more than a century. My avoidance of these old terms and introduction of a few new terms are likely to strain the reader's mind, but I urge him to follow my analysis of the village data with patience.

The terminological innovations are confined mainly to the taxonomy of households. All other terms and concepts and analytical procedures used in Part I are part of the common heritage of modern sociology and social anthropology. The households in the village have been classified into types on the

4

basis of their numerical and kinship composition, and the frequencies of households of the different types have been compared. An attempt has been made to show a developmental pattern in the types with the help of the idea of the developmental cycle of domestic groups formulated by Fortes and his associates (Fortes, 1949; Goody [ed.], 1958), although the idea is modified somewhat. The pattern of interpersonal relations in each type of household has been described in considerable detail, showing in particular the harmony and conflict among the general norms governing the formation of households and the norms of behaviour attached to different roles and relationships within the household. The household pattern is viewed in relation to other structures in the society such as caste, kinship, and rural and urban communities. And the past pattern has been compared with the present.

In brief, I have presented in Part I what is called an "analytical description" of the household pattern in the village. Although there is very little comparison with other studies, the description is made in such a manner that it can be used for comparative purposes. Issues have been raised and correlations have been established that can be taken up for comparison on an all-India level. The micro-study is executed in such a way, I submit, that it takes care of a number of things at the same time with reasonable consistency.

Almost the entire discussion of the significance, if any, of the analysis of the village data for the study of the family in India as a whole is presented in Part II. It includes a lengthy critique on previous studies of the family in India. The examination of other studies has of course to depend upon some ideas, and these are drawn mainly from the analysis of the village data presented in Part I.

The distinction Radcliffe-Brown made between *idiographic* and *nomothetic* enquiries is perhaps apt to describe the difference between Parts I and II respectively. He stated, "In an idiographic enquiry the purpose is to establish as acceptable certain particular or factual propositions or statements. A nomothetic enquiry, on the contrary, has for its purpose to arrive at acceptable general propositions" (1952, p. 1). There is only one qualification: the general propositions sought to be established in Part II are confined to different parts of a single though large society, namely, India, and are not extended to cover a number of societies.

There are two main reasons why the idiographic enquiry in Part I precedes the nomothetic enquiry in Part II and why the former is kept free from the terminology commonly used in the study of the Indian family. First, this is exactly how I proceeded in my study — I made an extensive review of the literature after I had made most of the analysis of the field data — and I think I should record this procedure. The second and more important reason is that in at least some of the fields of sociological enquiry in India it is necessary for the progress of the subject to have analytical descriptions which are free from the prevalent jargon and abstractions. I may repeat in this connection Louis Dumont's forceful words from the preface to his papers on "Marriage in India: The Present State of the Question":

> [In studies on India] it has become more or less the habit to reduce description to general propositions — therefore of doubtful validity — before proceeding to abstract considerations which are often as subtle as they are ambitious. Certainly it is impossible to eliminate the personal equation completely and provide descriptive material for others to use at will. But perhaps this has been repeated too often for, true as it is, we seem to be in danger of going to the other extreme: description begins to disappear to a point at which critical judgment becomes difficult. It is time to react against this tendency and it would be desirable, in the Indian field, to define what conditions a "mere" description has to fulfil in order to be collectively useful. At all events, as a counterweight to top-heavy generalizations, let us demand facts, more facts and always facts (1961, pp. 75–76).

It is mainly to facts, therefore, that I devote my attention in the following five chapters of Part I.

I took a census of the village of Radhvanaj at the beginning of my field work in August 1955. During the course of field work, however, I found that the information recorded in my census cards was far from perfect, and therefore, I took another census at the end of field work in February 1958. A field census of this kind is thus more intensive than the official censuses conducted under the Census of India. Although I have used data from both of my censuses, all the numerical figures about households in Radhvanaj presented in this book are based on the first census. It is scarcely necessary to mention that the census data are used along with other field data, such as genealogies, and facts collected through the method of "participant-observation." It may also be noted that in the presentation of numerical data, percentages have been rounded off to make totals of 100.

1
Preliminary Considerations

The Village and Its People

The village of Radhvanaj is situated in what is popularly known as the Charotar tract in Central Gujarat, Western India. (For a brief general account of the village, see Shah, 1956.) Administratively, the village falls within the jurisdiction of Matar Taluka of Kaira District. Charotar is one of the most populated areas in India, with a density as high as 950 people per square mile. It is also one of the most highly commercialized and urbanized areas in India, with 26 towns and 332 villages, or an average of one town for about a dozen villages. The towns are all small or medium-sized, distributed evenly all over the area, so that almost every village has several towns in its vicinity. Radhvanaj has three towns within a radius of four miles, and three more within a radius of ten miles. Two large cities, Ahmadabad and Baroda, are at a distance of about twenty-five and thirty-five miles, respectively, from the village. Almost all the villages and towns in the area are connected with each other by a network of railways and roads.

Radhvanaj has a population of 1,305 persons divided into 299 households.[1] The household is a residential and domestic unit composed of one or more persons living under the same roof and eating food cooked in a single kitchen. In Gujarati a household is called *ghar* (lit., house) as well as *chulo* (lit., hearth). The term "household unit" will be used in preference to "household group" as there are many single-member households in Radhvanaj.

[1] Source: Field census of 1955.

Of the 299 households, 263, made up of 1,185 persons, reside in Radhvanaj and spend most of their day-to-day life there. The remaining 36 households, with a population of 120, reside in other villages and towns but are domiciled in Radhvanaj and relate to it in many ways (see Chapter 2).

Radhvanaj has a village-site of about eighteen acres, on which about 350 buildings, residential and non-residential, private and public, are located, while fields lie all around. There are about 35 houses dispersed in fields away from the village-site, but the nucleus of all communal activities of the village remains the village-site. The buildings range from flimsy huts with walls made of branches and leaves, and thatched roof, through fairly substantial houses with mud walls and tiled or corrugated-sheet roof, to urban-style, brick and cement structures of two-or-three storeys. On the whole, as Indian villages go, Radhvanaj has a prosperous look. There is a complicated pattern of ownership and use of buildings, which I shall not describe here in detail; it is sufficient to mention only a few essential points. First, each of a half-dozen buildings is divided into two parts occupied by two separate households with separate kitchens, so that only a close observation can reveal their separation. Second, although a large majority of households own one building each and use it as a dwelling, a fairly large number of households each owns more than one building — and one household owns at least six buildings. In such cases, generally one building is used for residential purposes and the others are used for storage of agricultural produce, implements, and so on. What is most significant for my further analysis, however, are the possibilities of converting any additional building into a dwelling unit whenever necessary, and of renting or buying a house.

Table 1 shows the classification of households and population of Radhvanaj by caste and place of residence. There are twenty-one caste groups. The first eight — Brahman, Patidar, Rajput, Molesalam Rajput, Talapada Koli, Patanwadia Koli, Chamadia, and Senwa — are, in terms of number of households and popu-

Table 1

Caste and Place of Residence of Radhvanaj Households and Population

Caste	In Radhvanaj		Outside Radhvanaj		Total		Total HH as in Chapter 2
	HH	P	HH	P	HH	P	
Brahman (priest)	8	35	4	20	12	55	9
Patidar (peasant)	13	70	2	2	15	72	14
Rajput (warrior)	34	170	4	16	38	186	37
Molesalam Rajput (Muslim warrior)	15	76	1	1	16	77	15
Talapada Koli (peasant)	49	198	10	30	59	228	53
Patanwadia Koli (peasant)	72	315	2	11	74	326	73
Chamadia (leather-worker)	20	92	7	22	27	114	27
Senwa (rope-maker and menial servant)	15	70	—	—	15	70	15
Gadhvi (bard)	7	23	—	—	7	23	7
Luhana (trader)	2	7	4	12	6	19	4
Valand (barber)	4	14	—	—	4	14	4
Kumbhar (potter)	4	17	—	—	4	17	4
Suthar (carpenter)	3	11	1	2	4	13	3
Raval (drummer)	4	15	—	—	4	15	4
Vaghri (menial servant)	4	23	—	—	4	23	4
Bharwad (shepherd)	3	18	—	—	3	18	3
Ode (digger)	1	6	1	4	2	10	2
Bhoi (water-carrier)	2	9	—	—	2	9	2
Sadhu (mendicant)	1	4	—	—	1	4	1
Gosai (mendicant)	1	3	—	—	1	3	1
Bania (trader)	1	9	—	—	1	9	1
Totals	263	1185	36	120	299	1305	283

HH=Households; P=Population.

lation, the major castes in the village.[2] Although the traditional occupation of Brahmans is priesthood, their principal occupation today in Radhvanaj is agriculture. The Patidars are the traditional peasant caste of Gujarat, and the Rajputs were traditionally rulers and warriors but are now landlords and peasants. The Molesalam Rajputs, also peasants, are partly Hindu and partly Muslim: originally they were Hindu Rajputs, like the Rajputs, but they were converted to Islam during the rule of Muslim kings, although the caste has retained a number of Hindu institutions and ways of life. Practically all the villagers are thus Hindus. The Talapada and Patanwadia Kolis are two of the several major divisions of the widespread Koli caste of Gujarat. Most of them are small landowners, tenants, and landless labourers. The Brahmans, Patidars, Rajputs, Talapada Kolis, and Patanwadia Kolis have ritual status in the descending order in which they are mentioned, the Patanwadia Kolis being the least Sanskritized of the five.[3] The Chamadias (leather workers) and Senwas (labourers and rope-makers) are the Untouchable castes. The remaining thirteen castes are mostly artisan, servicing, and trading castes, each represented by a small number of people. I shall reserve for Chapter 5 the relation between household units and caste differences.

Definitions of Terms and Concepts

Table 2 shows the classification of households of Radhvanaj according to numerical size. It can be seen that there is a wide range from one to nineteen members per household. The mode is 5 and the arithmetical mean, 4.6. This mean is very close to the corresponding means for Gujarat and the whole of India arrived at by the Census of India.[4] Households with one

[2] For analyses of the caste system in Central Gujarat, see Pocock, 1955, and 1957; and Shah and Shroff, 1958.

[3] For an exposition of the concept of Sanskritization, see Srinivas, 1962, pp. 8-11, 42-62.

[4] The mean for Gujarat is 4.8 (Census of India, 1951b, p. 314, Subsidiary Table 6.3), and for India as a whole, 4.9 for villages and 4.7 for towns (Census of India, 1951a, p. 49).

11

Table 2

Numerical Size of Households in Radhvanaj

Numerical size			Households	
			Number	Percent
Small	1		34	
	2		25	
	3		38	
		Totals	97	34·27
Medium	4		45	
	5		52	
	6		36	
		Totals	133	47·00
Large	7		18	
	8		17	
	9		9	
		Totals	44	15·55
Very large	10		5	
	11		1	
	12		1	
	13		2	
	19		1	
		Totals	9	3·18
Totals			283	100·00

to three members have been considered as small, with four to six as medium, with seven to nine as large, and with ten and more as very large. Totals and percentages for households of each of these categories are shown in Table 2. These percentages are also very close to the corresponding percentages for Gujarat and India given in Table 3. They show that most of the people

Table 3

Household Size for Gujarat and India (in percent)

Household Size	Gujarat		India	
	Village	Town	Village	Town
Small	31·24	41·62	33	38
Medium	46·03	39·94	44	41
Large	18·31	14·19	17	16
Very large	4·42	4·25	6	5
Totals	100·00	100·00	100	100

Source: Gujarat: Census of India, 1951c, pp. 342-343, Table C-I.
India: Census of India, 1951a, p. 49.

of Radhvanaj live in small and medium households as in the rest of India.

The range in kinship composition of households is much wider than the range in numerical composition, and it presents some complicated problems for analysis. As a first step toward this analysis I shall classify the households in my census by kinship composition into two major categories, "simple" and "complex." To describe kinship composition I shall use the term "parental family," meaning a unit of a man, his wife, and their unmarried children.[5] (For convenience, throughout this book I shall use the plural forms for family members — children, brothers, sisters, etc. — whenever I mean "one or more." A parental family is thus composed of one or more unmarried children.)

[5] The conventional term "elementary or nuclear family" is often defined in a similar but not identical way, e.g., as "the unit consisting of a man and wife and all their children whether young or old, living at home or outside it, married or unmarried" (*Encyclopaedia Britannica*, XIII, Chicago, 1970, p. 372). See Part II, especially Chapters 6 and 9, for a fuller discussion and comparison of terminology.

A simple household may be composed of the whole or a part of a parental family.[6] There are six major possible compositions: (1) husband, wife, and unmarried children; (2) husband and wife; (3) father and unmarried children; (4) mother and unmarried children; (5) unmarried brothers and sisters; (6) a single man or woman. It is clear that the term "simple household" is not equivalent to "parental family," which is only a genealogical model and represents only one of the six types of simple households mentioned here.

For further delineation I shall use the following terms: "parental unit" to cover the three possibilities of father, mother, and father and mother (not to be confused with "parental family"); "fraternal unit" for a unit of two or more brothers; "sororal unit" for a unit of two or more sisters; and "sibling unit" for a unit of one or more brothers plus one or more sisters.

The nature of the simple households in Radhvanaj is discussed in Chapter 4. We shall classify the many other types of households — that is, those composed of more than one parental family, or of parts of more than one parental family, or of one or more parental families and parts of one or more other parental families — as "complex." Complex households are discussed in Chapter 3. Finally, within these two categories but resident outside Radhvanaj are thirty-six "emigrant" households, which are discussed in Chapter 2.

The classifications of households according to kinship composition is not an end in itself, however. The types are not discrete and haphazard; there is some order in them, and they are understandable only as parts of that order. All households

[6] There are only two households in Radhvanaj that include servants living with their masters. They are employed on an annual contract and spend most of their time on farms. They are not serfs or bonded labourers such as are found in South Gujarat and in some other parts of India. Although they get their food from the master's kitchen, they may not sit in the kitchen with members of the master's household, because they belong to lower castes. Thus, servants are marginal members of the household in Radhvanaj. I have therefore considered households as exclusively kinship units.

are constantly going through what has come to be known as "developmental process" in social anthropology (see Goody [ed.], 1958). (It is frequently termed "developmental cycle", but I prefer to use the term "developmental process" for reasons discussed in Chapter 5.)

Norms Governing Household Formation.

One of the major factors affecting the developmental process of households is the explicitly stated norms governing the formation of households. The norms are described here; their actual observance, influence, effects, and relations with other parameters are discussed in Chapters 2–5.

All marriages in Radhvanaj, and in Charotar in general, are virilocal; that is, in every marriage the bride leaves her parental home and goes to live in her conjugal home. But under certain circumstances, as when there are only daughters, one of the sons-in-law may agree to become a *ghar-jamai,* that is, become a member of his affinal home. In such a case the woman returns along with her husband and children to her parental home. Initially, however, every marriage is virilocal. The transfer of residence of a girl from her parental home to her conjugal home is the central theme of a number of wedding rituals. Although there is no rule of village exogamy as such, most marriages are inter-village, for reasons that need not be discussed here. A marriage therefore generally involves the bride migrating from her parental to her conjugal village.

The villagers say that a son and his wife should not only start their married life in his parental home but also continue to live there afterwards. This norm has a number of implications. For instance, if a man has more than one son, each son and his wife will live not only with his parents but also with his brothers and their wives and children, and there is indeed a saying that a man and his wife should live with his brothers and their wives. People also say that brothers and their wives should live together not only during the lifetime of the brothers' parents but also after their death, and that the brothers' sons and their wives should also live in the same household. Some-

15

times the norm is extended still further. Taking all these norms together, the central idea is that while the female patrilineal descendants of a male ancestor go away to live with their husbands, the male patrilineal descendants and their wives should live together. The wives should be so completely incorporated into their husband's kin group that they should not be divorced, and even after their husband's death they should stay on in the same household. Unmarried children should be with their parents. In the event of the divorce or death of their mother, they should stay with their father or his male patrikin. I shall call the central idea behind these norms *the principle of the residential unity of patrikin and their wives.* Because this principle is normative in nature, and there are deviations from it (as in the case of all norms), the measurement of conformity to and deviation from this principle is an important problem of enquiry.

The problem of the relation between the household and property-holding units is a complex one, particularly because the rules governing property are prescribed by custom as well as law (see Chapter 7). It is sufficient to mention at the outset only the basic rule that inheritance is patrilineal — from father to sons — and that all the sons of a man have equal rights in the inheritance of his property. The dominance of the patrilineal principle is also seen in the worship of patrilineal ancestors and in the existence of corporate patrilineages in almost all the major castes.

There is only one case of polygamy in Radhvanaj, that of a man living with two wives. As this case is an exception to the general rule, I have used the word "wife" in the singular in my formulation of the term "simple household." There are, however, a few cases in which a man takes another wife after the death or divorce of the first, and children by both the wives live with him; and there are a very few cases in which a woman marries another husband after the death or divorce of the first, taking her children by the first husband with her into the house of the second. Most of the marriages of the latter type are leviratic unions called *diyervatu* (lit., marriage with husband's younger brother). There are also a couple of cases of adoption. Thus, in the formulation of "simple household" the words "children," "mother," and "father" include also stepchildren and adopted children, stepmother and adoptive mother, and stepfather and adoptive father, respectively. This means the term "parental family" as used here includes not only the "elementary family" but also certain types of what is called the "compound family" (as defined by Radcliffe-Brown, 1950, p. 5).

There is also the custom of foster parenthood. One middle-aged couple in Radhvanaj have no child of their own and are acting as foster parents of the man's brother's daughter. It is not a formal adoption, the adoption of daughters being rare in predominantly patrilineal Hindu society. The girl was the only child, and her mother died a few months after giving birth. The father remarried later and had children by the second wife. The foster parents were guided in their action not only by the sentiment of bringing up a widowed brother's child but also by the idea of earning religious merit (punya). According to Hindu scriptures, a Hindu earns punya by giving away a girl in marriage, that is, by performing the ritual of the gift of bride (kanyadan). It has to be performed by a married couple, and normally they are the girl's parents. If the girl is brought up by foster parents they perform the ritual. If the girl's parents die after she has come of age, the ritual is performed by some other couple. Sometimes, even though parents are alive at the time of the daughter's wedding, they may allow some other couple to perform the ritual. This is particularly likely if they have more than one daughter and if there are strong ties between them and the childless couple who desire to perform the ritual. One may describe such couples as ritual parents and the girls as ritual daughters.

"Child marriages" are quite common in the villages of Charotar, particularly among the Kolis, Chamadias, Senwas and Bharwads, in spite of the existence of statutory laws prohibiting such marriages. A married girl, however, is not sent to her husband's home until she has attained puberty. Many boys and girls

17

who are formally married do not live together. I have recorded them as married in my census cards but considered them as unmarried for purposes of the present analysis.[7]

[7] The suspicion that my census cards might be passed on to government officials as evidence of child marriage caused many parents to give me false information about the ages of their children. The official birth and death registers of the village are helpful in finding the correct ages of only a few children because the births of many children have been registered in their mothers' parental villages where they were born. (Although residence is virilocal, wives return to their parental homes almost invariably for the first delivery and sometimes for subsequent deliveries also.) I have also considered for the present analysis a few adult married boys and girls as unmarried, because their weddings had taken place only a short time before my census and the wives had not joined their husbands.

2
Emigrant Households

Places of Residence and Occupations of Emigrants

There are thirty-six households resident outside Radhvanaj though related to it in a number of ways. Thirty-four of the thirty-six are in towns and villages in central Gujarat, and only two are in distant places beyond. This may seem inconsistent with the well-known fact that Gujaratis have migrated in large numbers to distant places in other parts of India and abroad, but this is more true of the urban than the rural populations, in which only a few castes have a tradition of migration. In central Gujarat the rural caste known for its distant migrations is the Patidar (see Pocock, 1955; Shah, 1956), and it has a very small population in Radhvanaj. The migration of most other rural castes is largely confined to central Gujarat: to the two cities Ahmadabad and Baroda, to the many small towns, and last but not least, to villages in the area. It is hardly necessary to point out that emigration to nearby places allows emigrants to maintain intimate contact with the original village.[1]

Of a total of thirty-nine earning men in these households, thirty-four are engaged in occupations forming part of modern industrial, commercial, and administrative growth: thirteen are policemen, four are clerks or peons in government offices, five are shop assistants, one is a school teacher, and eleven are workers in factories and railways. The remaining five men are engaged in traditional occupations: two are cultivators, two are shopkeepers, and one is an earth-digger.

[1] For an account of a different pattern of emigration from a Gujarat village, see I. P. Desai, 1964b.

19

Emigrant Households' Relations with the Village

There is a considerable variation in the nature of relations maintained by emigrant households with the village. To show the pattern in the variations, the thirty-six emigrant households are classified in Table 4 according to the kind of relatives each has in Radhvanaj, and the broad nature of the relation maintained with them.

Table 4

Relations of Emigrant Households with Near Kin in Radhvanaj

Category of Relation	Household
(A) " Independent " emigrant households	20
(i) Emigrant parents separated from a married son residing in the village	1
(ii) Emigrant men separated from parents and married brothers	9
(iii) Emigrant men separated from married brothers	3
(iv) Emigrant households having no near kinsman in the village	7
(B) " Linked " emigrant households	16
(i) Emigrant husbands each having wife and children in the village	2
(ii) Emigrant unmarried men each having parents and unmarried siblings in the village	2
(iii) Emigrant households each forming part of a joint unit of parents and one married son	4
(iv) Emigrant households each forming part of a joint unit of parents and more than one married son	7
(v) Emigrant household of a married man linked with parents but separated from a married brother	1
Total	36

There are four men who live alone outside the village. The two cases cited in Table 4: B–i are each composed of a single man who keeps his wife and children in the village and returns frequently to live with them. The two cases cited in B–ii are similar: one unmarried man living alone in a town has a widower father who lives alone in the village, and they visit each other frequently; the other unmarried man has a widowed mother and an unmarried brother and sister in the village, whom he visits frequently. In each of these four cases the emigrant and the village households together form a full or an incomplete parental family. That is to say, although they reside separately, they form a highly integrated kinship unit.

Of the four cases cited in B–iii, in one case the only son lives with his wife in a town while his old parents live in the village. In the second, one married son lives outside the village while his widowed mother and unmarried brothers and sisters live together in the village. In the third, an old couple and their one married son and another unmarried son live in a nearby town while the eldest son, a bachelor, lives in the village. And in the fourth, an unmarried man lives in a town while his widowed mother and married brother live in the village. In each of the four cases, the emigrant household and the related village household constitute a kinship unit of parents, their one married son and other unmarried children, and they all form an integrated group in terms of property, income, expenditure, rituals, and so on. We shall see that a kinship unit of this type is generally an integrated group, whether its constituent parts reside in the village or are divided between the village and the town.

In the single case in 4 : A–i, an old man and his wife (without children) live outside the village while the man's son by his first wife lives in the village, but they do not form an integrated group. The father and the son have quarrelled and divided their property, as usually happens when a man takes another wife while his adult sons by the first wife are alive.

In the seventeen cases cited in A–ii, B–iv, and B–v, each emigrant household forms part of a kinship unit composed of parents, two or more married sons and, in some cases, unmarried children. The details about them are described below.

21

One widow who lives in the village has her four married sons living in four different households in four different places outside. The sons have divided their ancestral property, each of them has a house and land in the village, and each is an independent income-expenditure unit. They have, however, agreed that the mother should live in one of their houses, derive income from some land allotted to her for her maintenance, and be provided with some cash by each son.

An old widower living alone in the village has both his married sons living in two different places outside, but in this case the village household and the two outside households form an integrated group in terms of income, expenditure, and so forth.

One village household of a widow and her young children and two outside households of her two married sons form an integrated group.

Another widow living in the village with her young children has two married sons: one lives outside the village; the other has a separate household in the village. The emigrant son provides money to his mother for maintenance of her household, and he and his wife and children live with her whenever they come to the village. That is to say, the emigrant son's household and the mother's household form an integrated group, while the non-emigrant son is dissociated for them.

In four cases a married man living outside the village has his parents as well as all his married brothers in the village. The parents live with only one or two of the married sons, but the other sons — including the one resident outside the village — each have a house, land and other property, and separate income and expenditure. That is to say, each emigrant son has his own house in the village which is opened when the members of his household visit it.

In five cases, one of the several married sons lives outside the village and the rest live with the parents in a complex household in the village. The emigrant son owns land and house in the village jointly with his parents and brothers, and contributes a part of his personal income to a pool for joint expenses. When the members of the emigrant son's household go to the village, they live with his parents and brothers in the same house. A complicated set of rules prevail regarding the management of property and the share of income and expenditure.

The description of these seventeen emigrant households shows that when a married man living outside the village has parents as well as married brothers, his relation with them may vary from that of integration into a single unit of property, income, expenditure, and so on, to that of separation in all respects. The nature of this phenomenon will become more clear when I discuss the nature of similar kinship units residing entirely in the village.

The three men living with their wives and children outside the village, cited in A–iii, each have one or more brothers and their wives and children residing in the village. The brothers are separated from one another after the death of the parents. Each outside brother has his own house in the village, which is opened only when he and his wife and children visit the village.

The seven emigrant households cited in A–iv do not have any near relative — wife, child, parent, or brother — in the village. Each of them has a house in the village, which is opened only when its members visit the village — during holidays, to supervise the management of their land, to celebrate calendrical festivals and rites of passage of the members of the household, to attend similar occasions in the life of the members of their lineage and caste, and to take part in village festivals and other village activities. Moreover, the village provides them with the locus for continuing their relationships with kin, affines, and caste members resident in other villages around the native village. Among the seven households, one is a single-member unit, four are full parental families, and two are complex units — one composed of a widowed mother and her married son, and the other composed of a couple and their two married sons, two unmarried sons, and two unmarried daughters.

It is evident from these descriptions that an emigrant household may maintain a house (including household equipment) of its own in the village and remain independent in terms of property, income, expenditure, and so on, or it may be linked with a village household to form an integrated group as shown in Table 4.[2] The terms "independent" and "linked" emigrant households refer not to the degree that the households are independent of the village as a whole but only to near kinsmen.

It can be seen from Table 4 that there is a definite relationship between an emigrant household's remaining independent or linked and its place in the kinship structure. Both the emigrant husbands and both the emigrant unmarried sons are linked with their wives and parents, respectively. In the same way, each of the three emigrant men having married brothers but not parents, and each of the seven emigrant households without any near kinsmen, is independent. On the other hand, of the five emigrant households forming parts of units composed of parents and one married son, four are linked and one is independent, and of the seventeen households forming parts of units composed of parents and more than one married son,

[2] It should be noted that for the sake of simplicity I have considered that all the six men living alone in towns constitute single-member households. In fact, only one or two of them really maintain households, in the sense that each man lives in a rented house and cooks his food himself. One or two others have rented small houses but take their meals in restaurants or other public eating places. And the rest live as members of hostels or messes, in what are called "institutions" in the Census of India. I have ignored these intricacies because the focus of my study is a village, although I agree that they cannot be ignored in a study of households in an urban area. If we take into account such temporary migrants from a number of villages, we can get an idea of the composition of floating populations in urban settlements.

seven are linked with parents and married brothers, one is linked with parents but not with brother, and nine are independent. With regard to the kinship units composed of parents and more than one married son, therefore, there is considerable flexibility as to whether an emigrant household remains linked or independent. It will become apparent, as I proceed with my analysis, that these variations of independent and linked emigrant households according to kinship relations are a reflection of established patterns of kinship relations in the village. Furthermore, it is obvious that within the category of independent or of linked emigrant households, the kind of contacts an emigrant household maintains with the village would depend on, among other things, the kind of kinsmen it has in the village.

Some Implications of the Analysis

On the basis of my study of the history of Radhvanaj during the last 150 years I may state that the phenomenon of independent and linked emigrant households is not entirely a modern one in India — by "modern" I mean the postindustrialization period.[3] Migrations used to occur in the preindustrialization period, and emigrants did not sever their relations with their original village abruptly. As a result of industrialization, however, migrations take place over wider areas and in larger numbers. The speedy and easy means of communication, which have helped these migrations, work in two ways: not only migration but also maintaining contact is easier. A new and increasingly important pattern of social relationships has therefore emerged in modern India, which is important for the social system of towns as well as of villages. The independent and linked households are as much a part of the village social system as of the town social system, and they affect the direction of social change in both. Any macro-study of the family and household in modern India should treat the pattern of interrelations between independent or linked emigrant households on the one

[3] The same point is made by I. P. Desai in his study of migration in a South Gujarat village (1964b, pp. 155-156).

hand and village households on the other as an inclusive network linking villages and towns. The focus of my study being one village, I shall ignore these intricacies. I shall consider every independent emigrant household as if it were a separate household resident in the village, and each integrated group of a linked emigrant household and the corresponding village household as if the whole of it were resident in the village. For example, the integrated group of each of the two emigrant husbands and his wife and children will be included among husband-wife-children households, and that of a "simple" emigrant household of a married son and the linked simple household of his parents in the village will be included among complex households composed of parents and one married son. The distinction made between households in the village and households outside the village will thus be removed in my further analysis, and the total number of households in the village will be considered to be 283 (see Table 1).

Another element of expediency may also be pointed out. Just as households originally belonging to or domiciled in Radhvanaj have left but have remained linked with households resident in it, there are also a few households — three I know for certain, and I suspect an additional two or three — who have come to live in Radhvanaj from other villages but remained linked with households resident in these villages of their original domicile. The number of such households is small because more people migrate from village to town than from town to village or from one village to another village. I shall not treat these households separately.

A migrant household may reduce its relations with its original village in course of time and settle down in its new place of residence, retaining in the original village only occasional relations with some people, and immovable property, if any, until it is sold. I have excluded from my census such erstwhile residents of Rahdvanaj; the line dividing these people from some of the independent emigrant households without any near kinsmen in the village is a very thin one.

3
Complex Households

Out of the total number of 283 households in Radhvanaj, 91 are complex. In this chapter the complex households will first be classified into certain types of kinship composition. The number of households and the pattern of interpersonal relations in them will then be considered in detail for each type in order to elucidate the nature of the developmental process of households and the operation of the principle of the residential unity of patrikin and their wives.

The composition of eighty out of ninety-one complex households is based on the principle of the residential unity of patrikin and their wives. The eighty households are classified by varying degrees of complexity of kinship composition in Tables 5–9, and the compositions are illustrated in the accompanying genealogical charts. (The other eleven households, which include members who illustrate the reversal of the principle of the residential unity of patrikin and their wives, are discussed in the last section of this chapter.)

Atypical Complex Households
As stated earlier, there is a certain pattern in the developmental process of households. This pattern can best be seen by first studying the six households that are atypical. They reveal, among other things, the maximum extent to which a household may, but does not normally, grow. In other words, they represent the limits within which the developmental process of most of the households is confined.

The composition of the six atypical households is shown in Table 5 and the accompanying genealogical chart.

Table 5

Households of Atypical Compositions

Composition	Households
(i) Eldest brother and his wife, younger brother and his wife, youngest unmarried brother	1
(ii) Man, his wife and unmarried children, and his father's widower brother	1
(iii) Man, his wife and unmarried children, his widowed mother and father's widower brother	1
(iv) Man, his wife, his two bachelor brothers, widowed mother, and father's brother's widow	1
(v) Man, his wife, and father's widowed mother	1
(vi) Man, his wife, his one married son and other unmarried children, and his widowed mother	1
Total	6

Genealogical Chart for Table 5

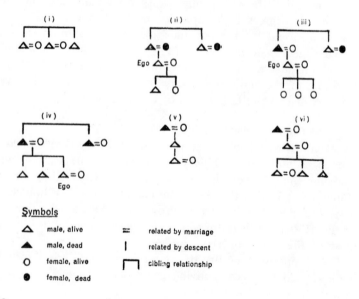

Symbols

△	male, alive	≈	related by marriage
▲	male, dead	│	related by descent
O	female, alive	⌐	sibling relationship
●	female, dead		

28

Household 5:i is the only one in the village in which two married brothers and their wives are living together after the death of the men's parents. On the other hand, there are many instances of married brothers living separately from one another after the death of their parents, which shows that such separation between brothers is quite normal in this village, despite the norms described in Chapter 1. In a household composed of two or more married brothers and their wives there is the likelihood of tension, first of all, between elder brother and younger brother. Srinivas has rightly observed:

> As long as the brothers stay united, the social personalities of the younger brothers do not attain completion. The younger brothers are husbands and fathers, and heads of elementary families. But as members of the joint family they are subordinate to the eldest brother. The headship of an elementary family and membership of a joint family are in some respects incompatible. [1952b, p. 30. "Joint family" means "joint household" here.]

There is also the possibility of tension between the wives of brothers. The younger brother's wife (*derani*) does not easily acknowledge the elder brother's wife's (*jethani's*) position as the chief housekeeper. The two generally come from different villages, sometimes from different social strata within their caste, and occasionally from different castes in the case of inter-caste hypergamy. Unless the brothers married two sisters, the social and cultural backgrounds of the wives tend to be so different that they rarely get along with each other in a joint household. The relationship between *derani* and *jethani* is characterised as one of perennial conflict in many folk songs and folk tales. It is a matter of comparative study whether the extent of tensions between the wives of brothers would be the same where, as in South India, cross-cousin and uncle-niece marriages are frequent and wives come from a more restricted circle than in the North (cf. Srinivas, 1952a, pp. 145–148; Gough, 1956, p. 844).

29

It is noteworthy that in household 5:i there is also an unmarried brother, and this seems to be an important reason why
the two married brothers live together. The married brothers
think that it is their joint responsibility to look after the unmarried brother until he marries. A household of brothers
breaks up after the marriage of all the brothers (cf. Srinivas,
1952b, p. 30). In my census *there is no household in which two
or more married brothers live together without their parents or
unmarried brothers and sisters.* We shall see that two or more
married brothers may start living separately even during the
lifetime of their parents. There are, however, always some cases
of two or more married brothers living together during the lifetime of their parents, whereas once the parents are dead and all
the sons and daughters are married, all the married sons establish separate households.

When brothers live in separate households it does not mean
that they sever all other social relationships. Household separation obviously involves partition of almost all the movable
property, such as jewellery, pots and pans, mattresses, furni-
ture, and other household equipment. In most cases it is also
accompanied by partition of immovable property, but this need
not always be so. Brothers may continue to own land and buildings jointly, and may even cultivate land or carry on some commercial or productive enterprise jointly. In this regard it is
necessary to distinguish between various forms of immovable
property, such as ancestral and self-acquired, corporeal and in-
corporeal (e.g., *jajmani* rights), dry land and wet land, cultivable
land and uncultivable land, sentimentally and ritually important ancestral fields, land under special tenures, and expensive
agricultural equipment, such as a well, particularly a well with
irrigation devices, a diesel or electric pump, a storehouse, a cart,
and so on. Brothers may partition property of only some kinds,
but remain joint with reference to others; that is, they may
partition different items of property at different times. Moreover, they may act together in political, ceremonial, and ritual
spheres, and they may be bound together by a number of mutual

rights and obligations. All these activities are oriented toward specific ends, are not very much charged with emotion and sentiment, and involve men rather than their wives and children. To live in separate households and cooperate in these activities is a different thing from living in a complex household and carrying on these activities as members of a single household. Complex households involve mutually satisfactory organization of a vast range of activities, adjustment of interests, emotions, and sentiments, and adherence to a certain pattern of authority. At least in this village society, there do not seem to be any influences that could lead married brothers to solve all these problems and continue to stay in a single household after their parents' death.

To conclude: the ideal that brothers should live together in the same household even after the death of their parents finds expression in informal conversation and in folklore but not in actual practice. It is therefore an ideal norm — a desirable but not expected mode of behaviour — in Radhvanaj and other villages around it.[1] The principle of the residential unity of patrikin and their wives becomes extremely weak when the parental link joining the sons is lost.

Atypical households 5:ii, 5:iii, and 5:iv are similar in certain important respects and may therefore be considered together. In these three households a man and his wife look after his old father's brother (*kaka*) or father's brother's widow (*kaki*). In Radhvanaj many men and women are looked after in their old age by their sons, and some old men by their brothers, but only a lucky man would be looked after in his old age by his brother's son (*bhatrijo*), and only a lucky woman, by her husband's brother's son (*bhatrijo*). We shall see in Chapter 4 that many widowers and widows live alone, even though relatives nearer than their brother's son or husband's brother's

---

[1] I have followed Elizabeth Bott (1957, pp. 193-194) in using the distinction between "ideal norm" and "expected norm." Gluckman (1955, pp. 125-129) makes essentially the same distinction by his concepts "upright man" and "reasonable man."

son (respectively) are alive. The three cases mentioned here are the only cases of the observance of the ideal that a man should look after his *kaka* or *kaki* in his or her old age. Normally the necessity for a *bhatrijo* to look after his *kaka* or *kaki* would not arise, because, as we have seen, the *kaka* and his brother (the *bhatrijo's* father) would almost always be living in separate households (after the death, if not during the lifetime, of their parents), and each would have sons or some other relative to look after him in his old age. Only when the *kaka* or *kaki* does not have sons may it become necessary for the *bhatrijo* (nephew) to look after them. The *bhatrijo* may also be interested, as in the three cases cited here, in inheriting their property, which would be conditional on his care. There are many cases in which the *kaka* or *kaki* is not looked after by the nephew, usually because all of them cannot live harmoniously in a single household. The conflict between brothers and their wives may show itself in the relation between the *kaka* or *kaki* and the *bhatrijo*. The *bhatrijo* and his wife may also not like to take up the burden of looking after the old *kaka* or *kaki*, who may simply be a very unpleasant character. In brief, in these cases the principle of the residential unity of patrikin and their wives is observed even beyond the phase of residential unity of two or more married brothers. In none of the three cases, however, is the principle observed to the extent that first cousins and their wives live together. The norm that they should live together finds expression only when villagers are engaged in informal talk.

In the fifth atypical household in the village, household 5:v, a man (Ego) and his wife look after his father's widowed mother even though his father is alive, that is, the widow lives with her grandson even though her son is alive. The separation of the father from his son and from his mother is like many other cases of separation between parents and sons described at a later stage, but I have no information as to why the duty of looking after the old woman has fallen on the grandson even though her own son is alive. The sixth atypical household, 5:vi, is the only household in the village where a grandparent lives with a married son as well as a married grandson. (There is also a household that includes a grandmother and her married grandson, but she is his mother's mother and not his father's mother; see p. 62.) Very few men and women live long enough to see their grandsons married; a person therefore considers himself very lucky if he is a witness to the wedding of his grandson. There are only three more grandparents having married grandsons in the village, but in accordance with the general practice the two do not live together in the same household. The grandparents live with the younger sons who do not have marriageable sons; the grandsons are sons of the elder sons. Generally, by the time grandsons are married the elder sons have separate households and the parents are left to the care of the youngest son. It is therefore rare to find a household composed of a grandparent and married son as well as married grandson.

We have seen how the six households discussed above are atypical in several respects: in that there is only one household of each type of kinship composition, in the developments in the life cycle of individuals, in the practice of the norms of household formation held by people, and in the pattern of interpersonal relations in the household. The discussion has also indicated the maximum limit to which a household usually develops in this village community in central Gujarat.

It should be noted that I have discussed above only the atypical aspects of the six households cited in Table 5; otherwise they are similar to many other households in the village. The father's brother in household 5:ii and the grandmother in household 5:v live with a full parental family and a husband-wife couple respectively, that is, with a simple unit; and the father's brother in household 5:iii and the father's brother's widow in household 5:iv live with relatives who themselves constitute a complex unit. I shall discuss the latter along with other similar complex units below, and also break household 5:iv into two complex units for further discussion (see footnotes to Tables 7 and 8).

Households of One Married Man and One or More Unmarried Siblings

The type of household compositions cited in Table 6 is within the maximum limit of the developmental process of households in Radhvanaj, but it is represented by only five households — a relatively small number. The distinguishing characteristic of the five households is the co-residence of one married brother with one or more of his unmarried siblings after the death of their parents (in contrast to the households in Table 8 in which one married brother co-resides with one or more unmarried siblings along with their parents).

In three of the five households (6:i) the members are the eldest brother, his wife and unmarried children, and one or more unmarried younger brothers, and in one case an unmarried sister. Such households are relatively few in number not because the norms governing them are weak or the interpersonal relations in them unmanageable but because their existence is due to the unusual coincidence of certain life-cycle events. They are mostly the result of the death of both parents at a relatively early age leaving one married son and other unmarried children. In rare cases the parents may die leaving all children unmarried, and when the eldest son marries, a household of the type described here comes into existence. In such a household it is considered to be the duty of the eldest brother and his wife to bring up his younger siblings and get them married. This duty is generally performed by eldest brothers, but when the younger brothers are married the household moves on to another phase of development, during which tensions between the brothers and between their wives come into play, leading to separation of the brothers. During my field work I saw this happening in one of the three households. In the case of another household with no less than five younger brothers, all the younger brothers as a group separated themselves from the eldest brother even before their marriages, because the eldest brother and his wife proved to be incapable of looking after them. (It is noteworthy

Table 6

Households of One Married Man and One or More Unmarried Siblings

Composition	Households
(i) Eldest brother, his wife and unmarried children, his unmarried younger brothers and sisters	3
(ii) Bachelor elder brother, younger brother, his wife and unmarried children	1
(iii) Widower elder brother, younger brother, his wife, one married son, and other unmarried children	1
Total	5

Genealogical Chart for Table 6

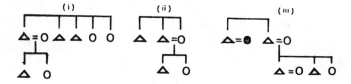

that one of the two households was composed only of unmarried children. Such households are discussed in Chapter 4.)

In household 6:ii a younger brother and his wife look after a bachelor elder brother. This household belongs to the Kheda-wal Brahman caste, which is hypergamous (i.e., girls marry in their own or higher social stratum but not in a lower one). In such a system the problem of finding husbands for girls of the highest stratum and wives for boys of the lowest stratum is particularly acute. In the past, in several hypergamous castes in Gujarat the highest stratum solved its problem by practising polygyny and female infanticide, and the removal of these customs has created much "hardship" at the present time. The lowest stratum cannot kill male infants, who are regarded as precious in a patrilineal society, and these castes also do not

35

practise polyandry. They follow either of the following courses:
(1) they get wives from acceptable lower castes, which is an
extension of intra-caste hypergamy into inter-caste hypergamy,
or (2) let some of the men remain lifelong bachelors.[2] The
Khedawal Brahmans of Radhvanaj belong to the lowest stratum
in their caste; being Brahmans they are deeply concerned about
polluting their caste by marriage into lower castes; and therefore they generally follow the course of letting some of their
men remain unmarried. V. H. Joshi, who has worked among
the Anavil Brahmans of South Gujarat, informs me that the
lowest stratum among the Anavils also follow this course.
Among the Khedawals, generally the eldest son remains unmarried and the younger sons marry; they show their indebted-
ness by looking after him throughout his life and acknowledging
him as the head of the household. In four out of five fraternal
units among the Khedawals of Radhvanaj, the eldest brother
is a bachelor, and there is genealogical evidence of a number of
bachelor eldest brothers in the past. This shows how household
composition is affected by customs and institutions peculiar to
a caste. It is important to note, however, that the eldest brother
is able to be the head of a household of all the brothers only
as long as just one younger brother is married. As soon as
another younger brother marries, tensions arise between the
two younger brothers and between their wives, leading to the
separation of one of the two from the complex household. This
is exactly what has happened in the case of the Khedawal household cited here.

In the last household cited in Table 6 (6:iii), a younger
brother and his wife look after his elder brother who is a
widower, childless and almost blind, and has handed over his
property to the younger brother in gratitude for his services.
Here again, the absence of the elder brother's wife — and consequently, of tensions between her and younger brother's wife —

2 This is a very brief and somewhat crude description of hypergamy, but it is sufficient, I hope, to explain the point I want to make
here.

is a crucial factor in maintaining residential unity. (It may be noted that in this household the younger brother has one married son and another unmarried son. It is therefore similar to the households in Table 8, and is included on this account in that table also.)

Interpersonal Relations in
Households including Parents and Married Sons

The composition of the sixty-nine households cited in Tables 7, 8, and 9 (plus five households included from Tables 5 and 6) is based on the dominant norm of co-residence of parents and married sons. These households will receive our close attention in this and the next three sections.

In each household shown in Tables 7 and 8 there is one married son (in a few cases, a widower) residing with his parental unit (father, or mother, or father and mother), whereas in each household shown in Table 9 there are two or more married sons (in a few cases, widowers) residing with their parental unit. In all the households in Table 8 and in six households in Table 9 there are unmarried children as well as married sons, whereas in all the households in Table 7 and in nine households in Table 9 there are no unmarried children. Within each of these three tables the households are classified on the basis of (1) the parental unit (father, or mother, or father and mother), and (2) the married sons having or not having children, that is, the households with or without grandchildren.

In twelve households in Table 7 and seventeen households in Table 8, where a father and a married son live together, the father is the formal head of the household and the son is supposed to have a subordinate position. Generally, however, the father tends to pass on gradually to his adult son the responsibilities of running the household, so that the relationship between them at any given time is subsumed under one of the following three phases: (1) the father does not allow the son to have much voice in making decisions and the son works according to the father's instructions; (2) the father and

Table 7

Households of Parental Unit and One Married Son

Composition	Households
(i) Father, mother, son and his wife	6
(ii) Father, mother, son and his wife and children	2
(iii) Widower father, son and his wife	2
(iv) Widower father, son and his wife and children	2
(v) Widowed mother, son and his wife	2
(vi) Widowed mother, son and his wife and children	11+2[a]
(vii) Widowed mother, widower son and his children	3
Total	28 + 2

[a] Units taken from Table 5.

Genealogical Chart for Table 7

the son work almost as equals in making as well as executing decisions; and (3) the father is mostly an adviser and benevolent supervisor of household affairs, while the son makes

Table 8

Households of Parental Unit, One Married Son, and Other Unmarried Children

Composition	Households
(i) Father, mother, unmarried children, married son and his wife	9 + 2[a]
(ii) Father, mother, unmarried children, married son and his wife and children	6
(iii) Widowed mother, unmarried children, married son and his wife	8 + 1[b]
(iv) Widowed mother, unmarried children, married son and his wife and children	3
Total	26 + 3

[a] 1 unit taken from Table 5 and 1 unit from Table 6.
[b] Unit taken from Table 5.

Genealogical Chart for Table 8

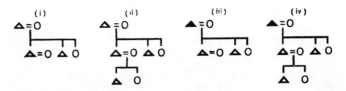

most of the decisions and executes them. As the father and the son pass through these phases there is a gradual change in the manners observed by them toward one another. For instance, in many cases the father begins to show respect toward the son by addressing him in the plural form and with the honorific *bhai* or *lal* suffixed to his name. If the father is permanently disabled by injury or illness, the son assumes full charge of the household and the father becomes dependent on the son.

Table 9

Households of Parental Unit and Two or More Married Sons

Composition	Households
(i) Father, mother, two married sons and their wives and children	3
(ii) Father, mother, unmarried children, two or more married sons and their wives and children	4
(iii) Widower father, two married sons, and their wives and children	1
(iv) Widowed mother, two or more married sons and their wives	5
(v) Widowed mother, unmarried children, two married sons and their wives and children	2
Total	15

Genealogical Chart for Table 9

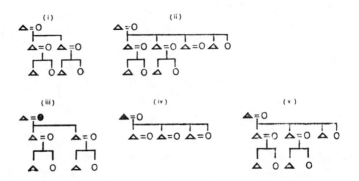

In all the households in Table 8 where there is a father and a married son there are also unmarried children; it is the joint responsibility of the father and the married son to look after the unmarried children. In such households the eldest brother is entitled to respect from his younger brothers and sisters and may even discipline them. Therefore, one of the important functions of the father is to restrain the eldest son when he tries to be unduly harsh toward his younger siblings.

In eighteen households in Table 7 and in twelve households in Table 8, where a married son lives with his widowed mother, the son is the formal head of the household. However, until the son becomes adult the mother plays a dominant role in running the household. On the death of her husband she knows much more than the young son about the husband's dealings with other people in the society, and it is only with her help that the son can deal with them effectively in the first few years after his father's death. The mother gradually passes on responsibilities to her son, but some clever and vigorous widows guide household affairs even after their sons have become adult. In nine of these households in Table 8 there is not only a married son but also other children; the married son is therefore not only the formal head of the household but also the eldest brother and has the added responsibility of looking after his younger siblings. Here the mother takes special care to see that the married son fulfils his obligations towards her unmarried children and she protects them against possible harshness and injustice.

In twenty-six households in Table 7 and in all the twenty-nine households in Table 8, where the *vahu* (daughter-in-law) lives with her *sasu* (mother-in-law), the *sasu* is the chief housekeeper and makes all the major decisions, which the *vahu* is supposed to carry out unquestioningly. The relationship between mother-in-law and daughter-in-law lacks the tendency for the older person to pass on power gradually to the younger person that prevails in the father–son and mother–son relationships. While the father and mother have a tendency to reduce voluntarily their authority over their son, the mother-in-law continues to wield authority even in her old age over her daughter-in-law (unless, of course, she is permanently disabled and therefore dependent on the daughter-in-law).

The relationship between *sasara* (father-in-law) and *vahu*

41

(daughter-in-law) is one of mutual avoidance in all households. She has to veil her face before him, and he has to see that he does not obstruct her movements in the house because of his presence.

A son has a difficult time in keeping the balance between his loyalty to his parents on the one hand and to his wife on the other. Srinivas and Dube have given vivid descriptions of these tensions (Srinivas, 1952a, pp. 143–144, 154; Srinivas, 1952b, pp. 29–30; Dube, 1955, pp. 141–156). As Srinivas has pointed out, marriage weakens not only a girl's ties to her natal kin group but also a man's ties to his. Like the peasants of Rampura (the village Srinivas has studied), the peasants of Radhvanaj remark that when a marriage takes place it is not only the girl who is lost to her parents but also the boy, to some extent, to his parents. There is a difference here, however: the conflict between a man's loyalty to his father and his wife is not as acute as that between his loyalty to his mother and his wife, because the father is not in as intimate a relationship as the mother with the daughter-in-law, and chances of quarrelling are therefore less.

In addition to tensions arising out of interpersonal relations, tensions may also arise because of alleged or real interference by the parents in the relationship between their son and his wife. Further, if the father has married a second wife, tensions are very acute between the son by the first wife and his stepmother, and also between him and his father.

In those households in which parents have unmarried children along with a married son, tensions may develop between the daughter-in-law and her unmarried *diyer* (husband's younger brother) and *nanand* (husband's sister). As long as the *diyer* and *nanand* are very young they are not a problem, but as soon as they begin to understand the relationships in the household, say, after their ninth or tenth year, they become a source of trouble for the *bhabhi* (brother's wife) and, therefore, her husband. While the *bhabhi* has a joking relationship with the *diyer* and the *nanand*, they are a source of tension for the *bhabhi* because of their loyalty to their parents. The *bhabhi* has always to see that she does not hurt their feelings even in her jokes, otherwise they would complain about it to their parents. They watch her actions in the absence of the parents, in and outside the house, and report them to the parents. The joking relationship exists alongside a respect relationship: the *bhabhi* on the one hand, and the *diyer* and *nanand* on the other, have to address each other respectfully in the plural. What is remarkable is that the *bhabhi* has to show respect toward the *diyer* and *nanand* even though they may be much younger, sometimes younger than even her own children. The *bhabhi* can usually tolerate the *nanand* because, after all, the *nanand* will marry and go away to her husband's village. A young *diyer,* on the other hand, is a potential rival; the *bhabhi*'s relationship with him becomes subject to further tension after his marriage.

In the four households in Table 7 where there is a widower father, the daughter-in-law is free not only from the authority of the mother-in-law but also from much of the control by the father-in-law, which he exerted through his wife. Conversely, the widowed father-in-law lacks influence not only because of the absence of his wife but also because of the avoidance relation between him and his daughter-in-law. He is also dependent on the daughter-in-law for many things in the house.

In two of the three households in Table 7 a widowed mother is the housekeeper for a widower son and his children. Thus the grandmother, as well as the father, performs some of the functions of mother toward the young children. In the third household the widowed mother is too old to look after the housekeeping, and her widowed daughter has come along with her children to look after her mother, brother, and brother's children.

In my census there is no household where a widower father and his young unmarried children live with his married son and his wife, but such households existed in the past in Radhvanaj and exist at the present in other villages in Charotar. They are much like the households mentioned in Table 6, but with the difference that the father restrains his eldest son and his wife from exercising their authority over the son's unmarried siblings. The daughter-in-law in such a household has to assume the role of mother toward her husband's younger siblings. This is considered to be a difficult thing to do, and in many cases the father tries to send his young children to be brought up under the loving care of their mother's brother, mother's father, mother's sister, or father's sister. If, however, a woman is able to combine the role of elder brother's wife and of mother, she is highly respected in the society as an exceptional person.

It is significant that in Radhvanaj there is not a single household in which a widowed daughter-in-law lives with her parents-in-law or brothers-in-law, and I have not found any such household in other villages in Charotar. She either goes back to her parental home or sets up a separate household with her children in the conjugal village, because with the loss of her husband she loses protection from the authority of in-laws in her husband's home.

In households composed of two or more married sons, which are shown in Table 9, tensions exist not only between parents and each son and his wife but also between brothers and between their wives (*derani* and *jethani*), and there are further irritations in households which also have unmarried sons and daughters: a younger son has to remain under the authority of not only his parents but also his elder brother or brothers, and a younger daughter-in-law has to remain under the authority of not only her mother-in-law but also her *jethani* — perhaps not one but even two or three *jethănis*. The occupation of the household — agriculture, trade, craft, or service — has to be organized to the satisfaction of each brother, and the numerous household chores have to be organized to the satisfaction of the mother-in-law and each daughter-in-law. The necessities — food, clothing, mattress, medicine, recreation, and so on — for everyone in the household have to be met. In sitting, speaking, eating, and many other "trivial" things of life, a number of rules of etiquette and ethics (all subsumed under

44

the term "proper conduct") have to be observed by each member toward all the others. Everyone in the household has his own likes and dislikes, habits, tastes, and idiosyncracies. The daughters-in-law differ markedly from their husbands and parents-in-law. Each son has his own cluster of affinal relatives (unless two sisters are married to two brothers); his and his wife's and children's relations with them have to be adjusted to their relations with other members of the household. It is impossible to describe here the complicated life of a complex household of parents and two or more married sons in all its detail. Either actual living in such a household, or reading biographies, novels, stories and folktales (particularly in the local language), and detailed descriptions of family disputes, like the one published by Srinivas (1952b), can provide some idea of the tensions I am referring to here.

Partition of Households of Parents and Married Sons
Whether it is a household of parents and one married son or of parents and more than one married son, there is always a possibility of the tensions rising to such a height as to lead to the partition of the household. That is to say, sons may start living separately from their parents. In the case of thirty-eight out of fifty-nine households cited in Tables 7 and 8, each parental unit (father, or mother, or father and mother) has only one married son and he lives with it, but in the case of the remaining twenty-one households, although each parental unit actually has two or more married sons, only one married son lives with the parental unit while each of the other sons has a separate household. Similarly, each of the fifteen parental units of the households in Table 9 has more than one married son, but only in twelve cases do all the married sons live with their parental units; that is, in the case of three parental units one or more of the married sons live in separate households. Thus, taking all the thirty-six parental units that have two or more married sons, in twelve cases all the married sons live with their respective parental unit, while in twenty-four cases

45

one or more of the married sons live separately from their respective parental unit. In fourteen out of the twenty-four cases, each parental unit has one separated son, in eight cases two separated sons, and in two cases three separated sons — thus making a total of thirty-six married sons each living separately from his parents as well as from his married brothers.

Whereas in the households of Tables 7, 8, and 9 each parental unit has one or more married sons residing with it, there are seventeen other parental units (included in the simple households cited in Table 18; see Chapter 4) with which none of the married sons resides. In twelve cases each parental unit has one married son, in four cases two married sons, and in one case four married sons, thus making a total of twenty-six married sons each living separately from his parents as well as from his brothers.

Table 10 shows the number of parental units living in single or separate households from their married sons. In 76 per cent of the cases of parental units with one married son each the parental unit and the married sons form a single household, while in only 24 per cent of the cases the parental unit and the married son live in separate households. On the other hand, only in 29.27 per cent of the cases of parental units with two or more married sons each all the married sons live with the parental unit in a single household, while in 70.73 per cent of the cases all or some of the married sons live separately from the parental unit. This shows that a married son may live separately from his parents even though he is their only married son, but such separation is much less frequent than in the case of parents having more than one married son. Tensions existing in a household composed of a parental unit and its only married son do not generally go to such an extent that the household breaks into two, whereas tensions existing in a household composed of two or more married sons frequently reach such a height that the household breaks into two or more separate households.

Table 10

Relations between Parental Unit and Married Sons

Category of Relation	Parental Units		Married Sons
	Number	Percent	Number
Parental units with only one married son	50	100·00	50
Parental unit and the married son living in a single household	38[a]	76·00	38
Parental unit and the married son living in separate households	12[b]	24·00	12
Parental units with two or more married sons	41	100·00	103
Parental unit and all the married sons forming a single household	12[c]	29·27	27
Parental unit and one married son forming a single household;	21[a]	51·22	21
with other married sons residing in separate households			31
Parental unit and two or more married sons forming a single household;	3[c]	7·32	7
with other married sons residing in separate households			5
All the married sons living in separate households	5[b]	12·19	12

[a] Included in Tables 7 and 8.

[b] Included in Table 18.

[c] Included in Table 9. These three cases are included in both single and partitioned household categories, thus making a total of 44 parental units with two or more married sons, in Tables 11, 13, 14, and 15.

We have seen, in the discussion of atypical households, that co-residence of married brothers after the death of their parents is an ideal norm — a desirable but not expected mode of behaviour — in Radhvanaj. This is not true, however, of the co-residence of married brothers during their parents' lifetime, and it is even less true when the parents have only one married son. Both these types of residence are held by the villagers to be expected modes of behaviour. But the problem is that, along with these two norms about the formations of households there are also norms governing the relations between persons forming part of the household — between father and son, mother and son, husband and wife, mother-in-law and daughter-in-law, *derani* and *jethani,* and so on. These norms are not always consistent with each other. Each person in the household has to enact several roles at the same time, and he is not always able to harmonize the expected modes of behaviour of all the roles. Hence tensions and conflicts arise, and therefore, the partition of the household during the lifetime of parents, that is, the non-observance of the overall norm. The frequency of non-observance is greater in the case of a unit consisting of parents and more than one married son than in the case of a unit consisting of parents and only one married son.

Factors Affecting Co-Residence
of Parents and Their Only Married Son

In this section we shall make a more detailed analysis of the factors encouraging parents and their only married son to reside in a single household and those encouraging partition of such a household. In the next section we shall do the same with regard to units of parents and two or more married sons. We shall thus obtain a deeper understanding of the developmental pattern of households and the operation of the principle of residential unity of patrikin and their wives.

The households in which the parental unit and its only married son live together can be classified into two categories mainly on the basis of age of married son, existence of unmarried sons, and existence of grandchildren. First, the married son may be one of several children of his parents, and if the children include more than one son the married son is usually the eldest, except among the Khedawal Brahmans. Generally he is young (between sixteen and twenty-five years old) and has not yet become a father: out of twenty-one households of this category, in four households the married son has children and in seventeen he does not. The daughter-in-law in a household of this category spent only a short time after marriage, not sufficient for intense tensions to develop, and there is also a positive norm that the daughter-in-law should be extremely docile during the first few years after marriage. At the same time, the son is under the firm authority of his parents. There are therefore very few chances of such a household partitioning. Of the twelve cases of partition of parental units with one married son, mentioned in Table 10, only in four cases does the son belong to the phase described here. In one case the son's mother is dead and the father has married again; separation between father and son in such a situation is considered quite normal. In another case the son is separated from his widowed mother but his father's widowed sister lives with him. In this case separation has taken place because of tensions not only between the mother on the one hand and the son and his wife on the other but also between the mother and her husband's sister, that is, between *bhabhi* and *nanand*. I have no information about the circumstances in which partition took place in the remaining two cases.

If the parents in a household of the category discussed above have an unmarried son in addition to the married one, it would become after the former's marriage a household of parents and more than one married son. However, in some cases the parents may not have an unmarried son in addition to the married one: either no other son was born, or if born, was dead. In these cases, the only married son usually continues to live with his parents. In such households, which form our second category, generally the parental unit is old or middle-aged, while the son is about to reach middle age and has children of his own. In nine out of seventeen households of this category the parental unit is constituted of the widowed mother, in four cases, of the widowed father, and in four cases, of father and mother. In thirteen cases the married son has children, and in four cases, no children. A crucial factor that keeps the tensions in control in these households is the son's strong sentiment that, being the only son of his parents, he should properly look after them in their old age, putting up with or ignoring the annoyances they cause, and a reciprocal sentiment on the parents' part that the son is their only legal and ritual descendant, and his annoyances should therefore be tolerated.

The strength of these sentiments is much less if the son's mother has died and the father has married another wife, or if the son is not a natural son but has been adopted. In eight cases the son belonging to the phase described here is separated from the parents, but in three of them he is a stepson or an adopted son. In the remaining five cases separation has taken place between parents and their own only son. Such separation is strongly disapproved by the people, and when it takes place the parents as well as the son and his wife become the targets of criticism.

Factors Affecting Co-residence
of Parents and Two or More Married Sons

The ideal is for all the married sons to live together in a single household with the parental unit. However, as was already mentioned, the fact that in only 12 out of 41 units of this kind do all the married sons live together with parents while the other twenty-nine have split up, speaks for itself. Nevertheless, it is significant that only in 5 of the 29 cases has "complete" partition taken place, that is, each of the married sons is living separately from the others and from his parents. In 21 cases at least one of the sons continues to live with his parents, and the other sons live separately; and in 3 cases, two or more sons live with parents and the remaining one or two live separately. These figures confirm the existence of a general feeling among the villagers that although sons may not get along well with each other in a household and partition becomes inevitable, at least one of the sons should remain with the parents to look after them in their old age. This fact, in turn, confirms the point made earlier that it is easier for a married man and his wife to live with his parents as long as he is the only married son in the household than when they have to live with his married brothers.

At what phase in the developmental process does the partition of a household of parents and two or more married sons take place? There seem to be several influential factors: when two or more married sons have children; after the marriage of the last sibling; and after the death of the father.

Table 11 contrasts the single and partitioned households of parental units and two or more married sons according to the numbers of married sons with children. Of the fourteen cases without two sets of children, in more than two-thirds the parents and all the married sons live in a single household, whereas in only a sixth of the cases with two or more sets of children, the parental unit and the married sons live in a single household. To put it another way, two-thirds of the single households have grandchildren by only one son or no grandchildren, and almost seven-eighths of the partitioned households have two or more sets of grandchildren. From this evidence it may be

Table 11

Relation of Number of Sons with Children to Co-residence of Parental Unit and Two or More Married Sons

Parental Units with Two or More Married Sons	Single Household	Partitioned Household	Total
No married son with children	1	0	1
One married son with children and one or two married sons without children	9	4	13
Two married sons with children and one married son without children	2	0	2
All married sons with children	3	25	28
Totals	15	29	44

inferred that two or more married sons of a parental unit tend to remain in a single household when none of them or only one of them has children, whereas partition tends to occur when two or more of them have children. This inference is related to three observable phenomena. First, it takes time for the newly wedded wife of the second son to become entrenched in the household and to begin to raise her voice against other members. Second, quarrels arise between brothers, and particularly between their wives, over their children. And third, quarrels arise over unequal disbursement of the joint income of the household between the emergent parental families. On the one hand the rules of inheritance lay emphasis on equality between brothers, but on the other hand the requirements of each brother and his wife and children may be unequal for various reasons — even such physical factors as the number of children and their age and health create inequality — and the brothers may therefore consume the joint income of the household in unequal proportion. Finally, with the birth of children the husband and wife acquire a new interest and an ambition to work for a future household for themselves and their married sons.

As for the twenty-four cases in which some of the married sons remain with parents while others live separately, we have to ask: who remains with parents and who moves out? It can be seen from Table 12 that when it becomes impossible for all the married sons to live under the same roof and one or two of them have to move out, it is mostly the eldest son or elder sons who move out (seven-eighths of the cases) while the younger sons continue to live with parents.

The fact that of the forty-one parental units with two or more married sons there are twelve cases of co-residence of the parental unit and all its married sons shows that partition of such a household is not a general phenomenon, which in turn means that it is not a general custom in this village for every eldest son to set up a separate household soon after his marriage. Partition may or may not take place when the parents are alive; if it does take place, then normally the eldest son moves out to

Table 12

*Relation of Age of Married Sons to Partition of Households of Parental Unit
and Two or More Married Sons*

Category of Relation	Cases
The youngest married son resides with the parental unit, and the elder married sons reside in separate households.	19
Four younger married sons reside with the parental unit, and the eldest married son resides in a separate household.	1
Two younger married sons reside with the parental unit, and three elder married sons reside in separate households.	1
The eldest or the second married son resides with the parental unit, and the remaining married sons reside in separate households.	2
Two elder married sons reside with the parental unit, and the youngest married son resides in a separate household.	1
Total	24[a]

[a] See Table 10.

set up a separate household and the youngest sons continue to
live with their parents. I must confess that I did not observe
this pattern of household partition when I was in the field; it is
the quantitative analysis of my data after coming back from
the field that has revealed the pattern. I am therefore unable to
relate this pattern of household partition in a definite way with
other phenomena observed in the field.

Another factor affecting partition of a complex household has
already been indicated. Two or more married brothers tend to
live together if they have unmarried brothers and sisters, and
they tend to break off when all the brothers and sisters are
married, as shown in Table 13. The existence of unmarried
sons and daughters is not considered to be an insurmountable

53

problem. After all, they continue to live with the parents, provision can be made for the expense of their marriage, and final partition of property can be postponed.

Table 13

Relation of Unmarried Siblings to Co-residence of Parental Unit and Two or More Married Sons

Parental Unit with Two or More Married Sons	Single Household	Partitioned Household	Total
Unmarried siblings	8	9	17
All siblings married	7	20	27
Totals	15	29	44

It has also been mentioned earlier that as long as either parent is alive they tend to serve as a binding force among their sons, and that brothers tend to separate when this force is removed. There is some difference, however, in the influence of the father and the mother. The figures in Table 14 show that a household composed of a parental unit and two or more married sons is more likely to be partitioned when the parental unit is the widowed mother than when it is the father and mother or

Table 14

Relation of Death of Parent to Co-residence of Parental Unit and Two or more Married Sons

Parental Unit with Two or More Married Sons	Single Household	Partitioned Household	Total
Father and mother	7	9	16
Widowed father	1	3	4
Widowed mother	7	17	24
Totals	15	29	44

the widower father. The main reason for this is that after the father's death the eldest brother becomes the head of the household, and his dominant position is shared by his wife. This change in the authority structure of the household heightens the tensions existing between brothers, between their wives, and between mother-in-law and the senior daughter-in-law, which in turn encourages partition of the household. As Srinivas has suggested, "the moral authority of the eldest brother or mother is *much less* than that of the father. It is only where the eldest brother is very senior to the others, and is also a man of exceptional character, that he commands the same moral authority as the father" (1952b, p. 29, italics mine). The figures presented here, however, suggest that the moral authority of the mother or the eldest brother is not as much less than that of the father as Srinivas's statement suggests, at least as far as household composition is concerned.

I have considered above three situations, each one separately, affecting co-residence of the parental unit and two or more married sons: (1) when the parental unit is the widowed mother rather than the father and mother or the widower father, (2) when all the children of the parental unit are married, and (3) when two or more married sons have children. Table 15 shows all the possible combinations of the three situations and gives their frequency in single and partitioned households.

All the households with these three situations are partitioned, and there is no single household with these three situations. That is to say, the largest number of partitions have taken place in those cases where the father is dead, all the children are married, and two or more married sons have children. In contrast, in only one case has partition taken place even though the father is alive, not all the children are married, and only one son has children. Of the remaining fifteen cases of partition, in eight cases two situations are combined, and in seven cases only one situation has been sufficient to bring about partition. It is significant that in twelve of the fifteen cases the existence of two or more sons with children is a constant factor, and in nine cases partition has occurred despite the existence of the father. The father's death (seventeen cases) is a less potent factor in partition than the marriage of all the children (twenty cases), which in turn is less potent than two or more married sons' having children (twenty-five cases).

Almost the same pattern emerges from households that have remained together. All but two possible combinations of the three situations are almost equally represented in Table 15. The effects of two situations, namely, the existence of the father and of unmarried children, in keeping a household united are almost evenly balanced (8 cases each). The inclusion of one or no married son having children in a household is again the factor with preponderating influence (11 cases).

To conclude: There is an overall norm that parents and all their married sons should live in a single household. It is supported not only by custom but also by religious scriptures. At the same time, however, all kinds of tensions arise in such a household that lead to the disregard of the overall norm. There is an important compromise with the overall norm: at least one son should remain with parents, thus avoiding complete dissolution of the parental household. Even this norm is disregarded in some cases. However, it is significant that there is always a considerable number of households showing the observance of the overall norm. In these households all, or a majority of the members are seized by the ideal of joint living and are prepared to endure a number of hardships and irritations for the sake of the ideal.

It has already been pointed out that after the parents' death, brothers may continue to form a joint unit for property and production even though they cease to live in a joint household. This is much more true of relations between brothers whose parents are alive. When a son sets up a separate household, he of course gets some household equipment and some cash and jewellery from the parental household, but the dwelling into which he moves may or may not become exclusively his own property. He may be allotted a few rooms in the parental house

Table 15

Relation of Combinations of Situations to Co-residence of Parental Unit and Two or More Married Sons

Situations	Parental Units with Two or More Married Sons		
	Single Household	Partitioned Household	Total
Father dead; all children married; two or more married sons with children	0	13	13
Father dead; some children married; two or more married sons with children	0	3	3
Father dead; all children married; no more than one married son with children	3	1	4
Father dead; some children married; no more than one married son with children	4	0	4
Father alive; all children married; two or more married sons with children	2	4	6
Father alive; all children married; no more than one married son with children	2	2	4
Father alive; some children married; two or more married sons with children	2	5	7
Father alive; some children married; no more than one married son with children	2	1	3
Totals	15	29	44

or another building owned by the parents. The ownership rights over it may remain with the coparcenary of father and all his sons, and not be transferred to the seceding son at the time of his separation. He may also not take any separate land for his own cultivation or set up a separate unit for the production of crafts or for the supply of services. That is to say, he may start living separately not because of dissatisfaction with the management of property and production but from dissatisfaction with the management of kitchen and other items of household expenditure and with the lack of harmony of temperaments in the household. He may only want to avoid the continuous "heart-burning" which he would suffer from if he remained a member in the household. Property and production may be managed on a commercial basis, which is not unusual in a region, such as Gujarat, dominated by commercial culture.

Summary

In the preceding sections I have tried to examine the relation between four factors: (1) overall norms about the formation of households, (2) numerical frequencies of the households of various types of composition, (3) patterns of interrelationships among members of each type of household, and (4) life-cycle events and other demographic phenomena. The most general norm about the formation of households is the principle of the residential unity of patrikin and their wives. The operation of this norm begins, for most of the simple households, with the first marriage of a son in the household. The norm that one or more married sons of a pair of parents should live together with them as long as either or both parents are alive is a strong ideal, but observance of the norm varies according to whether the parents have only one married son or more than one married son. These two situations are demographic in origin but social in operation. In the second situation, the partiton of the household during the lifetime of the parents occurs usually only if at least one son continues to live with them. As a result, the majority of complex households based on the principle of residential unity of patrikin and their wives, have each only one married son in addition to the parental unit. There are only a few households composed of a married man and his unmarried brothers and sisters staying after the death of their parents, because the demographic factors necessary for their existence occur but rarely, not because either the norm for such co-residence is weak or the tensions are great. The principle of the residential unity of patrikin and their wives becomes extremely weak when both the parents are dead and all the sons and daughters are married. While such households are demographically possible, very few do exist as a matter of actual fact. It is difficult to decide whether the norm is weak because the tensions are insurmountable, or vice versa.

Complex Households vis-a-vis Emigrant Households

This section is a brief intervention pointing out the implications of the above analysis of complex households *vis-a-vis* the question of independent and linked emigrant households mentioned in Chapter 2. I stated there that the relation between an emigrant household's remaining independent or linked with a village household and its place in the kinship structure is a reflection of the established pattern of kinship relations in the village. Just as in the village, married brothers do not live in a complex household after the death of their parents, the household of each of the three emigrant men having married brothers but not parents is independent (Table 4: A-iii). Kinship relationship beyond this phase is considered "distant" in the context of household formation; accordingly each of the seven emigrant households having no "near" kin in the village is independent (Table 4: A-iv). Just as most cases of parents with only one married son in the village have complex households, of the five emigrant households each forming part of a unit of parents and one married son, four are linked and one is independent (Table 4: B-iii, A-i). It has been pointed out that when a man takes another wife after the death of the first, the parents and the first wife's son live in separate households: this is exactly what has happened in the case of the independent household just mentioned. Finally, it has been shown that there is a low frequency of households of a parental unit with two or more married sons. In the same way, in the case in which the emigrant man has parents and married brothers there is low frequency of linked households: of seventeen such emigrant men, nine have independent households each separated from the households of parents and brothers (see Table 4: A-ii), one is separated from brothers but linked with parents (see Table 4: B-v), and seven are each linked with parents and brothers (see Table 4: B-iv).

It should be noted that in the case of some of the complex households included in Tables 5–9, what is considered to be one household is in fact divided into two or more households, one residing in the village and one or more outside the village. Tables 7 and 8 include five such integrated groups: four are each constituted of one household of parents in the village and the other of a married son outside the village, and one is constituted of a bachelor son in the village and the parents and a married son in the town. Table 9 includes five integrated groups: two are each constituted of parents in the village and two married sons in two different places outside the village; two are each constituted of parents and one married son in the village and another married son outside the village; and one is constituted of parents and two married sons in the village and another married son outside the village. As stated in Chapter 2, any macro-study of the family in India should treat the pattern of interrelations between linked and village households as an overall network linking villages and towns with each other, but I have ignored this fact and have considered the integrated group as if the whole of it is resident in the village, because the focus of my study is the village.

It has been mentioned in Chapter 1 that if the 36 emigrant households (both independent and linked) were excluded, there were 263 households residing in Radhvanaj at the time of my census. Of these, 174 (66.16 per cent) were simple, and 89 (33.84 per cent) complex. If the emigrant households are included and the integrated units of linked and village households are regarded as households of the village, there would be

192 (67.84 per cent) simple and 91 (32.16 per cent) complex households. There would thus be a slight decline in the percentage of complex households, because the majority of the independent emigrant households were simple. At the same time, the percentage of the complex households of the type shown in Table 9 would go up and that of the households of the type shown in Tables 7 and 8 would go down. In other words, the inclusion of emigrant households would show greater importance of households composed of parents and two or more married sons, and lesser importance of households composed of parents and one married son.

Reversal of the Principle of Residential Unity of Patrikin and Their Wives: "Core" and "Accretion" in Complex Households

It has been mentioned in Chapter 1, and it is also implicit in the discussion of complex households so far, that a woman leaves her parental home after her marriage and goes to live in her conjugal home. It may also be recalled that this rule has been considered a part of the principle of residential unity of patrikin and their wives. In certain circumstances, however, a married woman may return to her parental home, she may even take her husband and children with her, and after her death her children may go there. On the other hand, a woman may take some members of her paternal kin group to her conjugal home. Seventeen complex households in my census of Radhvanaj include one or more such relatives, which show what may be called the reversal of the principle of residential unity of patrikin and their wives.[3]

[3] Just as men, women, and children who ought to have lived in other villages according to the principle of the residential unity of patrikin and their wives have come to live in Radhvanaj by the reversal of the principle, in the same way men, women, and children who ought to have lived in Radhvanaj have gone out to live in other places. Some have gone permanently and others temporarily. None have been recorded as members of the households of Radhvanaj, although I have recorded them in genealogies and shall consider

In four of the seventeen cases, a widowed daughter or her children, or both, have come to live with one or both of her parents. In one of the four cases, a widowed daughter has come to live with her old widowed mother in order that they may support one another. On the one hand, the old lady does not have any other child or other near relative to whom she may turn for care in her old age, and on the other, the daughter is prohibited from remarrying by caste custom, and she cannot live with members of her husband's parental home because there would be nobody to restrain them in exercising their authority over her. In the second case an old widow has called a bachelor son of her daughter to live with her, while the daughter herself lives with her husband and other sons in a nearby town. (The old lady's only son died in his youth leaving a young widow, who consequently went back to her parental home and renounced her legal right to inherit her husband's property. The daughter's son then came to look after the old lady and inherit her property.) In the third case an old widow lives with a widowed daughter and a young son of another daughter, who lives with her husband and other children in another village. The boy has been called in order to look after the two widows and inherit their property. In the fourth case an old widow lives with a widowed daughter and her two sons, one married, and the other unmarried. In all four cases the relationship between a daughter or her children on the one side and her parents on the other is one of affection and not one of jural rights and duties, and therefore mutual adjustment does not pose a serious problem.

them in other contexts. It may only be noted that the temporary emigrants are similar to linked emigrants described in Chapter 2 but are not included among them.

I must make it clear that I have discussed only the problem of co-residence of certain kinds of relatives in a single household. I have not considered the relation between such relatives staying in separate households either in the same village or in different villages, including, for example, mutual exchange of gifts and help between them in ordinary circumstances.

In three cases, a widowed sister has come to live with her brother's family. In one, an old widowed sister is living with her brother and his wife and their sons, married as well as unmarried. In another, an old widow lives in a household which includes her mother, brother's wife, and his married and unmarried children. And in the third, a widowed sister lives with her brother and his young son. The brother has driven his wife out of his home and sent her to her parents' home on account of quarrels between his sister and his wife, that is between *nanand* and *bhabhi*. The brother, in his conflicting loyalties to the wife and the sister, chose to side with the sister and not with the wife. I found during my later visit to the village (January 1962) that the wife had come back to the husband as a result of reconciliation brought about by friends and relatives. Such a husband is indeed rare, but the case shows clearly that when a widowed or divorced sister returns to live with her brother, tension prevails between her and her brother's wife, and that the brother has a difficult time maintaining friendly relations with his wife as well as sister.

In one case, a divorced daughter and her children live with her parents, but her brother and his wife live in a separate household because of conflict between *nanand* and *bhabhi* as well as between parents and the son and his wife — one of the cases of separation between parents and the single married son mentioned above.

In one case, the brother with whom the sister and her son have come to live is a widower with two small children, and there is in addition the brother's (as well as the sister's) old, disabled, widowed mother. The widowed sister is therefore the chief housekeeper, looking after not only her own son but also her mother and brother's children. In this household there is no problem of conflict between *nanand* and *bhabhi*.

In two cases, a widow is being looked after by her brother's son (*bhatrijo*) and his wife. This shows that a widow may be looked after not only by her parents and brothers but, in their absence, also by her brother's sons. In one of the two cases,

while the man and his wife live with his father's sister (*foi*),
his own widowed mother lives in a separate household with her
young children — another instance of conflict between *nanand*
and *bhabhi* and between mother-in-law and daughter-in-law.

In three cases, the sister's children are living with her mother's
brother. In one case, three young children, after the death of
their mother, have come to live with their mother's widowed
mother and two mother's brothers, one married and the other
unmarried. In the second case, a nephew, aged fifteen, has come
to live with his mother's brother even though his parents are
alive, but I do not know the reasons for this. Similarly, I do
not have any information about the third household in which
a young nephew lives with his mother's brother. Generally
nephews and nieces come to live in their maternal uncle's home
for short periods of time, usually until they come of age or
until they complete the period of informal apprenticeship in the
traditional occupation of the caste.

In all the fourteen cases described above, a woman or her children, or both, have come to live in her parents' or brother's home.
There is, however, one case, and the only one of its kind, in
which not only a daughter and her children but also her husband are staying with his wife's widowed mother. The son-in-
law, a policeman, lives in his place of work and visits his wife,
children, and mother-in-law in Radhvanaj, and also his native
place where he has his kinsmen and some property. During my
later visit to the village (January 1962), he was planning to
retire from his job and settle down in his mother-in-law's home.
An uxorilocal son-in-law like this one is called *ghar-jamai* (lit.,
son-in-law in one's own home). This case of uxorilocality is,
however, qualified by the fact that it followed virilocality,
because all marriages are initially virilocal.

Cases of uxorilocal sons-in-law are few and far between.
First of all, when a couple has a son they naturally do not think
of inviting the son-in-law to stay with them: the son is their
rightful heir, successor, and supporter in old age. In all the
cases of *ghar-jamai* I know of in central Gujarat, the parents-in-

law do not have a son. Second, the relationship between father-in-law and son-in-law is one of mutual respect and avoidance, and each is always an honoured guest in the other's home. What is significant is that the son-in-law receives respectful treatment even though he is much younger. He would lose this respect if he settled down in his affinal home. Third, although the relationship between mother-in-law and son-in-law is also one of mutual respect and avoidance, it is somewhat freer than that between the father-in-law and son-in-law. Thus, in most cases of *ghar-jamai* the son-in-law goes to live in his affinal home if his mother-in-law is a widow, or when the father-in-law is so old that he is almost completely dependent on the son-in-law.

Finally, there are two cases in which a man's wife has brought a member of her parental home to live with her in her conjugal home: in one case, her brother's young daughter (with a view to performing her *kanyadan* ritual), and in the other, her old widower father. Cases of members of a woman's parental home going to live with members of her conjugal home are much fewer than cases of a woman and her husband and children going to live with members of her parental home. A woman acquires certain rights in her conjugal kin group at her marriage, but she also retains certain rights in her parental kin group of which she was a full-fledged member before marriage. These rights are shared by her children and to a certain extent by her husband. But the members of her parental kin group acquire few rights over members of her conjugal kin group, except over herself and to a certain extent over her children. This demonstrates how the patrilineal principle dominates even when the principle of the residential unity of patrikin and their wives is reversed.

It is rare indeed for a woman's father to go and live with his son-in-law. First, among the more Sanskritized groups in central Gujarat there is a belief that a bride is given away as a *dan* (gift), and just as one does not derive any material benefit from a thing given as a gift, one should not receive anything from one's daughter. Some parents do not even drink water in their daughter's home, let alone think of living there. This objection applies also to the elder brothers of a girl, particularly if they officiated at her *kanyadan* ritual, and also to any other relative who has performed the ritual in the absence of the girl's parents and brothers. The *kanyadan* ritual is common to upper caste Hindus all over India, but it is interpreted in the above manner only in the north where a girl's break with her natal kin is more extreme than in the south. It is also important to note that the father-in-law and, to a lesser extent, the mother-in-law find it difficult to adjust themselves in their son-in-law's home, mainly because, as was mentioned earlier, they have to show respect to him even though he is much younger. Thus, cases of fathers-in-law staying with their sons-in-law are fewer than those of sons-in-law staying with their fathers-in-law. Again, cases of fathers-in-law staying with their sons-in-law are fewer than cases of mothers-in-law staying with their sons-in-law.

Although in my census there is only one case of a child going to live with his father's sister, and there is no case of a younger brother going to live with his elder sister, I know of the existence of several such cases in the near past in Radhvanaj and at the present time in other villages. The relationship between brother and sister and between brother's child (*bhatrijo*) and father's sister (*foi*) is an affectionate one. The nephew may stay with his *foi* while going through his school or undergoing his informal apprenticeship, but very rarely does he settle down there for good. First of all, there are few chances of the nephew inheriting the *foi*'s property, and second, the nephew's kin group ought to give shelter to the *foi*'s affinal group and not vice versa.

When a man, woman, or child comes to live in a household by a reversal of the principle of the residential unity of patrikin and their wives, the incoming persons may be called "accretions" while the persons with whom they come to live may be called the "core" of the household. The accretions are usually simple units, a widowed or divorced woman and her husband and her unmarried children. In only one of the seventeen cases considered here is the accreting unit a complex one (see Table 16). Five of the seventeen core units are complex, based on the principle of the residential unity of patrikin and their wives and included in Tables 5–7. They may be considered to have become more complex by the accretion of simple units. In twelve cases the core units are simple: three husband-wife couples, three full parental families, one father-son unit, and five old widows. Eleven of them are combined with simple accreting units and have thus become complex, and one is combined with a complex accreting unit, thus making the household even more complex.

Table 16

Types of Core and Accretion in Reversals of the Principle of Residential Unity

Type of " Core "	Type of " Accretion "	Households
Simple	Simple	11
Simple	Complex *a*	1
Complex *a*	Simple	5
Total		17

a Included in Tables 7, 8, and 9.

Of the total number of 91 complex households in Radhvanaj, the kinship composition of 74 is based solely on the principle of residential unity of patrikin and their wives, 11 are complex only because of the inclusion of accretions, and 6 are complex in both ways. This means that out of 80 complex households included in Tables 5–9, 74 are based solely on the principle of the residential unity of patrikin and their wives, and 6 are complex in both ways. The frequencies of households of these three types are shown in Table 17. The term "complex household" thus covers households based on the observance of the principle of residential unity of patrikin and their wives as well as those based on the reversal of the principle. Our description has shown that both types form part of the entire dynamics of kinship and marriage in Indian society. They should not be considered as exceptional and therefore insignificant for the taxonomy of households in India.

Table 17

Bases of Composition of Complex Households

Bases of Composition	Complex Households
Principle of residential unity of patrikin and their wives	74
Reversal of the principle	11
Combination of the above two	6
Total	91

It is also noteworthy that the complex households based on the observance of the principle of residential unity of patrikin and their wives covers a wide range of kinship compositions: at one end the household may be composed of a man, his wife, and his widowed father or mother, and at the other end the household may be composed of two or more married brothers and their wives and children with or without the brothers' parents.

4
Simple Households

There are 192 simple households in Radhvanaj. As noted in Chapter 2, 174 are resident households in the village and 18 are independent emigrant households. The classification of the 192 simple households according to the six types presented in Chapter 1 is shown in Table 18, and the households of each type are then taken up for detailed description.

Table 18

Classification of Simple Households by Type of Kinship Composition

	Households		
Composition	Resident in Radhvanaj	Independent Emigrant	Total
(i) Single man or woman	33	1	34
(ii) Unmarried brother, sister	1	0	1
(iii) Mother, unmarried children	9	0	9
(iv) Father, unmarried children	6	0	6
(v) Husband, wife	11	6	17
(vi) Husband, wife, unmarried children	114	11	125
Totals	174	18	192

Single-Member Households

The thirty-three single-member households resident in the village are each composed of an adult man or woman. Of these, twenty-one are either old widows or widowers; nine are young or middle-aged men who, though eligible for marriage or re-marriage, are not married or re-married for various reasons; one young man is married, but his wife has not joined him because of her extreme youth; one old man has driven out (though not divorced) his wife and children to her natal home because of her "misbehaviour"; and one middle-aged widow has returned to the village and is living the life of a wandering ascetic, only occasionally residing in her village home.

It is noteworthy that there is no young woman living alone in the village. It is only in large towns that young women pursuing careers are found living alone. In villages and small towns there is always someone to look after a young unmarried woman, and a woman may live by herself only in her old age. In lower castes the institution of remarriage of widowed and divorced women obviates the need for them to live alone; and in both higher and lower castes a young woman can always look forward to living with members of her parental kin group until she becomes old, when she is allowed to live by herself.

Three old men and seven old women live alone even though each of them has at least one near relative living in the village itself. Two of these three men have adult and married sons, while the third has no son but does have a married brother. Five of the seven women have married sons; the sons of the two other women died leaving widows and children, that is, the two women each have a daughter-in-law and grandchildren. The norms concerning the care of aged parents are quite strong, and the principles are adhered to in practice. Generally every father and mother expect that they will be looked after in their old age by their son. In the absence of a son, men look forward to the services of a son's son or a brother; women also look forward to the services of a son's son but not to services of the husband's brother. A man is not very much looked down on if he does not take care of his brother, but he becomes an object of severe criticism if he does not look after his aged parents. On the other side, an aged father or mother would consider it a misfortune not to be taken care of by their son. Widowed daughters-in-law and their children living separately from parents-in-law have been discussed above. The old men and women have to do most domestic chores themselves, but their near kin provide them with maintenance in cash and kind, take care of them during illness, and bring them to live in their households when they are disabled. There are also three other old or middle-aged persons residing in single-member households in the village who are taken care of by their "linked" near kin living outside the village and on that account are not included in Table 18.

All these old men and women are fortunate in that they have near kin, but there are five other old men and six old women without any near relative. Either no son was born to them, or sons were born but died before the parents became old. A few of them have daughters, but they have not been able to return to their natal homes with their husbands and children. The old men do not have other patrilineal kin such as grandsons or brothers to look after them, and the old women are unable to go back to their parental homes for various reasons. The old people themselves, as well as others, consider their lot an unhappy state of affairs. They have to do some work for their livelihood in addition to domestic chores at a time when they are physically declining. Moreover, men are required to do household work which they consider to be women's work and therefore degrading, and women have to do several things for which they are not generally trained in their youth. They frequently attribute the cause of their unhappiness to the religious doctrines of *maya, karma, dharma,* and so forth. There are always rival claims to the property of such old persons, and it is the claimants who take care of them during serious illness and arrange to perform funerary ceremonies.

Among the nine young or middle-aged men living in single-member households, two are considered to be unfit for marriage because of physical defects, and neither is fortunate enough to have near relatives. Two young men were divorced by their wives, who have since remarried; both these men have parents and brothers, but are living separately because of disputes with them. One man is a widower and is living alone because he has no near relative; his young son is being brought up by his wife's parental kin group. Finally, four men are victims of the social structure. They have not been able to marry because they have neither a near relative to help them get married nor enough money to pay for the bride price and other marriage expenses. They have a low status in their respective castes. The fact that they do not have parents or brothers is itself a disqualification for marriage. One young man living in an "independent" household outside the village is also in this category.

Brother-Sister Households

The one brother-sister household cited in Table 18 is a simple household of the rarest variety. The brother is aged fifteen, and the sister, twelve. They had lost their father a couple of years before the census, and the widow had eloped with a man of a lower caste soon after the husband's death. (Some villagers stated that she had died after elopement.) The dead man's property is managed by a distant agnate under the general supervision of the other members of the lineage. He provides money to the children for running the household. The boy is studying in the village school and is also learning to cultivate the family land under the supervision of his agnates. The girl has left the school and is doing all the household chores — most girls in the village have learned domestic chores by the time they are twelve.

A similar household of young unmarried children that came into existence because the eldest married brother and his wife proved incapable of looking after his younger brothers was cited in Chapter 3. I may describe here another case of neglected children that occurred during my field work. Soon after the death of her husband, a woman with two young children remarried a man having a job in a town and carried the children with her. But a few months later she came to the village, left the children with the village leaders, and went back. After much deliberation the leaders decided to hand over the children as well as their father's property to the care of a bachelor who was the father's distant cognatic relative. These three cases of neglected children show clearly the importance of the rule that children should live with their father's kin group even after the father's death or after the mother's death or divorce.

Mother and Unmarried Children Households

In each of the nine mother-children households mentioned in Table 18 the mother is a young or middle-aged widow. When a man dies leaving behind a widow and young children, she has not only to earn her livelihood, like widows living in single-member households, but also to support her children until they marry. When the children grow up they help the mother in earning. If the widowed mother has only daughters and no son, the daughters go away after marriage and the mother has to lead a lonely existence, unless a daughter comes back. If the widow has a son, he gradually becomes the chief earning member, marries, and takes over the position of the head of the household (see Chapter 3). For some period of time, however, the responsibility of running the household is shared by the mother and the adult son; they are jointly responsible for the care of the younger children and for getting them married. When the mother becomes old and all the children are married, she ceases to take much interest in the management of the household, although some intelligent and vigorous widows continue to guide household affairs until they are disabled. With the marriage of sons, tensions begin to develop between mother-in-law and daughter-in-law, between brothers, between their wives, and also between mother and son. As a result, some or all of the married sons live separately from the mother.

In eight of the nine cases considered here the widowed mothers have only unmarried children: in four cases a mother has one working son; in one case a working son in the village and another working son in town (both bachelors); in one case a working daughter; and in two cases no child is old enough to work. In the remaining case, the widow has one married son, but he lives in a separate household in the village, providing money to the mother to run her household. Two units constituted of a mother and her children living in the village and her husband living in a town are included among husband-wife-children households, and three units constituted of a mother and her children resident in the village and her married sons living in linked households outside the village are included in Tables 8 and 9.

Father and Unmarried Children Households

In five of the six father-children households the father is a widower, and in the sixth the wife is divorced and has remarried. In three cases the household includes at least one daughter capable of doing almost all the domestic chores a woman is required to do in village society. The daughters, however, will soon be married away, and if the father does not remarry, or if a son does not marry (where there is a son), the father and the son would have to do many feminine domestic chores. The remaining three households are such father-son households. After the son's marriage the father would look forward to receiving the care and service of the son and daughter-in-law and to becoming the head of the complex household. There is no father-daughter household, but in such a case the father would be left alone after the daughter's marriage.

Husband and Wife Households

In nine cases the husband and wife are old or middle-aged, and only in two are they young. Among the nine old or middle-aged couples, one couple has a married son living in a separate household in the village. In the case of another couple, the husband has no child by his present wife, but he has a son by the first wife who lives in a separate household in the village; the daughters of this couple are married and have joined their husbands. Two couples have no son but do have daughters who are married away; and five couples have no child at all. To have a son living separately from parents in their old age is considered to be unfortunate, but it is well known that among patrilineal Hindus not to have a son is considered a great misfortune, and not to have any child at all is an even greater misfortune. A daughter and her children and husband may be, to some extent, a surrogate for a son — the son-in-law may even be persuaded to become a *ghar-jamai* — but not to have a child at all means deprivation of even this source of solace. Among the six independent emigrant couples one is old (the husband's son by the first wife is living separately in the village), and five are young and expect to have children.

Husband, Wife and Unmarried Children Households

Among the 125 households composed of husband, wife, and unmarried children, that is, complete parental families, six are compound families. In the case of three of them, the husband's first wife is dead, he has married a second wife, and children by both the wives live together. In one case the dead wife has left children but there is no child by the second wife. In another case a widow has remarried and brought her children by the first husband with her. Finally, there is one leviratic union (*diyervatu*), where children by the first and the second husband live together.

Some of the 125 households include only sons, some only daughters, and some both sons and daughters, and the number of sons and daughters varies from household to household. Some couples may not get any more children in the future, some may get only sons, some only daughters, and some both sons and daughters, and again, the number of sons and daughters will vary from household to household. It may seem trivial to mention these simple facts, but they are important in the developmental process of households. If a couple has only daughters, they will all go away after their marriage and the household will never develop into a complex household. It has already been shown how the number of sons is an important factor in the development of complex households. Furthermore, it is important to realise that although for our definition of parental family it is sufficient to have only one child of either sex, in social reality parental families differ from one another because of differences in the sex and number of chidren. A parental family without any male child is definitionally complete but socially incomplete.

Simple Households and the Norm of
Co-residence of Parents and Married Sons

It is clear that the term "simple household" covers a considerable number of socially distinct types of kinship compositions. First of all, it is necessary to distinguish the simple households composed of the complete parental family from those composed of the various types of the incomplete parental family. The latter form a significant proportion of households in Radhvanaj: 34.89 per cent of the total number of simple households, and 23.67 per cent of the total number of households of all types in the village. I shall later consider the question of evidence for the frequency of such households for the whole of India, but I may mention here that the available evidence shows them as forming almost the same percentage in the whole country as in Radhvanaj. Second, it is necessary to recognize not only the six types mentioned in Table 18 but also to differentiate further certain of these types on the basis of sex and number of children.

In Radhvanaj the simple households of all types form 67.84 per cent, and the complex households of all types 32.16 per cent, of the total number of households. This is not, however, the surest measurement of the relative importance of the two types of households. It is also necessary to take into account, as I. P. Desai has pointed out (1955, p. 101), the number of people living in the households of each type. Accordingly, the simple households account for 56.45 per cent and the complex households 43.54 per cent of the total population of the village. Thus, the simple households are relatively more important than the complex households in the village community in both number of households and number of people residing in them.

It is necessary to keep one more consideration in mind while assessing the importance of the simple versus the complex households. Every simple household belongs to one of the phases in the developmental process along the line set by the principle of residential unity of patrikin and their wives. We have seen that among the series of norms subsumed by this principle, the co-residence of parents and married sons is the dominant norm in Radhvanaj. Every simple household belongs to one of the phases in the process of progression toward or regression from such a household. Table 19 shows the classification of simple

Table 19

Classification of Simple Households by Phases in Developmental Process

	Phase	Households
A	Simple household either composed of one man or headed by a man	$169+7^a$
	(i) Man's parents are alive but reside in a separate household, and he has no married son	53
	(ii) Man's parents are dead, and he has married sons residing in separate households	$7+2^a$
	(iii) Man has parents as well as married sons residing in separate households	2
	(iv) Man's parents are dead, and he has no married son	$107+5^a$
B	Simple household either composed of a widow or headed by a widow	$23+4^a$
	(i) Widow has married sons residing in separate households	6
	(ii) Widow has no married son	$17+4^a$
	Total	$192+11^a$

^{a} Taken from simple core units (see Table 16).

77

households according to the principal phases to which they belong.

In 68 cases the simple household is a result of partition of a household of parents and one or more married sons (19: A-i-iii, B-i). In other words, these households represent contravention of the dominant norm of co-residence of parents and married sons. In addition, among the eleven simple core units mentioned in the preceding chapter, the married sons of two men live in separate households.

The remaining 107 men (Table 19: A-iv) have lost their parents and have no married son of their own. Similarly, none of the remaining 17 widows (19: B-ii) has a married son. Thus, in 124 cases there is no question of the simple household living in contravention of the dominant norm of co-residence of parents and married sons at the present moment (19: A-iv, B-ii). In addition, there are five men and four women of this type among the eleven simple core units. Most of these 112 men and the husbands of most of these 21 widows must have married during the lifetime of their parents and lived with them in complex households for shorter or longer periods of time. It is also probable that some of them had separated from their parents, like the 55 men mentioned above. Most of these simple households would also become complex when their sons are married, though in a few cases the sons may be separated from them, like the 7 men mentioned above. All the same, the phenomena of sex, age, birth, death, marriage, and partition occur simultaneously in the society as a whole, and therefore there are always some men belonging to a phase when their parents are dead, brothers (if any) are separated, sisters (if any) are married away, and sons (if any) have not yet married, and similarly there are always some women whose husbands are dead, who cannot therefore reside with their parents-in-law or brother-in-law (if alive), and whose sons (if any) are not yet married. At the present time, the households that are simple because of the coincidence of certain demographic and social conditions form 64 per cent of the total number of simple households and 43.6 per cent of the total number of households of all types in the village.

The point is that, although the majority of the households in Radhvanaj are simple in composition and the majority of the population also reside in them, all of these simple households should not be considered as wilfully contravening the norm of joint residence of parents and married sons. In fact, for most of them the question of wilful contravention of the norm is irrelevant. This point is important because, as we shall see in Part II, there is a tendency in the literature on the family in India to consider the frequency of simple households as indicative of the strength or weakness of the norm of the residential unity of patrikin and their wives. The demographic as well as the developmental dimensions of the norm are frequently forgotten in making the assessment.

5

Conspectus: The Household, Other Social Structures, and Social Change

The Developmental Process of Households

It is clear from the previous chapters that every type of kinship composition of the household — from the simplest one-member to the most complex multi-member type — is significant in the household life of the people of Radhvanaj. The structure of the household relations becomes more complex as more categories of relatives are included. In a one-member household there is no relationship; in a two-member household there is one relationship; but in households of three or more, the addition of one relative means an addition of multiple relationships. For example, the addition of the son's wife to a simple household of father, mother, and son means the addition of relationships not only between the son and his wife but also between father-in-law and daughter-in-law and between mother-in-law and daughter-in-law. The addition of the son's wife to a household of father, mother, son, and one or more other children brings about a different configuration of relationships from that of her addition to a household of father, mother, son, and no other child, because of the additional relationships between the son's wife and her husband's younger brothers or sisters. In the same way, a household including one married son has a different configuration of relationships than a household including two or more married sons.

Each person in a household is involved in a complex pattern of behaviour with every other member. There is a tendency in the literature on the Indian family to focus on the economic aspects, but this is a narrow view of household life. Although economic activities form an important component of household activities, they cannot be separated out: distinction between household chores, economic activities, and kinship roles is not as easy to make as is generally believed. The widely prevalent idea that in patrilineal Hindu society only men work and earn is true only of the small section of higher income groups; in most sections of Hindu society, women and children also take part in productive work. Even if we leave aside the fact that in many sections women work regularly on farms and in factories and offices, a number of women's activities generally called household chores are in fact productive economic activities. Because economic activities and household chores have to be organized to the mutual satisfaction of the members of the household, kinship positions of the members play a very important role in such organization. Kinship positions are also relevant in planning the expenses of the household.

What is far more important, as I have already pointed out, is that, in sitting, speaking, eating, and many other so-called "trivial" things of life, a number of rules of etiquette and ethic (all subsumed under the term "proper conduct") have to be observed by one member toward another, and every kinship relationship has a code of "proper conduct" attached to it. Frequently the code one has to adopt toward another is in conflict with the code one has to adopt toward the rest of the members. Everyone in a household has his own likes and dislikes, habits, tastes and idiosyncracies, which have to be harmonised to a reasonable extent. Life in a household is marked by sentiments, emotions, and tensions, which are related to its kinship composition. The point I want to make is that if our aim is the analysis of household life in its entirety, then the classification of households should take into account all the relatives in a household.

However, as we have seen, such classification is not an end in itself; the compositional types are not discrete and haphazard but are interrelated in a developmental process. There is always some pattern in the developmental process of households. It is affected by three major factors. The first is the demographic factor, which includes not only the phenomena of birth, adult-hood, and death but also the sex and number of members. While these phenomena are demographic in origin, they are social in operation. The second factor is the series of explicitly stated norms regarding the residence of various relatives in a household. The third is the pattern of interpersonal relations in a household, largely dependent on norms or codes of proper conduct attached to kinship relationships in the household.

This process may be in progression or in regression. The pro-gressive development of a household takes place with an increase in membership, mainly by birth, in-marriage of women, and return of out-married women and their husbands or children. The regressive development takes place with a decrease in membership, mainly by death, out-marriage of women, return of in-married women and their husbands or children, and partition.

It is noteworthy that a good deal of developmental process, both progressive and regressive, goes on at the level of simple households. For example, a single-member household of a man becomes a husband-wife household at his marriage, but may become a single-member household in regression. Both progres-sion and regression are possible between husband-wife and husband-wife-child households. A mother-child or father-child household becomes a single-member household at either's death, or at the offspring's marriage if the offspring is a daughter. It develops into a complex household only if the offspring is a son. Similarly, a husband-wife-child household may not develop into a complex household if the child is a girl and not a boy, or if the boy dies prematurely. The point is that not all simple house-holds develop into complex ones, and when they do develop into complex households, they are not all of the same type; the type of a newly developed complex household would depend on the type of the simple household from which it developed.

Compared with the developments at the simple-household level, the developments at the complex-household level are indeed complex in nature, and their analysis presents certain special problems. The first major problem is : What is the maximum limit to which the progressive development goes along the line of the principle of the residential unity of patrikin and their wives ? This problem is complicated by the fact that the villagers have a variety of norms, the operational efficacy of which needs to be evaluated with reference to the numerical data on their observance in practice. Such evaluation is all the more necessary because, as we shall see in Part II, a number of facile notions about the efficacy of norms governing the formation of households have prevailed in the literature on the Indian family for over a century. We have seen that the norm that two or more married brothers should continue to live in the same household even after their parents are dead is only stated in gossip, folklore, and mythological stories of the villagers; it has no operational value in the village. It can be easily understood why the villagers do not even mention the norm that married first cousins should live together after the death of their grandparents and parents, although it is frequently mentioned as an important norm in the literature on the Indian family. Even when norms have an operational value, it is necessary to examine the degree to which they are observed. All villagers say that the ideal course of life for a man and his wife is to have more than one son and at least one daughter, to see all of them married, and to preside over a large household composed of themselves (the father and mother), all the sons, and their wives and children. The ideal, however, may not be realised for a variety of reasons. The parents may not have any children; they may have only daughters and no son; there may be only one son; one of the parents may die before any of the children is married; and even if all the demographic conditions for an ideal full-fledged household are fulfilled, the sons may be separated from one another and from the parents. We have seen how the ideal is observed in only a small proportion of cases, and how partitions take place. We have also seen how the villagers themselves distinguish between the situation in which the parents have only one son and the one in which they have more than one son.

All this shows that the developmental process is not a mechanical one. Although the demographic factor has an important role, the question of norms and their observance arises at every stage. And the consideration of this question shows that norms form a hierarchy.

As the entire process of development — progressive and regressive taken together — is spread over a number of years, the whole of it is not observable by a student in the field; its description has necessarily to be reconstructed by him on the basis of observations made in the field over a short period of time. The basic data are in fact provided by a census of households taken on a particular day. While the census data are not sufficient, they are absolutely indispensable. Other data — genealogies, biographies, and people's own views of the process — are also essential, but they would not by themselves allow us to reconstruct a comprehensive view of the process. It is impossible to collect accurate long-range biographical data for more than a few households. In the first place, a large number of people would have grown up in such circumstances that accurate knowledge about the past is not passed on to the growing generation, and there would be a tendency to use statements about the past as a charter for the present. Second, biographical data would be available only for those households that have had an unbroken line of existence, and these data could therefore be useful for an understanding of the developmental process of only such households. They will not show how households become extinct.

We may consider here the question whether the developmental process of households is cyclical. The idea of developmental cycle may mean that *each* household begins its development as a household of one type, expands through a regular sequence of phases, and is dissolved and replaced by one or more households of the original type. Meyer Fortes, the chief exponent of the concept of developmental cycle, seems to hold this belief. He states : "Each domestic group comes into being, grows and expands, and finally dissolves" (1949, p. 60). "The domestic group goes through a cycle of development analogous to the growth cycle of a living organism. The group as a unit retains the same form, but its members, and the activities which unite them, go through a regular sequence of changes during the cycle which culminates in the dissolution of the original unit and its replacement by one or more units of the same kind. These so-called types are in fact phases in the developmental cycle of a single general form for each society" (1958, pp. 2-3).

My interpretation of Fortes is substantially the same as that of Edmund Leach's: "Fortes' case is that if we are to understand the set of data observable simultaneously at any one point of time we must take account of the fact that each of the individuals whom we observe is separately progressing through a developmental cycle from infancy through adulthood to death, and that the groupings directly observable by anthropologist (e.g., domestic groups) are themselves passing through a derivative sequence of phases" (1964, p. xi). Fortes also does not seem to take account of social change. As Leach remarks, "Fortes' developmental cycles take no account of history; they are conceived of as sequences within a total system that is static and 'integrated' in Malinowski's sense of the term" (1964, p. xii). Surely, then, the developmental process is not cyclical. It is impossible to decide, first, where exactly the cycle of a particular household begins, second, how far it will expand, and third, the precise sequence of phases.

In another sense, however, the developmental process can be considered cyclical: if we take the frequency percentages of households of all the types in the society at one point of time and find the same percentages for all the types at another point of time reasonably removed from the first, although the developmental process for all the individual households cannot have been the same, we can say that the process has been cyclical for the society as a whole, because all the factors affecting the process have acted in such a manner that the total effect is always the same. While there is a possibility for the developmental process to be cyclical in this sense, there are two important

85

reservations. First, it is rare to get the kind of comparative data we need for two points of time. Second, there is hardly any part of the world at the present time — certainly not India — which is so static as to have such a cyclical developmental process, because social change is everywhere taking place.

Indices of Pattern of Developmental Process: Relation between Numerical and Kinship Composition

One of the problems I shall discuss in the rest of this chapter is that of comparisons — between the household pattern in Radhvanaj and in other villages, between the rural and urban patterns, between the patterns in different sections of the society, between the present and the past patterns, and so on. The principle of the residential unity of patrikin and their wives can be taken as the main basis of these comparisons. We start with the idea that differences exist in the extent to which the principle is observed, and then try to find if there are differences in the maximum extent to which the developmental process goes in progression, differences in the frequencies of the households of various types within this extent, and differences in the frequencies of cases of observance and non-observance of the dominant norms of residence. To find these differences it is of course necessary, ideally, to have not only a census of households but also a considerable amount of genealogical and other data. If, however, genealogical data are not available, we should enquire whether it is possible to derive any inferences from the census data alone.

We may enquire whether we can derive any meaning out of a simple ratio between simple and complex households. Take the case of Radhvanaj. If the total population of the village and the influence of the demographic factors are taken as constant, then a reduction in the number of households composed of parents and two or more married sons from 15 to, say, 5, will lead to an addition of 10 to 15 simple households and of an almost equal number, if not more, of households composed of parents and one married son, which in turn will alter the overall ratio between simple and complex households. Not only that such a small number of households of parents and two or more married sons will lead to the conclusion that they do not represent a prominent norm in the village. And if such households are completely absent, the proportion of simple households would increase further. Conversely, if there is a fairly large number of households composed of two or more married brothers residing together after the death of their parents, the number of simple households will be substantially reduced. As the norm represented by these households would be fairly strong, the norm of co-residence of married brothers during the lifetime of their parents would be even stronger, thus leading to a larger proportion of complex households. In this way, it is possible that a certain ratio between simple and complex households may prove to be a rough index of a certain pattern of households; another ratio may indicate another pattern.

The relative frequencies of households of different numerical sizes may also be a rough index of a certain pattern of kinship composition of households. Table 20 shows the classification of simple and complex households in Radhvanaj according to numerical size. It can be seen that while roughly nine out of every ten simple households are "small" or "medium," nine out of every ten complex households are "medium," "large," or "very large." A change in the ratio between simple and complex households would, therefore, affect the frequencies of the households of various numerical sizes.

The average larger size of the complex household has an important implication. In Radhvanaj, while the simple households form a higher percentage of the total number of households (67.84 per cent), the number of persons living in these households form a smaller percentage of the total population (56.45 per cent). Conversely, while the complex households form a lower percentage of the total number of households (32.16 per cent), the number of persons living in them form a larger percentage of the total population (43.54 per cent).

87

Table 20

Classification of Simple and Complex Households by Numerical Size

Numerical Size			Households		
			Simple	Complex	Total
Small	1		34	0	34
	2		23	2	25
	3		31	7	38
		Totals	88	9	97
Medium	4		29	16	45
	5		38	14	52
	6		20	16	36
		Totals	87	46	133
Large	7		7	11	18
	8		5	12	17
	9		3	6	9
		Totals	15	29	44
Very large	10		2	2	4
	11		—	1	1
	12		—	1	1
	13		—	2	2
	19		—	1	1
		Totals	2	7	9
Totals			192	91	283

The Household Pattern in Radhvanaj in
1825 A.D. and its Comparison with the Present Pattern

Although it is difficult to get the kind of data we need to compare the household patterns at two points of time, luckily some useful data are available about Radhvanaj's household pattern in the early nineteenth century. Radhvanaj was one of the many villages in the Charotar region acquired by the British in 1803. There are voluminous records about these villages for the period 1801–30 (for a detailed description see Shah, Shroff, and Shah, "Early Nineteenth Century Village Records in Gujarat" [1963]). The most important of these are records of a survey of villages and towns conducted by a special official organization called the Revenue and Topographical Survey of Gujarat. The survey records of Radhvanaj include a Census Register of 1825, which contains information about each household in the village tabulated in fifteen columns, seven of which are relevant for the present analysis: (1) serial number of the household, (2) name of the head of the household, (3) houses and huts, (4) men, (5) women, (6) servants and slaves, and (7) total number of persons. Names of heads of households are listed according to caste and religion, and a table at the end of the Register shows totals for the various columns and for each caste and religious group.

In 1825 Radhvanaj had a total population of 720 persons divided into 157 households. Table 21 shows the classification of 157 households according to numerical size (excluding servants and slaves), in the same way that Table 2 shows the classification of the households at the present time. A comparison of the two tables shows that there was almost as wide a range in the numerical size of households in 1825 as at the present time. The mode was also 5 members per household as at the present, and the arithmetic mean (4.54) was only a little less than the mean at the present (4.61). The difference in the mean was caused by the slightly smaller percentage of "small" and "medium" households. All this evidence about the numerical size of household suggests that relative frequencies of various types of simple and complex households were also nearly the same in the past as at the present time.

The Census Register does not contain any direct information about the kinship composition of households. However, it is possible to make some inferences from the information about

89

Table 21

Numerical Size of Households in 1825

Numerical size			Households		in 1955[a]
			in 1825		
			Number	Percent	Percent
Small	1		11		
	2		17		
	3		27		
		Totals	55	35·03	34·27
Medium	4		25		
	5		32		
	6		17		
		Totals	74	47·14	47·00
Large	7		14		
	8		4		
	9		4		
		Totals	22	14·01	15·55
Very large	10		2		
	11		2		
	12		2		
	13		0		
	19		0		
		Totals	6	3·82	3·18
Totals			157	100·00	100·00

[a] Cf. Table 2.

the numerical and sex composition of households, the names of heads of households, and some information in other records of 1825. It is safe to assume that the principle of the residential unity of patrikin and their wives was as prevalent in the early nineteenth century as at the present time.

Of the 157 households in the village, four were each composed of only one woman, a widow; one was composed of two women, most presumably a widow and her unmarried daughter; one was composed of three women, most presumably a widow and her two unmarried daughters; and one was composed of a widow and her one unmarried son and one unmarried daughter: thus a total of seven households were either composed of a widow or headed by a widow.

All the remaining 150 households were each either composed of an adult man or headed by an adult man. Seven were each composed of a single adult man; and four each, of two men, most presumably a widower father and his unmarried son, or two unmarried brothers: thus a total of eleven households were composed only of men.

Of the remaining 139 households each composed of members of both sexes and headed by an adult man, twelve were each composed of one man and one woman, mostly a husband and his wife or a widower father and his unmarried daughter. Another twelve households were each composed of one man and two women, the latter being most presumably the man's wife and unmarried daughter, or his wife and his widowed mother. Further, twenty-four households were each composed of one woman and two or more men: a majority of them must have been composed of an adult man, his wife, and one or more unmarried sons. Finally, twelve households were each composed of one man and three or more women: a large number of them must have been composed of a man, his wife, and unmarried daughters.

The point I want to make is that, out of 78 households considered above (49.68 per cent of the total), a very large majority were simple households, each composed of a complete or an incomplete parental family. In addition, among the remaining 79 households each composed of two or more men and two or more women, there must be a considerable number of simple households composed of either the complete parental family with two or more unmarried children of both sexes, or the incomplete parental family with three or more unmarried children of both sexes. This evidence supports the suggestion derived from the evidence regarding the numerical size of household, namely, that the relative frequencies of various types of simple and complex households were nearly the same in the past as at the present time. It is reasonable to estimate that there were 106 simple and 51 complex households in 1825.

How were these complex households distributed among the compositional types ? We are helped here by the evidence about partitioned households. The Census Register records sixteen partitioned fraternal units, fourteen each of two brothers, one of three brothers, and one of four brothers, thus making a total of thirty-five brothers. It is not possible to know for all these cases whether the brothers were living in separate households during or after the lifetime of their parents. As against sixteen partitioned fraternal units, there was no case of the only married son of his parents living separately from the parents. This evidence suggests that the majority of complex households must have been composed of parents and one married son in 1825 as at the present time. As regards households composed of parents and two or more married sons, while their proportion was certainly smaller than that of the households composed of parents and one married son, it is difficult to decide whether it was higher or lower than the proportion of such households at the present time. On the one hand the evidence on the numerical composition of households suggests that the proportion was slightly lower in the past than now; on the other hand all the statements of the villagers suggest that the proportion was higher. The statements also suggest that there were probably a few — and only a few — households composed of two or more married brothers living together after the death of their parents.

All in all, while the developmental process of households has not been absolutely cyclical during the last century and a half in Radhvanaj, there has been very little change in its nature.

Apart from whether the developmental process has been absolutely cyclical or not, one thing is abundantly clear: the widespread notion that all the villagers in traditional India lived in large and complex households composed of two or more married brothers is not true of Radhvanaj. In fact, small and simple households were predominant, and even among the complex ones the large majority were composed of parents and one married son.

Caste and the Household Pattern

In the analysis so far, the village has been considered mostly as if it were a social entity isolated from the wider society and also as if it were internally undifferentiated. This has been done for convenience of analysis, but both these assumptions have no basis in fact and may now be discarded.

While all Hindus living in an area share certain common institutions, there are undoubtedly important differences among them according to the caste to which they belong. This is particularly true in the sphere of household life, because caste determines the broad framework of kinship within which households operate as kinship units. The kinship system of each caste possesses certain distinctive features which have an important bearing on the nature of household life. A reference has already been made to the strong emphasis on intracaste hypergamy among the Khedawal Brahmans leading to bachelorhood of senior members of the fraternal unit. I have also suggested the possible effects of cross-cousin and uncle-niece marriages on the nature of relationships in households composed of parents and one or more married sons and in those composed of married brothers after their parents' death.

While the need to study household life in relation to caste is undeniable, there are certain problems inherent in such a study. First, usually the population of a caste is spread over a number of villages and towns, which means the fullest understanding of the relation between caste and household would be possible only if castes were studied and compared as "horizontal unit."

Second, while the population of a village or town is divided into castes, each caste is also internally differentiated. Frequently the members of a caste are divided into rural and urban sections, the former being considered lower in status than the latter, and the rural section itself forms a hierarchy, each village having a distinctive culture and status. Results of village-wise and caste-wise studies have therefore to be coordinated. My own data are about only one village, but I shall try and examine whether, and how far, they allow us to draw any significant conclusions about the relation between caste and household.

Table 22 shows the distribution of simple and complex households among the twenty-one castes in Radhvanaj. Figures for the thirteen minor castes are shown collectively, because each

Table 22

Distribution of Simple and Complex Households among Castes

| Caste | Households | | | | | |
| | Simple | | Complex | | Total | |
	Number	Percent	Number	Percent	Number	Percent
Shahukar	30	50·00	30	50·00	60	100·00
Brahman	2	22·22	7	77·78	9	100·00
Patidar	7	50·00	7	50·00	14	100·00
Rajput	21	56·76	16	43·24	37	100·00
Koli	94	74·60	32	25·40	126	100·00
Talapada	36	67·92	17	32·08	53	100·00
Patanwadia	58	79·45	15	20·55	73	100·00
Untouchable	30	71·43	12	28·57	42	100·00
Chamar	19	70·37	8	29·63	27	100·00
Senwa	11	73·33	4	26·67	15	100·00
Molesılam	11	73·33	4	26·67	15	100·00
Minor castes	27	67·50	13	32·50	40	100·00
Totals	192	67·84	91	32·16	283	100·00

of them consists of one to five households (except one caste, Gadhvi, constituted of seven households) and cannot therefore be compared meaningfully with other minor castes or with any of the eight major castes. The minor castes include at one end the wealthy and highly Sanskritized caste of Banias and at the other end the poor and ritually very low caste of Vaghris. The eight major castes are classified into certain categories: Talapadas and Patanwadias are "sub-castes" of the Koli caste; Chamars and Senwas are Untouchables; Brahmans, Patidars and Rajputs belong to a category called variously as *shahukar varna* (lit., creditworthy caste), *ujali varna* (pure caste), or *unchali varna* (high caste); Molesalams are partly Islamic and partly Hindu.

If one compares the percentages of simple households in the different categories of castes, the *shahukar* castes have a very low percentage of 50.00, the percentage for the minor castes is 67.50, and the remaining three categories have each a percentage above 71.00. This suggests that the lower percentage of simple households among the *shahukar* castes is related to their higher ritual status. Between the different non-*shahukar* categories of castes, however, there is a reverse relation between ritual status and the percentage of simple households: for example, the Untouchables have a lower percentage of simple households than the Kolis and Molesalams, who are of higher status. But between the three *shahukar* castes, between the two Koli castes, and between the two Untouchable castes, higher status corresponds with lower percentage of simple households.

At the end of the preceding chapter, simple households and core units were classified into two more major classes: (1) those that result from partition of the household of parents and married sons, that is, those who live in contravention of the dominant norm of co-residence of parents and married sons, and (2) those that are simple because of the coincidence of certain demographic and social conditions. Table 23 shows the distribution of these two classes of simple households among the castes in Radhvanaj. The gradation of status among the

Table 23

Distribution of Two Major Classes of Simple Households and Core Units among Castes

Caste	Simple Households and Core Units					
	Result of Partition		Result of Coincidence		Total	
	Number	Percent	Number	Percent	Number	Percent
Shahukar	10	28·57	25	71·43	35	100·00
Brahman	0	0·00	4	100·00	4	100·00
Patidar	3	42·86	4	57·14	7	100·00
Rajput	7	29·17	17	70·83	24	100 00
Koli	34	35·05	63	64·95	97	100·00
Talapada	15	39·47	23	60·53	38	100·00
Patanwadia	19	32·20	40	67·80	59	100·00
Untouchable	17	56·67	13	43·33	30	100·00
Chamar	12	63·16	7	36·84	19	100·00
Senwa	5	45·45	6	54·55	11	100·00
Molesalam	2	16·67	10	83·33	12	100·00
Minor castes	7	24·14	22	75·86	29	100·00
Totals [a]	70	34·48	133	65·52	203	100·00

[a] Cf. Table 19.

shahukar castes, the Kolis, and the Untouchables is reflected in the percentages of simple households living in contravention of the norm: the higher the ritual status of a caste category, the lower the percentage of such households. The status of each individual caste, however, does not correspond exactly with the percentage of such households. The Molesalams have a much lower percentage than that of the *shahukar* castes even though they have a lower status, and the Untouchable Senwas have a lower percentage than that of the Chamars.

Table 24 shows, for each category of caste, the distribution of units of parents and one married son and of parents and two

Table 24

Relation of Caste to Co-residence of Parental Unit and Married Sons

Caste Category	Parental Unit and One Married Son		Parental Unit and Two or More Married Sons	
	Single	Partitioned	Single	Partitioned
Shahukar	13	1	5	6
Koli	7	9	8	14
Untouchable	7	0	1	7
Molesalam	2	1	1	0
Minor castes	9	1	0	2
Totals [a]	38	12	15[b]	29[b]

[a] Cf. Table 10.

[b] The three cases in which two or more of the married sons live with the parental unit and one or two live separately are included in both single and partitioned household categories. Thus the actual total number of parental units with two or more married sons is 41.

or more married sons, according to whether they have single or partitioned households. In the case of units of parents and one married son, the *shahukar* castes, the Untouchables, the Molesalams, and the minor castes all have a very high proportion of single households; only the Kolis are an exception. With regard to units of parents and two or more married sons, the *shahukar* castes have the largest proportion of single households and the Kolis and the Untouchables follow them in order of ritual status.

It is possible to establish only one correlation between caste and household composition from the evidence presented above: the *shahukar* castes in general practise the norm of co-residence of parents and married sons more strictly than the other castes. I would relate this to the higher degree of Sanskritization of these castes. The principle of residential unity of patrikin and their wives, of which the unity of parents and married sons is a part, is strongly emphasised in Sanskritic Hinduism, and the highly Sanskritized castes are strongly influenced by Sanskritic norms. It is extremely significant that the Brahmans, the most Sanskritized caste, have the highest percentage of complex households and not a single simple household contravening the norm of co-residence of parents and married sons. While there are differences between the castes in Radhvanaj in the frequencies of various types of households, it is noteworthy that there is no caste that does not place at least some emphasis on the norm of co-residence of parents and married sons. The norm exists in all the castes; the differences are found only in the extent to which it is observed.

The above remarks about the relation between caste and household apply only to the sections of the various castes resident in Radhvanaj. The population of every caste is found, as was already mentioned, in a number of villages and towns. There may be differences in the relative frequencies of households of different types between the sections of the same caste living in different villages and towns. For example, it is very likely that the Rajputs living in some other village may have a higher percentage than those in Radhvanaj of households composed of parents and two or more married sons. Not only that, they may also have a considerable number of households composed of two or more married brothers living together after their parents' death. In brief, the principle of the residential unity of patrikin and their wives may be observed in different degrees in different sections of the same caste. It is hardly necessary to point out that the degree to which the principle is observed in any one village or town will depend to a great extent on the degree to which it is observed by the sections of the different castes composing its population.

Rural-Urban Differences and the Household Pattern
How far the household pattern in Radhvanaj is different from the household pattern in towns is an important question, but I have no comparative data to consider it with any degree of

adequacy. However, I shall list a few general facts to place the village pattern in the proper perspective.

It is now well recognized that urban areas in India do not have the same kind of social system as the urban areas in the West. There were towns and cities in India before the process of industrialization began, and excepting a few towns such as Jamshedpur, Chandigarh, Bhilai, and Rourkela, which have come into existence in recent times owing to the establishment of modern industrial and administrative centres, every present town and city has old and modern sectors.

One notion looming large in discussions on urbanization in India is that the growth of urban areas is fed by migrants coming only from villages, but it is necessary to note that migrations have taken place not only from villages to towns but also from one town to another. In fact, in the earlier phases of industrialization (at least in Gujarat) the growth of urban centres was fed more by migrants from smaller towns than by those from villages.

If I use the terms discussed in Chapter 2, any one town or city would have the following main types of households: (1) the permanent resident households of the town; (2) its own "independent" and "linked" emigrant households residing in other towns; (3) emigrants who retain in the town only property and occasional caste and kinship relations, that is, those who are on the verge of becoming permanent residents of another town; (4) immigrants similar to the emigrants mentioned in (2), that is, immigrants residing in the town but as "independent" or "linked" emigrants of another town or village; and (5) immigrants similar to the emigrants mentioned in (3), that is, immigrants who retain in their original town or village only property and occasional caste and kinship relations, and who are thus on the verge of becoming permanent residents of the new town.

It will be readily agreed that the household life of the permanent resident population of the town has been governed by the same general principle of the residential unity of patrikin and their wives as that prevailing in villages, except in the case of those who have been thoroughly Westernized. What was the maximum extent to which the principle was carried out in observance and what were the frequencies of various types of households within this extent is a matter of investigation. Nevertheless, we may derive a few inferences from certain related facts. It seems to me from my study of the social history of Gujarat that in the past the Sanskritized castes formed a much greater proportion of the population in towns than in villages. This means that the principle of the residential unity of patrikin and their wives was practised to a much greater extent in towns than in villages. And this in turn means that (1) a town included a considerable number of households composed of two or more married brothers living together after their parents' death; (2) it also included probably a few large households where married cousins lived together in the same household even after the death of their father and grandfather, the kind of households about which we read so much in the literature on pre-British India; and (3) the households composed of parents and two or more married sons formed a greater proportion of the households in the town than in Radhvanaj. The point is that the ideal of joint households was stressed strongly in towns, particularly among its elite population, and not in villages as is generally believed. The strong impact of Westernization on large towns must have affected the household life of their older population, but every large old city, even such a metropolitan city as Bombay or Delhi, even now includes a sizeable population governed by older ideals. And smaller towns have a much larger population governed by these ideals. This point is important because it shows how two notions widely prevalent in discussions on urbanization in India are facile: (1) the notion that the people who migrate from villages are governed by strong emphasis on the principle of the residential unity of patrikin and their wives, and (2) the notion that the urban area into which they come to live is necessarily an area having a weak emphasis on the principle of the residential unity of patrikin and their wives.

Finally, the developmental process of households, both progressive and regressive, operated in the town as well as in the village. Simple households of all kinds would therefore be found in the town as part of the normal process of development. If, therefore, simple households are found today among the urban population governed by older ideals, they should not be confused with the simple households found among the urban population governed by the Western ideals.

Part II

The Study of the Household
and Related Dimensions
of the Family in India

Introductory Note

I would like to preface this part of the book with an apology.[1] After having analysed households in Radhvanaj, I am faced with this question: What, if any, is the significance of my analysis for the study of the household and related dimensions of the family in India as a whole? I am afraid I must devote a lot of space to an answer.

So far few attempts have been made to systematically review the literature for arriving at general formulations about the Indian family. As I stated in the Introductory Note to Part I, there does not exist a sufficient body of systematic generalizations based on the large number of reports on empirical investigations made in different sections of society in different regions of India. As Louis Dumont has rightly and bluntly stated about Indian sociology, "Writers too often do not take the trouble to relate their work to that of their predecessors or contemporaries, disregard precise description, underestimate the difficulties inherent in the definition of the subject, and finally push on to their conclusions, all this as if the work could stand by itself while in such conditions, it can be but ephemeral" (1961, pp. 75-76). I was therefore forced to first find out the general characteristics of the available studies before I could relate my study to them. To perform this task with any degree of satisfaction, it was necessary to examine each study internally, that

[1] Part II is a revised and enlarged version of my two papers (1964, 1968a). I am encouraged in this venture by the reception accorded to the papers by a number of friends and colleagues. I would like to thank in particular Dr. Adrian Mayer and Dr. (Mrs.) C. Vreede de Stuers for detailed comments on the first paper.

105

is to say, to analyse the terms and concepts used, the nature of the data collected, the analytical procedures, and the relation between all these and their conclusions.[2] The analyses of individual modern works are given in Appendix 1.

It may also be added here that the present state of the study of the Indian family is intimately related to earlier studies, and any attempt to comprehend the former must involve an evaluation of the latter. Part II has tended, therefore, to become a rather lengthy review of the literature on the Indian family since Sir Henry Maine first wrote about it in the middle of the nineteenth century.

Although I have given only the minimum documentation necessary, it is possible that I shall be straining the reader's patience. But sacrificing the minimum documentation would be unfair to the authors whose writings I have considered.

[2] Recently two important comparative works by Pauline Kolenda (1967, 1968) have appeared. I have not been able to give as much attention to them as they deserve, since they reached me after I had written this book.

6
Basic Terms in the Sociological Study of the Indian Family

Introductory

The term "joint family" is prominent not only in sociological and social anthropological but also in legal and jurisprudential literature on the Indian family. It has become a part of the vocabulary of educated Indians. Scholars have considered the joint family to be one of the three most fundamental structures in Indian society — the other two being caste and village. It is widely believed to be a unique, ancient heritage of the Indian people, so much so that its alleged disintegration evokes emotions in many an Indian. A great deal of confusion prevails, however, regarding the meaning of this term. Aiyappan has rightly said, "When, in the Lok Sabha, a member says 'joint families have broken down,' in nine cases out of ten, he is repeating a slogan" (1955, p. 118). We should examine whether social scientists are also doing the same thing.

First of all, it is absolutely necessary to recognize that the term "joint family" has different meanings in law and in sociology. In sociology "joint family" is always understood in relation to "elementary (or "nuclear" or "individual") family," while the latter does not exist in Hindu Law (the legal definition is discussed fully in Chapter 7). In this chapter I discuss the most generally accepted definitions of these two terms in sociology, and the logical implications and inherent difficulties in these definitions.

The Elementary Family

The generally acknowledged meaning of "elementary family" is "a group composed of a man, his wife, and their children."

It is assumed by many writers on the Indian family, as well as by those on the family in general, that the members of an elementary family always live together in the same household, either by themselves or as part of a wider household group such as a joint or extended family. However, modern social anthropologists have shown, from researches in many different parts of the world, that this need not always be the case. In India itself, among the Nayars and a few other castes of Kerala, not very long ago the husband resided with his matrilineal kin but not with his own wife and children, whom he visited only occasionally. In most sections of Indian society, however, the members of an elementary family generally live together, and this book is also concerned with only these sections of the society. Nevertheless, the term "elementary family" does not by itself carry any implication of transfer of residence, at marriage, of one spouse to the parental family of the other (i.e., virilocality or uxorilocality), or the transfer of both to a new home altogether (i.e., neolocality). The elementary family is in fact a genealogical model.

In ordinary English parlance as well as in sociology the word "family" is used in the sense of a household as well as of a wider kinship unit whose members may be living in more than one household. When it is used in the former sense it is generally assumed that the elementary family is the antithesis of the joint family. This would mean that all households that are not joint families are composed only of parents and children. This is not so, as a matter of fact. We have seen in Chapter 4 how simple households in Radhvanaj include not only those composed of the complete elementary family or parental family but also those composed of the incomplete elementary family, how the latter are divided into five different types, how they form as much as 23.67 per cent of the total number of households, and how a household of each of these types has a distinctive pattern of life, with important consequences for further development of its members. What is found in Radhvanaj is not at all atypical. This is another reason why the elementary family is only a genealogical model. It is necessary to distinguish the complete elementary family from the incomplete one, and one form of the latter from another. All of them should not be lumped together in a single type as the elementary family.

We shall see that only a few scholars of the Indian family refer to incomplete elementary families. Each of them, moreover, refers to only a few of the possible types, and none, except Ram Krishna Mukherjee (1962), tries to assess their significance. This unjustifiable attitude to incomplete elementary families is, as we shall see, a result of the pivotal position accorded to the dichotomy of elementary and joint family in the study of the Indian family.

Frequently, the elementary family is defined as a household composed of a man, his wife, and their unmarried children plus one or more persons not belonging to it, for example, the man's widowed mother, father, or sister, or unmarried brother or sister. It is noteworthy that Murdock's definition belongs to this class: "The nuclear family consists typically of a married man and woman with their offspring, *although in individual cases one or more additional persons may reside with them*" (1949, p. 1, italics mine). This tendency to include in the elementary family persons who do not really belong to it is also unjustifiable. It is also, as we shall see, a result of the use of the dichotomy of elementary and joint family in the classification of household compositions.

The Joint and Extended Family

"Joint family" means "two or more elementary families joined together." It is called "patrilineal joint family" when based on the principle of patrilineal descent, and "matrilineal joint family" when based on the principle of matrilineal descent. Frequently the term "extended family" is used in the place of "joint family." The former may be regarded as making explicit the implicit meaning of the latter — that the combination of two or more elementary families is based on an extension of the parent-child relationship. The patrilineal extended family

109

is based accordingly on an extension of the father-son relationship, and the matrilineal extended family, on an extension of the mother-daughter relationship. Recently, Madan has argued in favour of making a strict distinction between joint family and extended family (1962b, p. 13), but I shall discuss his views at a later stage and in the meanwhile use the two terms, as usual, as synonyms. The term "Hindu or Indian joint family" generally implies a patrilocal (or virilocal) patrilineal joint family, and I shall also follow this usage.

An important problem arises from this meaning of joint family. What is the limit of the extension of patrilineal descent in the formation of the joint family ? In many writings the term "generation" is used to define the limit. For example, the joint family is frequently defined as a three-generation or a four-generation group. There is, however, no unanimity about the meaning of "generation" or about the method of counting the number of generations. In some writings the number of generations refers to both the dead and the living generations, and in some others, only to the living generations. Some include, while others do not, the common ancestor's generation in the number of generations. For example, it is quite accurate to describe a group composed of a man, his sons and son's sons as a three-generation group, if all of them are alive and if the common ancestor's generation is included in the number. Frequently, however, a group including only living brothers and their sons and excluding the brothers' dead father is described as a three-generation group because the dead ancestor's generation is included in the number of generations. Frequently, it is also not clear whether daughters are included among patrilineal descendants. For example, some describe a group composed of a man, his son, and son's daughter as a two-generation and not a three-generation group.

A further problem is whether "generation" has any reference to the wives of patrilineal descendants. If we want to describe a group consisting of patrilineal descendants and their wives, should we include the wives in counting the number of generations? In this regard, the general anthropological practice is to include both the parents in a single generation: Ego's own parents in the first ascending generation, grandparents (father's father, father's mother, mother's father, mother's mother) in the second ascending, and great-grandparents in the third ascending (see, for example, Radcliffe-Brown, 1950, pp. 27–39, and Murdock, 1949, p. 102). This means that if a widowed mother or grandmother is included in a family, her generation should be counted, but this is not always done in discussions of Indian family. For example, a family composed of a widow, her sons and grandsons is frequently described as a two-generation and not three-generation group.

How should we describe a group composed of a male Ego, his wife, their son and his wife (but not son's child)? We may argue that if Ego's parents are included in a single generation, we should also include Ego's son and his wife in a single generation, and the group is therefore a two-generation group. This creates confusion, because the elementary family is a two-generation group, and a family composed of two or more brothers and their wives and unmarried children may also be considered, as mentioned above, a two-generation group. A two-generation joint family would thus be composed of three different types of family. The same problem arises in the description of a family as a three-generation group, four-generation group, and so on. Mukherjee (1959) has shown with the aid of mathematics how a large number of different types of families are possible within a generation span and how the definition of the family in terms of the number of generations can have several interpretations.

To sum up, it is not meaningful to describe the composition of a joint or extended family merely in terms of the number of generations, unless certain clarifications are made about the use of the term "generation" and about the method of counting the number of generations.

I have discussed so far only the genealogical problems involved in the definition of the joint family. There are also problems concerning the definition in terms of activities or functions. After the genealogical composition of the joint family is defined, the next question is whether it is a household group, property-holding group, ritual and ceremonial group, group for some other function, or group for two or more of these functions combined together.

Let us first consider the joint family as a household group. If it is defined as the patrilocal (or virilocal) patrilineal joint family, then it does not take into account what I have called the reversal of the principle of the residential unity of patrikin and their wives. For example, the custom of *ghar-jamai* leads to the formation of a joint family, but it is only patrilineal (regarding the daughter as belonging to a patriline) and not virilocal. When a man's widowed or divorced daughter or sister or father's sister comes to live with him, that is, comes back to her parental home, it is not correct to place her in the same category as "unmarried children" because that will mean reversal to her premarital status. We have seen that she may also bring her children to her natal home, or her children may come even after her death. Sometimes, a man's mother's brother's or mother's sister's children, wife's unmarried brother or sister, wife's married brother's or sister's children, or wife's father or mother may come to live with him. None of these relatives belongs to the male Ego's patriline, and therefore none can be fitted into "virilocal, patrilineal family." When any of the relatives mentioned above comes to live in a household that is already a virilocal, patrilineal joint family, one may by-pass the problem of terminology by calling the resultant household a joint family, but the problem of explaining the position of the non-virilocal, non-patrilineal relatives in the household still remains. A real problem of terminology arises, however, when these relatives come to live with a complete or an incomplete elementary-family household. Is the resultant household a joint family or not ? It is definitely neither an elementary family nor a virilocal, patrilineal joint family.

If the definition of the joint family as a patrilocal, patrilineal group, genealogically more extended than an elementary family, is strictly adhered to, then certain implications follow. First of all, it should be asked whether it is possible to lay down the maximum genealogical range of the joint family on an a priori basis for the whole of India, or to maintain that the range may vary in different sections of Indian society at different periods of time. Second, with the need to find variations in the range goes the need to find the concomitants of the variations. Third, within the maximum genealogical range of household composition defined for a section of the society there is a large number of possible types of composition. If even a single relative who does not belong to it is added to an elementary family, then the resultant unit has to be described as constituting a joint family. We have seen in Chapter 3 how the structure of the household becomes more and more complex when more and more categories of relatives are included, and how therefore the classification of households should take into account all the relatives in a household. If this ideal way of defining the composition of the joint-family household is followed strictly, there would be no difference between "joint family" and my term "complex household."

It is very rarely that the term "joint family" is used only for the household group, however. Usually it is considered to be a multi-functional group of three or more generations, with all its members living under one roof, eating food cooked at one hearth, holding property in common, pooling incomes in a common fund, incurring expenses from the same fund, participating in common family worship, and working under the authority of the senior male member. In a given section of the society, such as a village, town, or caste, there would certainly be some groups of this description, but there would also be cases in which the members of the defined genealogical unit are divided into separate households, although holding property in common, carrying on joint occupational activities, and participating in some common rituals and ceremonies. Even this is a simplified

113

description, because household separation may coincide with separation of property and occupational activities but not with separation of ritual and ceremonial activities. There are also many forms of property, and there may be partition of property of some kinds but not of all. Therefore, the definition of the maximum genealogical range of the multi-functional joint family is actually another genealogical model, like the elementary family. Some households would be found conforming to this ideal, but within the same genealogical limit there would be separate households interrelated by only some of the activities associated with the ideal type. If the term joint family is used for both the former and the latter indiscriminately, it becomes a source of confusion.

Lineage and Joint Family

In modern anthropological usage a lineage is considered a descent group. A patrilineage, which is the only relevant lineage group in most of India, includes male as well female descendants, in male line, of a recognized common ancestor. Although the female descendants are members, their children are not. The female descendants of the lineage may marry and join the male descendants of other lineages, but they do not cease to be the members of their   fathers' lineages. Wives do not acquire membership of their husbands' lineages even after they become mothers. The patrilineal joint family, on the other hand, recruits members by descent as well as by marriage. Daughters and sisters become members of their husbands' families after marriage. The patrilineage and the patrilineal joint family are thus defined on partly different criteria and should not be confused with each other. Moreover, the male members included in a patrilineage have a greater generation depth than those included in a joint family.

Nevertheless, there is a continuation between the male members of the joint family and the patrilineage. And as the wives of the male members stay with them, we find large lineage-based groups which look like extensions of joint family. As a result, there is a tendency in the literature on the Indian family sometimes to use the term "lineage" (= patrilineage) and sometimes "joint family" for such groups. Use of the former does not create much confusion, but use of the latter is a source of much confusion. This is another reason why it is necessary to define the maximum genealogical depth of the joint family.

7

The Indian Family in
Law and Jurisprudence

Introductory

An elaborate system of family law has existed in India from ancient times, mainly as a part of what is called Hindu Law.[1] Hindu Law is divided into three historical phases: Classical or Shastric Hindu Law, Anglo-Hindu Law, and Modern Hindu Law. There is a vast and complex literature on this subject, of which I shall touch only the fringe. In restricting my discussion to a few basic problems of terminology and approach I shall give special attention to two recent papers on the legal joint family by J. D. M. Derrett (1960, 1962), a distinguished scholar of Indian law and jurisprudence. In the first he made some remarks on the relation between the lawyer and the sociologist (pp. 17–18), and about the second the sociologist Louis Dumont states, "This is likely to be the 'open sesame' of that difficult subject [of joint family] and one of the major insights in these studies" (1961, p. 82, n. 8). One of Derrett's remarks is worth noting here: "To historians of legal exposition the older books on Anglo-Hindu Law are of interest, but they can be misleading to non-lawyers, and to see them cited in all seriousness by sociological writers of today induces a smile" (1961, p. 18). In order that my ignorance of legal works may not induce a smile in Derrett, I shall quote mostly him and P. V. Kane, whose works he considers superior to those of Jolly and more up-to-date than those of Trevelyan, Bhattacharya, Mulla, and Mayne (1962, p. 18, n. 3).

[1] Modern income tax law has also something to do with the Hindu family (see Gulati and Gulati, 1962), but I shall ignore this complication.

Meaning of "Joint Family" in Law

Hindu Law distinguishes between the joint family and the coparcenary. Kane states: "Under the *Mitaksara* [the most prevalent school of Hindu Law] a Hindu coparcenary strictly so called is a much narrower group than the joint family. It comprises only those males who take by birth an interest in the joint or coparcenary property, i.e., a person himself and his sons, son's sons and son's grandsons form for the time being a coparcenary" (1946, p. 591). Derrett states the same thing in the form of a generation formula: "There is no doubt that the notion that three generations of descendants owned *in some sense* the acquisitions of their common ancestors in the male line was older than the *Mitaksara*" (1962, p. 36). The same coparcenary may be described as a four-generation group, if the common ancestor is included. As Derrett puts it, "Membership of the coparcenary is confined to the male descendants in the male line from a common male ancestor up to *four degrees inclusive*" (1963, p. 249, italics mine).

Under the *Mitaksara*, as each son acquires by birth an interest in joint or coparcenary property, even a father and his unmarried son are sufficient to constitute a coparcenary. That is, a coparcenary may exist even within what sociologists call an elementary family. It is presumed in law that every Hindu male is a member of a joint property group within the defined limit of the coparcenary. As Derrett remarks, "One was either in the family or not" (1960, p. 309). ("Family" here denotes the coparcenary. Lawyers frequently use "joint family" or "family" for "coparcenary." This is perhaps the reason why Kane states "a Hindu coparcenary *strictly so called* is a much narrower group than the joint family" in the quotation above.) Under the *Dayabhaga* (the Bengal school of Hindu Law) there is no coparcenary between a man and his sons, married or unmarried, during his lifetime, even though they may be living in a single household. The point is that, under the *Mitaksara* as well as under the *Dayabhaga, Hindu Law is not concerned at all with the distinction between the elementary family and*

117

the joint or extended family. Otherwise we would not find Derrett making such a statement as the following about what he calls the non-Aryan family: "Their joint family was the elemental or natural family of the father and mother and children. The joint property of the home was made up of the ancestral property of the father, and the *stridhana* or paraphernalia of the mother" (1960, p. 309). This statement ought to make the sociologist smile.

"A Hindu joint family," Kane states, "consists of all males lineally descended from a common ancestor and includes their wives and unmarried daughters" (1946, p. 590). This statement does not refer to the generation depth of the joint family, but it may be assumed that the joint family consists of all the men constituting the coparcenary and their wives and unmarried daughters. Derrett's explanation of the law is illuminating: "The joint family consists at any one time of at least two related persons (within a prescribed circle). Thus a childless widower, sole surviving coparcener, and holder and ostensible owner of joint-family property does not himself constitute a joint-family. *Yet two widows, whether they be co-widows of the same deceased coparcener, or mother-in-law and daughter-in-law, may constitute a joint-family*" (1963, p. 244, italics mine). The female members of the joint family are not coparceners, but the wife, widowed mother, and widowed daughter-in-law have the right to maintenance, and even to a share in property according to some *shastric* texts and modern statutes, and unmarried daughters and sisters have the right to maintenance and wedding expenses from the joint family property (see Kane, 1946, pp. 592, 594, 605, 803–815). Derrett summarizes the position: "If one was a male, then one was an 'owner', a coparcener, subject to the very varied and fluctuating rights of the non-coparcener members of the family. One was proud to be almost their trustee, or even their manager" (1960, p. 305). The law does not lay down the rule that the joint family of the legal conception should always be a joint household. "Even if the members live apart and never correspond they may still be joint" (Derrett, 1963, p. 244). A son may live separately from his father, and one brother from another, but they continue to be members of the joint-property group. Although a widowed mother may live separately from her sons she can claim maintenance or even a share in property (see Kane, 1946, pp. 605, 803–815). The law is concerned primarily with the constitution of the property-holding group and with the persons having rights of maintenance from the property-holding group, and not with the constitution of the household group.

It must have become clear from the above that there are basic differences between the meanings of the legal and the sociological "joint family."

"Joint Family" in Law and Custom

The problem of the relative roles of law and custom in regulating social behaviour arises with regard to every field of social behaviour, but it is particularly important in the field of the family in India. Jurists and lawyers themselves now recognize that there has been a chasm between law and custom in the field of social relations governed by Hindu Law (see Derrett, 1961, pp. 38–40). Classical Hindu Law consisted mainly of *Dharmasastra* texts written in Sanskrit by sages (*rishis*). It was understood by and administered to a tiny section of the Hindu society, mostly the Brahmans and some other highly Sanskritized castes, who lived mostly in large towns. It did not reflect the divergent rules and regulations prevalent among the multitude of sects, castes, clans, and lineages in Hindu society. It is doubtful if it was administered even to all the Brahmans and other Sanskritized castes, by all kings, in all parts of India, throughout the pre-British period. For example, it seems it was hardly ever administered in Gujarat, either by the Muslim kings or by the numerous Rajput chiefs, before it was imported into the region by the Maharashtrian *pandits* who accompanied the Gaekwads in the last half of the eighteenth century (see Rangaswami Aiyangar, 1946). The multitude of the people solved their family disputes through caste, village, and kin councils (*panchayats*) and not through kings' courts.

When the British courts began to administer personal law to Hindus, they consulted Brahman *pandits* for expounding the law, and the latter stated and interpreted the Sanskrit texts. Although Hindu Law developed during British rule because of the accumulation of case law and the importing of English procedural and other laws, the ancient texts (including their commentaries) remained the principal source of law. While codification of Hindu Law after Independence has changed its nature in many respects, its position vis-a-vis custom has remained almost the same. It is presumed in the law that all Hindus are governed by the legal rules unless it is proved to the contrary. If an individual wants to be governed in a given lawsuit not by law but by custom, the onus of proving the existence of the custom and its applicability to him rests on him. Although customs are recognized, they are looked down on as inferior to the law. As Derrett remarks, "Custom is not *part* of the Hindu law, thus must be visualised as its opponent, not component" (1963, pp. 12–13).

Thus, not only is the legal definition of "joint family" highly specialized but its applicability to Hindu society is also highly restricted. If the sociologist is concerned with the study of the system of inheritance and succession in actual operation in Hindu society, he would not presume that all Hindus are governed only by the legal rules. He would investigate customary rules operating in different sections of the society. Second, he would study, on the one hand, property disputes taken to law courts as well as those settled by non-official *panchayats*, and on the other hand, partitions settled amicably by the members of the family. Third, he would study lawsuits in the total social setting. To him the law court is a social institution like many other institutions. Finally, legal norms are after all only one of the many kinds of norms operating in a society, and individuals may experience conflict between different kinds of norms. For example,

Srinivas has shown how, in the joint-family dispute he has reported, a custom overrides a legal right in certain circumstances (1952b, p. 29; see also Mayer, 1960, pp. 239–247). The consideration of customary norms brings us back to the problem of codes of "proper conduct" attached to kinship relationships.

8

The Sociological Study
of the Indian Family

Sir Henry Maine on the Hindu Family

The Indian family figured to a greater or lesser extent in many of the general works on the family during the nineteenth century which modern sociologists and social anthropologists consider to be their classics. It figured most prominently in the writings of Sir Henry S. Maine, and no other writer exercised a greater influence on his followers. His influence was due not only to the scholarly character of his works and the academic positions he held at Cambridge and Oxford but also, it is important to note, to his being the Law Member of the Government of India in 1862–1869, a member of India Council in London in 1871, and the vice-chancellor of Calcutta University in 1864–1866.

Throughout Maine's works, the Hindu family meant only the joint family of Hindu Law; and the principal, if not the only, source of his information was the existing literature on Hindu Law. This is not strange, because he was primarily a jurist. His interest in Hindu Law, however, was not that of a professional practitioner in the courts but that of a student of the wider subject of comparative jurisprudence. He treated Hindu Law as one of the many systems of law to be compared in order to arrive at generalizations about law, and he always tried to look for its connection with other social institutions.

Like other students of social institutions employing the comparative method during the nineteenth century, Maine had his paradigm of the evolution of social institutions. In this paradigm the earliest and most primitive form of the family is what he called the Patriarchal family (1861, p. 101; 1871, p. 15; 1875, p. 116). It is, as he described it, "a group of natural or adoptive descendants held together by subjection to the eldest living ascendant, father, grandfather, or great-grandfather" (1875, p. 116). "The eldest male parent — the eldest ascendant — is absolutely supreme in his household" (1861, p. 102). The joint family is also a primitive but slightly evolved form of the family. It "springs universally out of the Patriarchal family" (1875, p. 116) and marks a stage in "the gradual transmutation of the Patriarch into the Chief" (pp. 116–117).

Maine regarded as archaic not only the form of the Hindu family but also all other institutions associated with it, such as adoption, primogeniture, low position of women, and religious sanction of family law. Not only that, he regarded these, as well as most institutions in other sectors of Hindu society, as morally inferior. On the other hand, he maintained that the divided or individual family of Europe and America was civilized and represented the final stage in evolution (1861, pp. 16–17, 104, 124, 136, 138–140, 152, 160, 189–195; 1871, pp. 13–14): "The rule throughout most of the civilized world is that, for all purposes of law, families are broken up into individuals or dissolved into a number of new families by the death of their head" (1875, p. 106). Maine was representative of his era in this respect. As Evans-Pritchard has pointed out (1951, p. 41), the nineteenth-century anthropologists and sociologists were not only conjectural but also evaluatory. They believed that the social institutions and ideologies of Europe and America in their time were good in themselves, and consequently in their evolutionist paradigms they placed these social institutions and ideologies at one end and their antitheses at the other.

Although the Hindu family about which Maine wrote was mostly the family as depicted in Hindu Law, the comparative and evolutionist framework within which he placed it provided a sociological perspective to the study of the Hindu family; its legal as well as non-legal aspects could be discussed within this framework. More significant, however, is the fact that even

123

when in recent time sociologists and anthropologists discarded the evolutionist approach as such, they retained the typological and conceptual distinction between the joint family of India and the divided or individual family of the West that under-lay the evolutionist theories of the family.

Indological View of the Hindu Family

One of the significant characteristics of the study of the Indian family has been its inclusion in the study of ancient Indian society and culture by historians, Indologists, Orientalists, and Sanskritists (all referred to hereafter as Indologists) for over a century. The Indological view of the Indian family was in fact the dominant view until recently, in the same way that the Indological view of caste and many other Indian social insti-tutions was dominant. It is possible for me to present this view only in a summary form here.[1]

The Indological view of the family was constructed mainly from two kinds of information provided by classical literature. We have seen in the preceding chapter how the main concern of Classical Hindu Law was the definition of the property aspect of the family, and how the family unit it defined was not con-cerned with the household unit, nor with customary rules of different castes and other groups in the society. The second kind of information was the discussion on the *shraddha* (ritual in propitiation of dead ancestors) and other scriptural rituals. After a survey of these discussions K. M. Kapadia concludes: "The closest group bound by mutual ties of giving and receiving the funeral oblation included a person and his three immediate ancestors" (1947, p. 43). This means that a particular ancestor received oblations from his patrilineal descendants up to the third generation from him. They together formed a three-generation group if the common ancestor was excluded, and a four-generation group if he was included. This unit was not necessarily the same as the household unit, and the definition

[1] A good bibliography of Indological literature on the Indian family is to be found in Kapadia, 1947.

of the ritual group would apply only to those castes who performed the prescribed rituals. Not only was the ritual unit the same as the property unit, many writers of classical texts discussed the property question in relation to the question of who should perform the *shraddha* for whom. They argued that a man inherited property from an ancestor because he propitiated him. The legal definition of the joint family therefore tended to coincide with and be sanctioned by the definition of the circle of persons required to perform the *shraddha*. It seems to me that this coincidence of the legal and the ritual definitions of the joint family in the classical literature led Indologists to conceive of a composite definition of the classical Indian family: a multi-functional joint family composed of three or four generations of patrikin and their wives.

In the Indological view of the Indian family was also subsumed the legal view. And Maine's use of the latter in his comparative and evolutionist theories made it a part of sociological discussions of the Indian family. It is no wonder that a view with such a strong support gained wide popularity.

The Family in the Census : 1867–1941

Another significant feature of the study of the Indian family has been the use of the data provided by official censuses. Local, irregular, non-synchronous censuses began to be conducted from the beginning of British rule in India. For example, censuses of villages and towns were conducted in the British territory in Gujarat in 1820–1830, like the census of Radhvanaj analysed in Chapter 5. The first attempt at a countrywide census was made between 1867 and 1872, but it was also non-synchronous and unsatisfactory in many other ways. The first systematic census of the whole of India was carried out in 1881, and since then censuses have been taken regularly every ten years. While there was a minimum uniform pattern for the country as a whole, the census of each province and state had its peculiar features, and each census superintendent interpreted the data in his own way. It is not possible for me to attempt here a review of the

extensive and varied material on the subject of the In⌐
family in the censuses.[2] I offer here only a few remarks on
nature of the census data concerning the family prior to
census of 1941, and their bearing on the concept of the In⌐
family.

In all the censuses up to 1941, except a few local ones⌐
as the census of Gujarat in 1820–1830, the distinction betw⌐
"household," "house," and "building" was not follo⌐
uniformly in all the provinces and states, and sometimes eve⌐
all the different parts of a single province or state. No atte⌐
whatever was made to collect information on the kinship ⌐
position of households. There was also no all-India plar⌐
collect information on even the numerical composition of ho⌐
holds. Census reports presented figures on the average size⌐
the household, but the average was calculated by dividing⌐
total population of an area by the total number of house⌐
households.

Even these limited data posed certain intriguing problems⌐
the student of the Indian family. While the Indological⌐
legal literature dealt mostly with the property-holding and ri⌐
group, the censuses dealt with the household group. While⌐
former pictured the Indian family as if it were a single typ⌐
group with a large number of members, the census data⌐
gested that there were households of various sizes, from⌐
smallest households of one member to very large ones with n⌐
than a dozen members, and that the proportion of sma⌐
households was higher than that of larger ones. E. A. Gait⌐
Census Commissioner of India for 1911, went to the exten⌐
pointing out that "the average population per house is 4.9⌐
much the same as in European countries. In the British Isla⌐
it ranges from 4.8 in Scotland to 5.2 in England and Wa⌐
(Census of India, 1911a, p. 47).

Because of the dominance enjoyed by the Indological vi⌐
the authors of almost all the census reports felt a need⌐

[2] For a useful guide to the census material on the Indian fam⌐
see Khera, 1969.

explain the divergence between the Indological view and the census data by suggesting that the ancient joint-family system of the Indological view was disintegrating, but the decennial censuses themselves did not provide any comparative data to verify the suggestion.[3] Although this suggestion was not empirically justifiable, it should be recognized that the censuses did introduce empiricism into the study of the Indian family,[4] and the raw data are still useful for more sophisticated studies.[5]

L. S. S. O'Malley on the Indian Family

In the 1930s there appeared a few general works on the Indian family that put together the ideas thrown up by the legal, historical, census, and other literature. Foremost among these were the works of L. S. S. O'Malley, who was not only a superintendent of census operations and compiler of gazetteers in Bengal but also an author of several general books and articles on India. His ideas on the Indian family gained wide influence among scholars of all kinds, including sociologists and social anthropologists (see, for example, Mandelbaum, 1948, passim; Davis, 1942, pp. 96, 98; 1948, pp. 418–422; Bailey, 1957, p. 10).

O'Malley's *India's Social Heritage* (1934) includes a chapter

[3] The following are some of the reports that discuss the problem of the family at some length: Census of India, 1911a, pp. 46–47; 1911b, pp. 48–51; 1911c, pp. 22–23; 1911d, p. 12; 1911e, pp. 25–30; 1911f, pp. 30–32; 1921a, pp. 46–47, xix–xx; 1921b, pp. 21–22; 1921c, pp. 39–41, lxxxii–xcv; 1921d, pp. 90–94; 1921e, pp. 21–22; 1921f, pp. 51–52; 1931a, pp. 55–59; 1931b, pp. 56–58; 1931c, pp. 68–69; 1931d, p. 21; 1931e, pp. 47–50; 1931f, pp. 33–34.

[4] Another though minor source of empiricism was the socioeconomic surveys, mostly of villages but some also of towns, in different parts of the country, the results of which began to be published from the second decade of the twentieth century. They were conducted by economists and agricultural experts, but they included data very similar to those provided by the censuses and posed the same problems as the censuses. For a bibliography on the survey literature, see N. C. Desai, 1936.

[5] For examples of such studies, see Orenstein, 1961, and Khera, 1969.

entitled "The Family," which describes both the patrilineal and the matrilineal family among Hindus as well as among Muslims and the tribal groups. At the very outset of his description of the Hindu family he expresses his faith in Maine's evolutionist theories: "Maine's description of the early type of family applies precisely to the Hindu family today" (p. 118). Although O'Malley's description includes more details than Maine's, it is placed entirely within the framework of Maine's dichotomy of the joint and separate family. He also passes value judgements similar to Maine's. For example, he also considers the joint family an archaic form of social organization (p. 118). His catalogue of demerits of the joint family also follows from Maine's basic dichotomy of the group versus the individual although, unlike Maine, he points out a few merits as well (pp. 127–128).

O'Malley describes briefly "the complete form" of the joint family (pp. 120–121), which he assumes throughout to be the traditional or premodern form. It is a multi-functional group with "a common property, a common house with a common kitchen, and common worship of a family idol or idols." Its total membership may be "a hundred and even hundreds," and it may be composed of "a man and his wife, his brothers and their wives, his sons and their wives, and his grandsons." This would be a three-generation group if the common ancestor is excluded, and a four-generation group if he is included, which is the same as the group described in the Indological-cum-legal definition. Moreover, when O'Malley speaks of a common house for such a family, he adds that it requires "large convent-like mansions in towns and a number of straggling buildings in villages" which may look "more like a colony than a household." This shows how loosely he uses the terms "house" and "household."

He also describes at considerable length (pp. 121–126) how the members of a joint family may live in separate households but remain joint in property, worship, and other activities. However, he considers this to be a phenomenon of only the modern time. On the one hand he does not support his contention by any historical evidence except the evolutionist dogma and the provisions of Hindu Law, and on the other hand his own statements about the premodern family imply that this phenomenon did prevail in the past.

In his essay "Family and Religion" in *Modern India and the West* (1941) O'Malley is concerned more with the nature and causes of "disintegration" of the joint family than with the nature of the traditional family, for which he more or less summarizes the description given in his earlier book *India's Social Heritage,* and assumes throughout that all Hindus lived in multi-functional families of three or four generations during the pre-British period. In his account of disintegration he introduces an important structural difference, that between the higher castes, where separation is rare during the father's lifetime, and the lower castes, where separation takes place even during the father's lifetime (p. 383). He does not, however, probe further into this problem. He also observes that among the higher castes it is becoming increasingly common for the sons to establish separate families after their father's death, but they do not abandon the joint-family system, because they are separated only in residence, not in property, worship, and celebration of ceremonies (p. 383). However, he assumes here, as in *India's Social Heritage,* that this is entirely a modern phenomenon.

O'Malley believes that the disintegration of the joint family is due to changes in economic conditions. The entire description of earlier economic conditions, however, refers only to the unity of the joint family in property and production, thus assuming its coincidence with residential unity (p. 384). He considers the second major factor in disintegration to be psychological. Here he mentions the various "constant factors" showing "the difficulty of adjusting the conflicting interests of members and the frequent clashes to which the system lent itself" — such factors as the friction between different members of the family with different temperaments, the trouble caused by the work-shy, quarrels among women, mismanagement of

129

property by the head of the family or his inability to control those under him, and so on. O'Malley believes that these factors became effective in the disintegration of the joint family only with the onset of the spirit of individualism encouraged by Western influences (pp. 385–386). His belief in the correctness of the Indological-cum-legal view of the traditional Indian family is indeed the major obstacle in his attempt to understand the reality of the Indian family.[6]

Two Phases in the Sociological Study of the Indian Family
The history of the sociological study of the Indian family could be divided into two main phases. We have just concluded the discussion of the first phase, which covers roughly the period from the middle of the nineteenth century to the 1930s. It was dominated by the Indological-cum-legal view, based on historical and legal material, and held that the Indian family was a mono-type, large, multi-functional, and three-or-more-generational group. The prominence of the small household in contemporary India, revealed by the census and other data and the personal observations of scholars, was somehow seen as fitting neatly into the evolutionist view of change from the joint family of India to the nuclear family of the West.

In the second phase, which we shall discuss now, the contributions have come mainly from scholars who have had a formal training in modern sociology or social anthropology and seek to portray a more realistic view of the Indian famliy.

Indologically Oriented Sociological Studies
The studies of the Indian family during the second phase fall into two main categories: (1) those based on the same classic sources used by Indologists, and (2) those based on empirical or

[6] *Report on the Hindu Joint Family System: Its Economic and Social Aspects* by N. C. Desai (1936) was another general work on the Hindu family published at the same time as O'Malley's works. It was in many ways better than O'Malley's works but remained neglected until recently.

field investigation. Writings under the former category were the first to appear and continued to be prominent until about 1950: Ghurye's several early papers (1923 and 1946), Karandikar's *Hindu Exogamy* (1929), Karve's early papers (1938-1939a & b, 1940, 1941, 1943-1944), Valavalkar *alias* Prabhu's *Hindu Social Institutions* (1940), and Kapadia's *Hindu Kinship* (1947). Large portions of Karve's *Kinship Organization in India* (1953), the portion on India in Ghurye's *Family and Kin in Indo-European Culture* (1955), and large portions of Kapadia's *Marriage and Family in India* (1955b), though published after 1950, belong in the same category. It is likely that these works have made valuable contributions to Indology, especially as they applied the approach and concepts of sociology and social anthropology to historical and literary material (see in this connection "Introduction" in Kapadia's *Hindu Kinship* [1947], and my paper "Social Anthropology and the Study of Historical Societies" [1959]). However, a discussion of the exact nature of the contribution made by these works to Indology is not called for here. I shall discuss, in a summary way, only their contribution to the sociological understanding of the Indian family.

We shall soon see that these sociologists as well as many others tended to regard the classical literature as portraying the true state of the family in pre-British India and to use it as the base for the study of changes during the modern time. However, as a matter of fact, the classical literature does not provide the kind of information that is needed for the study of changes in the family in modern times. It does not distinguish between "family" and "household"; nor does it contain any information on the different types of households and the frequencies of households of different types; and it does not reveal the differences that must have existed between the different sections of Indian society at different periods of time. Although at best it may give us an idea of the ideal family according to early Indian lawyers and social thinkers, even the information it provides regarding the composition of the ideal family lacks the necessary precision. The sociologists referred to above discussed

131

the composition of the classical family in terms of the number of generations, and most of them have confirmed the old Indological formula of three or four generations. Thus their definitions contained the same inadequacies as the earlier definitions.

Earlier Empirical Studies

Sociological works on the Indian family based on the study of empirical data or on direct field investigations began to appear somewhat later than the works based on classical literature, and were few and far between until about 1950. Perhaps the first publication based on empirical investigation is K. T. Merchant's *Changing Views on Marriage and Family: Hindu Youth* (1935), which reports the results of a questionnaire administered to a sample of educated young men and women belonging mainly to higher castes and middle classes in some towns in western India. While Merchant's was perhaps the first attempt to use the questionnaire method, Karve's "Kinship Terminology and Kinship Usages of the Maratha Country" (1940, 1941) and Srinivas' *Marriage and Family in Mysore* (1942) were perhaps the first works based on ethnographic material including folk and other literature.

The three studies have their limitations. Merchant's book in particular suffers from serious methodological and conceptual weaknesses. He repeats the idea of the studies of the first phase that the joint family of the past is disintegrating in the modern times. Although Karve's and Srinivas' works contain some useful descriptions of interpersonal relations in the joint family, they neither distinguish between household and family nor define the composition of the family. Nevertheless, the three studies show how, at the beginning of the empirical study of the Indian family, attempts were made to use the so-called sociological as well as anthropological methods. It is worth noting that these three scholars did these studies while they were Professor G. S. Ghurye's students at the University of Bombay. The foundations for the sociological study of the Indian family were well and truly laid with Ghurye's encouragement of diverse methods and approaches in the study.

During the 1940s two general accounts of the Indian family by professional sociologists appeared, one, the section on India in Kingsley Davis' "Changing Modes of Marriage: Contemporary Family Types" (1942), and the other, David Mandelbaum's essay "The Family in India" (1948). These articles, particularly the latter, remained for a long time the only writings of this sort and came to be widely read and used. In Davis' piece the conceptual framework is the same as that of Maine's and O'Malley's. He thinks every classical family system is moving toward the standard Western type, "a part of highly transmissible culture which Americans and Englishmen diffuse wherever they go" (p. 92). The sources of his information are also hardly any different from O'Malley's. His work, however, shows the continuing interest in the Indian family for cross-cultural studies.

Mandelbaum's essay, published six years later, is perhaps the first attempt to use the new sociological works — Indological and empirical — mentioned above to depict the Indian family in general terms. The major part of the paper, however, is devoted to "the model of the orthodox, scriptural family" (p. 123), the definition of its composition follows the three or four generation formula of Indologists, and the brief account of changes assumes the existence of the family organization of the Indological type in former times and its inevitable change to the elementary family in the modern times. The major, and most valuable, part of the paper is the description of interpersonal relations in the joint family, although it covers only a few of its members.

The Family in the Census: 1951–1961

Before we go on to the empirical studies of the 1950s and 1960s, let us look at the census material of 1951-1961. The 1951 census made a departure from the previous censuses in two important respects. First, a clear distinction was made between "house" and "household", and all households were enumerated throughout the country (except West Bengal). Second, information was also collected about the composition of the household, under what was called the National Register of Citizens. All the members of the household were enumerated, and their sex and relationship to the head of the household were recorded. Although this information is valuable, we should consider how it has been used by census officials and sociologists in the analysis of the Indian family.

While the enumeration was exhaustive, data were compiled for presentation on the basis of a sample and tabulated according to categories devised by census officials. On the numerical composition of the household, I have come across only one census publication, *Characteristics of Family Households, West Bengal* (Census of India, 1951c), in which the frequencies of households of all the different numerical compositions, from uni-member onward, have been presented for 5 per cent of the households recorded in the National Register of Citizens. In all other census publications, data is presented for a sample of 0.1 per cent of the households, and the households are classified into the categories already stated in Chapter 1, namely, small (one to three members), medium (four to six members), large (seven to nine members), and very large (ten or more members). It is clear that frequencies presented according to these categories are not as useful for sociological analysis as frequencies for all the sizes.

The Census Commissioner of India, R. A. Gopalaswami, presents figures separately for rural and urban areas, for the country as a whole, according to the above categories, and then makes a general observation:

> Of the four types, medium households are most numerous, which is what one would expect. That "very large" households with 10 or more members number only about one in sixteen is also not unexpected. But it seems a *little surprising* that every third household in a village should

be a "small household" with three members or less. Such a large proportion of small households is a *prima facie* indication that families do not continue to be "joint" according to the traditional custom of the country and the habit of breaking away from the joint family and *setting up separate households* is quite strong. Unfortunately we do not have similar information for past censuses. So, we cannot say whether the percentage of "small households" has or has not been increasing and we cannot measure the differences in the rate of change in different parts of the country (Census of India, 1951a, p. 50, italics mine).

As this statement has evoked much criticism from sociologists, I shall analyse it in detail. (1) There is a confusion in it between "household" and "family" — the two are used as synonyms — but the concrete referent of "family" is the household. The referant of "joint family" is likewise joint household. In this connection the phrase "the habit of ... setting up separate households" needs special attention. (2) The Census Commissioner does not define the kinship composition of the joint family, nor does he contrast it with the elementary family, but he is right, on the whole, in regarding large households as joint families. (3) His empirical finding that a large proportion of households are small, and therefore not joint, must be accepted as correct. (4) He has erred, however, in assuming that the traditional custom of the country, particularly in villages, was that of joint households. This shows an acceptance of the Indological view of the traditional Indian family. And that is why he finds it "a little surprising" that every third household in a village should be a small household.

The Census Commissioner presents information regarding relationships within the household for every unit of 100 households (drawn proportionately from villages as well as towns). Every unit of 100 households has a total of 487 persons, and their relationship is that shown in Table 25. The Census

Table 25

Distribution of Household Relationships in the Census of 1951

Household Relationship		Numbers in 100 Households
A	Heads of households : Male (Married)	71
	Male (widowers)	19
	Females	10
	Wives of heads of households	71
	Total	171
B	Sons of heads of households	108
	Daughters of heads of households	81
	Total	189
C	Male relatives of heads of households (other than sons)	48
	Female relatives of heads of households (other than daughters)	72
	Total	120
D	Persons unrelated to the head of the household : Males	4
	Females	3
	Total	7
	Grand Total	487

Source : Reproduced from Census of India, 1951a, pp. 130–131.

Commissioner does not make any comment whatever on these figures. Let us see, however, if we can derive any meaning from them. If we deduct 7 persons who are unrelated to the head of the household — they are mostly servants and friends — there are 480 persons related by kinship and marriage. Of these, 360 persons in categories A and B are members of a complete or an incomplete elementary family. How the remaining 120 persons are distributed among the 100 households is a question to which the census report does not provide any direct answer. However, if we consider the fact that the numerical size of the household ranges from small to very large, and that small and medium households have a much larger proportion than that of large and very large ones, we can infer that most of the 120 persons must be living in large and very large households along with the relatives in categories A and B, thus making joint households. This, in turn, supports the contention that households composed of a complete or an incomplete elementary family form a very large proportion of households in India.

The census superintendents of various states have also presented the information on the numerical and social composition of the household according to the same categories as those above, but only a few of them have attempted to interpret the information. They have followed the Census Commissioner of India in concluding that the joint family is disintegrating (see, for example, the discussion of the problem by J. B. Bowman, Census Superintendent of Bombay, Saurashtra, and Kutch, in Census of India, 1951b, pp. 105–108).

Although much more information about the household was collected in the 1951 census than in the earlier ones, the way in which the data were compiled and presented left much to be desired, and practically no progress is made in the interpretation of the data. The Census Commissioner's complaint about the unavailability of comparative data for the past censuses is of course true, but the real difficulty lies in the conceptual framework used in interpreting the data.

In the 1961 census the data on the numerical and kinship composition of the household was presented for a much larger sample — 20 per cent of the households in the country — than in the 1951 census (see Census of India, 1961b, Table C–I, Statements I and II). The data, however, is meagre. For the numerical composition, only the figures of the average size of the household are presented: 5.20 for villages and 4.97 for towns, a little higher than the corresponding figures in 1951 (4.91 and 4.71, respectively). On the kinship composition, tables very similar though not strictly comparable to the ones in 1951 are presented, and they indicate only that the elementary-family households are preponderant in villages as well as in towns. The census officials have not provided any comments on the household data, nor have the sociologists. On the whole, the 1961 census has not made any progress on the 1951 census as far as the study of the household is concerned.

Modern Empirical Studies

In the last two decades a large number of empirical studies of the Indian family have been carried out, and there are also a few general and theoretical works. I have examined most of them individually in Appendix I. In the rest of this chapter I synthesize the examination of the individual studies.

Distinction between Household and Family

We have seen that in the literature of the first phase there is a recognition of the situation in which the members of a three-or-more-generational genealogical unit live in two or more households but are bound together by a number of activities. Not only have empirical investigations of the last two decades confirmed the widespread existence of this situation, a few have also endeavoured to analyse it, either wholly or in part (Agarwala, 1955; I. P. Desai, 1964a; Gore, 1968; Kapoor, 1965; Madan, 1965; Mayer, 1960; Nimkoff and Gore, 1959; Ross, 1961; Singer, 1968; Srinivas, 1965). A few have chosen to delineate only the property-holding group which is frequently composed of two or more households (Bailey, 1957, 1960; Nicholas, 1961). A few have also given attention to relations between emigrant households and the households residing in the original village or town (Cohn, 1961; I. P. Desai, 1964a; Gough, 1956; Madan, 1965; Rao, 1968). The distinction between household and family is fundamental to these analyses, whether the distinction is made explicitly or not. Many investigations are concerned only with the households, but even those not specifically concerned with them have had to accord them a crucial place in observation and analysis. For example, even though I. P. Desai's investigations (1956, 1964a) are avowedly concerned with inter-household relations, he has had to take the household as the basic unit of observation and the starting point of analysis.

The recognition of a distinction between household and family is indeed a major achievement of the studies of the Indian family during the last two decades, and writings on households have been preponderant during this period. A considerable confusion, however, still persists because of the tendency to use the words "family" and "household" as synonyms. It is impossible to accept many statements about the family on their face because of this confusion.

Taxonomy of Households

Compared to the uniform view of the Indian household prevalent until about 1940, the empirical studies of the last two decades portray diversity of forms — another major achievement. However, in their attempts to grapple with the diversity of forms they have produced a plethora of typologies, ranging from the simplest classification of households into nuclear and joint (or extended) to the elaborate typology involving mathematical formulae developed by Mukherjee (1959, 1962). It is no exaggeration to state that no two scholars' typologies agree with one another. Sometimes the same scholar uses different typologies in different studies (Kapadia, 1956, 1959).

Multiplicity of typologies is not necessarily undesirable if the types are sufficiently and accurately defined so that one could be translated into another's terms. Such typologies are rare, however. In some studies the types are not defined at all (Epstein, 1962). In some typologies the use of such words as uncle, aunt, cousin, grandfather, and grandson (Agarwala, 1955), "families" (Cohn, 1961), and "other related persons" (Conklin, 1968) makes the types inaccurate. In many, the use

139

of the term "generation" is a source of much inaccuracy (Cohn, 1961; I. P. Desai, 1955, 1964a; Dube, 1955; Kapadia, 1959; Kapoor, 1965; Karve, 1953; Madan, 1965; Ross, 1961; Sarma, 1951; Shahani, 1961; Srinivas, 1952a).

The dichotomy of elementary and joint (or extended) family forms the foundation of every typology. In most typologies, the joint family is considered, explicitly or implicitly, a group based on patrilineal descent and virilocal (or patrilocal) residence. Consequently, these typologies do not take care of the non-patrilineal and non-virilocal (or non-patrilocal) relatives found in many houeseholds. Some scholars note the existence of households including such relatives, usually a married daughter and her husband and their children (the cases of *ghar-jamai*), but they do not make the definition of the joint family consistent with these households, and they carry on the general discussion of the joint family with its conventional definition (Cohn, 1961; Madan, 1965; Mayer, 1960; Sarma, 1964). A few scholars have modified the definition of joint family to accommodate such relatives — they define it as composed of two or more related couples — but they also carry on the general discussion in terms of the patrilineal, patrilocal unit (Kolenda, 1968; Conklin, 1968). The only scholars who give full recognition to non-patrilineal, non-patrilocal relatives in their typologies in an accurate way are Mukherjee (1962) and his associate Pakrasi (1962). Unfortunately, neither of them has gone beyond the formulation of the types to throw any further light on this important aspect of the Indian family.

After the use of the term "joint family" in the sense of the patrilineal, partilocal group, very little concern is shown for a definition of the maximum genealogical depth — the outer limit — of patrilineal descent in the formation of households. Most of those who do show concern provide only imprecise definitions (Cohn, 1961; I. P. Desai, 1964a; Dube, 1955; Karve, 1953; Ross, 1961; Srinivas, 1952a). A major source of this imprecision is the use of the term "generation" in defining the depth. In some writings the joint family is not clearly distinguished from the lineage (Dube, 1955; Karve, 1953; Srinivas, 1952a). The only scholars who define the outer limit with considerable accuracy are Madan (1965) and Mayer (1960).

Although in all general discussions the joint family is considered to be a group wider than the elementary family, we rarely find this distinction applied consistently in the actual typologies. The joint households actually taken into consideration are usually of three types: (1) parents and one or more married sons; (2) two or more married brothers; and (3) members mentioned in the type (1) or (2) plus one or more married sons in the next generation. The general tendency to consider only these units as joint households is so general that most scholars have had difficulty in classifying the households falling between the elementary family and the "real" joint families (Cohn, 1961; Conklin, 1968; I. P. Desai, 1964a; Dube, 1955; Gore, 1968; Madan, 1962b, 1965; Morrison, 1959; Ross, 1961; Sarma, 1951; Sengupta, 1958; Shahani, 1961; Srinivas, 1952b). These neglected households are of two major types: (1) a married man (with or without children) plus his widowed mother, or widower father, or unmarried brothers and sisters; and (2) a complete or an incomplete elementary family plus one or more non-patrilineal or non-virilocal or both, relatives. Some or all of these households are sometimes totally neglected in classification (Cohn, 1961; I. P. Desai, 1964a; Dube, 1955; Epstein, 1962; Karve, 1953; Madan, 1962b; Nimkoff and Gore, 1959; Sengupta, 1958). Sometimes some or all of them are placed in the pigeon-hole of the elementary family (Cohn, 1961; Gore, 1968; Morrison, 1959; Sarma, 1951; Shahani, 1961; Srinivas, 1952b). And sometimes some or all of them are placed in a new pigeon-hole (Conklin, 1968; Gough, 1956; Kolenda, 1968; Morrison, 1959; Ross, 1961; Shahani, 1961). Whatever their fate in classification, the general discussion of the Indian household is carried on in terms of two ideal types, the elementary and the "real" joint family.

Only a few works give attention to the distinction between households composed of complete elementary family and those

141

composed of the various types of incomplete elementary family. Cohn distinguishes three sub-types of nuclear family: (1) single aged adult, (2) wife and unmarried offspring, and (3) husband and unmarried offspring (1961, p. 1052). Conklin has a type called "subnuclear" for households of one member and of one parent and children, but husband-wife households are included in "nuclear family" (1968). Kolenda's "subnuclear" type includes only households of one parent and children, and adds a separate type for single-member households, but husband-wife households are included in "nuclear family" (1968, p. 346). Kulkarni separates uni-member households from all other households (1960). Nicholas distinguishes two types called "irregular family" and "nuclear family"; the former includes "only the widow, or the widow and her children, or occasionally also a man who resides with her." Nicholas does not specify the relationship of the man with the widow, nor does he tell us why he considers such families "irregular" (1961, p. 1057). Mayer includes the complete elementary family and the family of a widower and his children among what he considers to be important types of households, and refers casually to households composed of a widow (1960, pp. 179–180). Madan mentions "non-familial households" of a man and his adopted son, or a widow and her son, or a childless couple (1962a, p. 89). I. P. Desai's typology in his Mahuva book includes the types "uni-member" and "husband-wife" (1964a, pp. 153–154). Ross defines "nuclear family" as including "one or both parents with children" (1961).

Each of these writings refers at best to only a few of the possible types of the incomplete elementary family, and none tries to assess their significance. Mukherjee (1962) and Pakrasi (1962) are the only scholars who recognize almost all of the various types of the incomplete elementary family, and among them only Mukherjee tries to assess their significance. All the scholars, however, tend to neglect the households composed of the incomplete elementary family in the general discussion of the Indian household. The households of some or all of the various types of the incomplete elementary family are regarded as "irregular" (Nicholas, 1961), "unimportant" (Mayer, 1960), "non-familial" (Madan, 1962a; Mukherjee, 1962; Pakrasi, 1962; Kulkarni, 1960), or "families only through courtesy" (I. P. Desai, 1964a). This is an unrealistic attitude.

Recently, Kolenda has introduced another complication. She defines the nuclear family as "a couple with or without unmarried children." That is to say, a husband-wife unit is also a nuclear family. And this is done deliberately. She states, "We should use the same definition for the nuclear family in India as in the United States, if we are ever to compare the Indian family structure with American family structure" (1968, p. 346). This means she abandons the standard anthropological definition in favour of a definition of just one culture. This is not likely to facilitate scientific discussion.

While the elementary family, of whatever definition, is considered a characteristic of Western culture, no attention whatever is given to a crucial fact of Indian culture that an elementary family may be *genealogically complete* but *socially incomplete*.

Thus, while a great deal of effort has gone into the classification of household compositions, the typologies used in the classifications suffer from a number of deficiencies.

The Developmental Cycle of Households

Compared to the enormous attention devoted to the taxonomy of households, the idea of the developmental process has received little attention. The essence of the idea, that a household of one type develops in course of time into one or more households of another type, is present in many works, and many have also pleaded for studying the Indian family in the framework of the developmental cycle and employing the idea to gain a fuller understanding of the Indian family.

Cohn (1961) rightly considers the type of family existing at a certain time not a fixed entity but rather a structural contingent resulting from the operation of a combination of several factors, such as life expectancy, economy, interpersonal relations in the family, and migration. His description of the developmental process, however, is sketchy. Conklin (1968, 1969) cogently emphasizes the importance of the role of the cycle of births, marriages, and deaths in the formation of households, but does not describe the formation process at any length and completely neglects the role of partitions in the process. Ross states that "the typical middle and upper middle class urban Hindu moves through a series of family forms during his lifetime," (1961, p. 37) and describes a few forms, but does not use the idea for any other purpose. Epstein (1962) views the cycle as having only two phases, the elementary family and the joint family. Although I. P. Desai (1964a), Gore (1968), and Sarma (1964) formulate a number of types of households, they freeze them into two types, elementary and joint, while describing the developmental cycle. Gould's description of the developmental cycle of the north Indian family (1968) includes only one cycle comprising three types of households, namely, the nuclear family, which develops into the family of the father and his two or more married sons, which after the father's death splits into as many nuclear families as there are brothers. In effect this cycle is composed of the dichotomy of the nuclear and the "real" joint family.

Madan's is the only work (1965) that describes the developmental cycle in greater detail and also uses it to gain a deeper understanding of other aspects of the household and family. He describes three courses of development: one arising out of the absence of a son in a nuclear family, the second arising out of the presence of only one son, and the third arising out of the presence of two or more sons. All other courses of development are considered "unusual" and are therefore neglected.

Recently, Kolenda has rightly questioned the idea of a single family cycle (1968, p. 347). She has also indicated certain factors making for a multiplicity of cycles, most of which are strikingly the same as those which I have discussed in my analysis of the developmental process of households in Radhvanaj: the time of a man's death in relationship to the ages and marriages of his children, the number of years between the latter in their ages, variation in obligation of children to parents and to each other depending upon birth-order and sex, and a number of norms — for example, those concerning the proper time for married sons to break away from parents, or married brothers to break away from each other. Unfortunately, Kolenda has not yet applied these ideas to an analysis of the developmental cycle in a field situation.

Use of Numerical Data on the Household

Data on numerical frequencies of households of different types have been increasingly used in the study of the household. Besides the Census of India, the Sociological Research Unit of the Indian Statistical Institute has collected such data on a macro level (see Mukherjee, 1959, 1962, 1965; Pakrasi, 1962). Some sociologists have used the macro data provided by the Census (Kapadia, 1955a, 1956; Kulkarni, 1960; Orenstein, 1961), and I. P. Desai (1955) has commented upon the census officials' use of their data. A large number of scholars have collected and analysed numerical data at the micro level: for one or more villages (Epstein, 1962; Ghurye, 1960; Mayer, 1960; Morrison, 1959; Nicholas, 1961; Sarma, 1964; Sengupta, 1958) ; for a small caste group in a village (Cohn, 1961; Gough, 1956; Madan, 1965) ; for a caste group living in a city and neighbouring villages (Gore, 1968) ; for a small town or a section of a large town (I. P. Desai, 1956, 1964a; Kapadia, 1954a, 1954b, 1959; Conklin, 1968; Kapoor, 1965; Lambert, 1963; Ross, 1961; Sarma, 1964; Shahani, 1961). Kolenda (1967, 1968) has recently tried to compare the numerical data of a number of studies.

The use of the numerical data has been confined mainly to assess the prevalence of the joint versus the elementary family, either in a population in general or in a sector of it. In most of these attempts the weaknesses of sampling, or of typology, or of both, have worked as obstacles to achieving significant results (see in particular Gore, 1968; Ghurye, 1960; Kapadia, 1955a,

145

1956, 1959; Kulkarni, 1960; I. P. Desai, 1964a; Morrison, 1959; Pakrasi, 1962; Sarma, 1964). Except Madan (1965) and to a lesser extent Cohn (1961), no one has yet used numerical data to reconstruct a detailed picture of the developmental process of households.

Changes in the Household

We have seen how from the time of Maine to that of O'Malley it was believed that the joint family, a characteristic of traditional India, would change to the elementary family, a characteristic of the modern West. The Indologically oriented sociological studies strengthened the belief in the prevalence of the joint family in traditional India. The initial empirical studies by professional sociologists, such as Merchant, Davis, and Mandelbaum, continued to maintain the belief in the change from the joint to the elementary family in modern times. And the officials of the 1951 census were guided by the same belief in their interpretation of their data on the household.

During the last two decades also, most of the discussion of changes in the Indian household has been carried on in almost the same old framework. Of course, in the place of the simple evolutionist dogma that the joint-family system will somehow change to the elementary-family system, it is now believed that the processes of industrialization and urbanization would bring about the change. The direction of change, however, is supposed to be the same. Some studies recognize that the elementary-family as well as the joint-family households exist at the present time, but they continue to assume that only the joint-family households existed in the past (Gough, 1956; Karve, 1953; Morrison, 1959; Ross, 1961). Some scholars, such as I. P. Desai (1955, 1956, 1964a) and Kapadia (1955b), contest the theory of disintegration of the entire joint-family system, but are silent about changes in the household pattern. They agree that although the elementary-family households have emerged as preponderant, their relations with the households of other members of the joint family remain strong. This argument,

146

however, assumes the former preponderance of the joint-family households. Evidently in response to the fact that both the elementary and the joint households always form part of a developmental cycle, some scholars have put forward a somewhat modified and sophisticated version of the old theory: a cyclical process of the periodic break-up of joint families and the emergence of new ones gives way to a process of change in which joint families break up and no new ones emerge (see Epstein, 1962; Goode, 1963; Gore, 1968). Goode agrees that the changes in the joint family are not as yet great, but asserts that the "direction of change" toward the conjugal family is clear (1963, p. 247). Maine's evolutionist idea has only taken new forms.

Recently a few scholars have challenged the presumed consequences of industrialization and urbanization for the family in India, as well as the framework within which they are studied. Orenstein (1961) has done this with the help of the Census data. He poses his problem as follows: If the widespread belief that the modern processes of industrialization and Westernization of traditional societies, such as India's, led to the emergence of small and elementary families is true, then these should be reflected in a decreasing average size of the household. He presents the Census figures for most of the states in India to show that not only has the average size of the household not decreased from the 1871 to the 1951 Census but there has been, on the contrary, a slight tendency — very slight indeed — toward an increase. This suggests that the processes of industrialization and Westernization have not brought about the expected disintegration of the system of large and joint households. Orenstein tries to support this inference with the data on infant mortality as compared with general mortality and on the number of married and widowed males per household. They show respectively that probably there are more adults as well as more married and widowed males per household, suggesting higher incidence of joint households, at the present than in the past. Orenstein therefore concludes that "it is incumbent upon those who defend the hypothetical relation between industrialization and the small family to clarify their terms, else we have another of those 'hypotheses' so vaguely conceived as to be subject neither to proof nor disproof" (p. 349). He also conjectures that the belief about the wide prevalence of large and joint households in pre-British India is false.

In his study of factory workers in Poona, Lambert has pointed out how his data show just the opposite of the presumed consequence of industrialization: the growth of the small, nuclear family (1963, pp. 38–43, 56). The average size of the household among the workers is 5.2 compared with 4.5 for the general population of Poona. The mean number of earners per household is also greater (1.6) than in the general population (1.3), and the additional earner in the household is usually a man rather than a woman, which suggests the presence of more than one adult male in the household.

Conklin has shown how in the study of changes in the Indian family, scholars have too often assumed what they set out to prove, and how the practice of today is being compared to a very idealised pattern of the past, and the necessary differences interpreted as a change over time (1969, p. 1447).

Caste, Rural-Urban Community, and Household

Very few works have tried to seek interrelation between caste and household, and they mainly offer qualitative observations rather than any hard quantitative data. All of them support the interrelation I have sought to establish in Chapter 5: emphasis on the joint family households is stronger among higher and more Sanskritized than among lower and less Sanskritized castes. In the Tamil village studied by Gough (1956), among lower castes a man's sons, once married, move into separate houses, while among the Brahmans there is a great deal of emphasis on co-residence of parents and married sons during the lifetime of parents. At the other end of the country, among the Brahmans in a Kashmir village studied by Madan (1965), the average size of the household is 6, appreciably higher than 4.91, the all-India rural average in 1951; the percentage of the "large" and "very large" households taken together is 32.4, higher than the all-India average; the complex households constitute 59.7 per cent of the total; and among them there is a greater emphasis on households composed of two or more married brothers with or without their parents. Cohn (1961) reports that in his village in Uttar Pradesh the high caste Thakurs reached the cultural ideal of the joint family more often than the low caste Chamars. In several large samples in eastern India studied by Mukherjee (1965) the upper castes and economic classes place a greater emphasis on joint households than the lower castes and econo-mic classes. In the three villages in the same region studied by Sengupta (1958) there is a greater tendency on the part of sons to establish separate households during the lifetime of their father among the lower castes. In the western Indian town studied by I. P. Desai (1964a), separation after marriage is more common among the Harijans than among others. Kolenda (1968) has also arrived at the conclusion that the joint family is somewhat more characteristic of higher "twice-born" castes and the least characteristic of the Untouchable castes.

A large number of empirical studies have sought to examine the relationship between the household and the rural-urban community. There is a tendency in almost all of them to view the relationship as part of the processes of industrialization and urbanization, and to make three interrelated assumptions: (1) Traditional India was village India, and the joint house-hold was a characteristic of village India; (2) contrariwise, urban areas are new and characterized by the elementary house-hold; and (3) urbanization, therefore, leads to disintegration of the joint household and preponderance of the elementary household.

The data reported by empirical studies, however, go against these assumptions. In Conklin's sample from Poona town (1968), the non-nuclear households constitute 42 per cent. We have already noted how in the same town, Lambert's sample of industrial workers reveal considerable emphasis on the joint household. In I. P. Desai's sample from Mahuva town (1964a), the joint households constitute as high as 58 per cent; among these there is a larger proportion of households with greater genealogical depth; and 6 per cent of the sample households are composed of four or more than four generations. Dube (1955) reports that while the four-generation and five-generation households are almost impossible to find in villages in Telangana, they are found in small number in towns and cities. Kapadia's surveys in villages and towns in western India (1954a, 1954b, 1955a, 1956, 1959) show higher proportions of joint households in towns than in villages, and among the towns, the larger the town the greater is the incidence of joint households. In Kapoor's sample from the Khatris in the heart of the metropolitan city of Delhi (1965), the complex households constitute at least 43.3 per cent. Mukherjee's several large samples from eastern India (1965) show that the emphasis on the joint household increases progressively as one passes from villages through small towns to large cities, or from non-industrial through partly industrial to highly industrial towns. Sarma's sample taken from villages in West Bengal and the two samples taken from the metropolitan city of Calcutta (1964) show higher percentage of joint households in the city than in the villages, and within the city, in newer residential localities than in the older.

While it is widely recognized that the assumptions regarding the effects of industrialization and urbanization on the household are not supported by empirical data, very few attempts have been made to view the emphasis on joint households in urban areas in a proper sociological perspective. In his first survey (1955a) Kapadia frankly admits his inability to explain the existence of greater emphasis on joint family in towns, in the second (1956) he tries but fails to explain it with reference to caste and economy, and in the third (1959) he changes the typology to suit the the assumptions. I. P. Desai tries to explain the facts with interesting polemic: "The belief that the nuclear type of family is consistent with urban area may not be true. Or *the urban area we have investigated is not urban*. If we think of

Mahuva in terms of its social structure and functional systems, Mahuva is not very much different from the surrounding rural area. It is a *rural town*. The population can be characterised as *urban-dwelling ruralities*" (1964a, p. 124, italics mine). The discrepancy between the assumptions and the facts thus remain a puzzle.

As I have shown in Chapter 5, the solution to this puzzle lies in the fact that urban communities in traditional India had a higher proportion of the population of higher and more Sanskritized castes and therefore a greater emphasis on the principle of residential unity of patrikin and their wives. In modern India small towns and older sectors of enlarged towns have more or less the same traditional characteristics. (I have excluded the new sectors in enlarged towns only because I want to be cautious, otherwise they too may show a higher degree of joint residence.) It is significant that in almost all the works that have reported greater emphasis on the joint household in urban areas, the samples are drawn from small towns or older sectors of enlarged towns, and in some cases we are informed that they include a large proportion of higher castes. I. P. Desai's Mahuva and Kapadia's Navsari are small towns with predominantly higher caste population in Gujarat. Conklin's and Lambert's Poona is a large town with an old core. Kapoor's sample consists of high caste Khatris in the old core of Delhi. Mukherjee reports that the incidence of joint families increases progressively from villages to small towns to large towns. Sarma reports higher incidence of joint families in the Calcutta samples taken from older as well as newer sectors.

9
Conclusion

"Elementary" and "Joint" Family
versus "Simple" and "Complex" Household

We have seen in the preceding chapter how the study of the household dimension of the Indian family has gained prominence during the last two decades, but the typologies used in the classifications of household compositions suffer from a number of deficiencies. The main source of these deficiencies is the use of the traditional dichotomy of elementary and joint family as the main basis of classification. If the taxonomy of household compositions has to take into account each member and if this dichotomy is based on the current definitions of "elementary family" and "joint family," then the confusion I have referred to above is inevitable. In my view this is a sufficient justification for rejecting the current terms in my analysis of Radhvanaj households.

It may be recalled that I have classified the households in Radhvanaj into "simple" and "complex," and have defined the term "simple household" as "a complete or an incomplete parental family," and the term "parental family" as "a unit composed of a man, his wife and their unmarried children." The category "children" includes adopted children, ritual children, and a remarried woman's children by her first husband carried to the second husband's home. The term "parental family" thus accommodates a few "compound families" in the village.

I admit that the term "parental family" used in my analysis is very similar to "elementary family." I would myself have used "elementary family" if I had not had a few compound families in my census. However, as I have made it clear, I have used the term "parental family" only as a genealogical model. It is only a tool to describe the genealogical composition of households. The term "elementary family" can be used in the same way as "parental family," but then it will have an altogether different role from what it has had so far: "simple household" will be dependent upon but not the same as "elementary family." I do not see any possibility of using "elementary family" in the sense in which I have used "simple household."

If "joint family" is defined as a household composed of two or more elementary families, or of parts of two or more elementary families, or of one elementary family plus part or parts of another elementary family, then there is no difference between "joint family" and "complex household." But then "joint family" will be very different from what it has been so far. It will include, for example, patrilineal and virilocal as well as non-patrilineal and non-virilocal relatives. And a household composed of a widow or widower and one married son will also be a joint family. The point is that, although my labels "simple household" and "complex household" are, I claim, more suitable than the current labels, and my labels may probably be replaced by more suitable ones, what is important is the reality subsumed by the labels.

Some may argue that my two terms "simple household" and "complex household" are only an improved version of the established terms "elementary family" and "joint family," and that I have also been discussing the Indian household within the framework of a dichotomy, however improved it may be. I want to make it clear that I have devised these terms only with a view to maintaining a continuity between my study and the preceding studies. Otherwise, I do not consider the dichotomy of "simple household" and "complex household" absolutely necessary. In any case, I have not attributed any special social quality to these terms as are attributed to "elementary family" and "joint family." I have used them as simple tools to aid exposition. Even the apparent qualities of simplicity and complexity, suggested by the adjectives "simple" and "complex," prove to be sociologically insignificant when we take into account the vital differences in simplicity and complexity among the various types of simple and complex households respectively. There does not seem to me to be any proper substitute for taking into account every member of the household in the taxonomy of household compositions and for recognizing the importance of all types that exist in the society.

Some may argue that such a classification is possible only in a micro-study such as that of a village and not in a macro-study such as that of a whole district or region where there would be so many types of households that it would be impossible to see the wood for the trees. If the definitions of simple and complex households are applied mechanically, there will surely be a large number of types resulting from permutations and combinations of parental (or elementary) families and their parts. In social reality, however, the number of types is bound to be limited because of the principle of the residential unity of patrikin and their wives and the demographic factor. And even if the number of types is very large, it would be, I presume, well within the range of a computer. In any case, it is necessary to formulate types as they emerge from the social reality rather than as they are constructed by the sociologist on the basis of preconceived notions about the nature of the Indian family. Only when we have such "natural" types will it be possible to compare in a fruitful way the results of investigations conducted by different scholars in different sections of society and in different parts of the country. At the present moment almost every scholar has his own typology, usually imprecisely formulated, which makes it impossible to compare the results of his investigation with those of others (see Kolenda, 1968 for nearly the same conclusion).

The Developmental Process and the Norms of Residence

We saw in the preceding chapter that while the need to view the different types of households in the perspective of the developmental process is widely recognized, there are scarcely one or two works dealing with the process. A number of studies of the developmental process in different sections of society in different regions of the country will be crucial for the progress of the study of the Indian family. This endeavour will be helped, I submit, by the conceptual clarification about the nature of the developmental process I made in Chapter 5, namely, that it is not cyclical but moves in progression and regression. This will take care of the valuable point made by Madan (1965) and Kolenda (1968) that there is not one but a multiplicity of courses of development. It is also hardly necessary to reiterate that the developmental process is dependent not only on the demographic factors of birth, marriage, and death but also on the norms of residence and the degree of observance of the norms.

The norms of residence can be conveniently summarised under the principle of residential unity of patrikin and their wives rather than under the confusing dichotomy of elementary and joint family. The observance of the principle can be distinguished from the reversal of the principle, and in the latter case "cores" can be distinguished from "accretions" in the composition of households. The different degrees of observance of the principle can be seen in different sections of society in different regions of India.

Use of Numerical Data on the Household

It has become common in sociology and social anthropology, and my analysis of Radhvanaj households also shows, that numerical data are essential to the understanding of the develomental process of households. Increased attention to the developmental process in the study of the Indian family will therefore involve increased attention to numerical data. Such data will have to be collected and analysed at every level from the village to the countrywide Census of India, and then coordinated for gaining a comprehensive perspective of the household pattern in the country.

I. P. Desai's discussion (1955) of the 1951 Census data created an impression that census data on the household do not and cannot have any sociological value, although in his later book on Mahuva he has expressed the possibility of improving the nature of the data collected at the censuses (1956, pp. 27, 60). Kapadia (1956) and Kulkarni (1960) have used the primary data of the 1951 National Register of Citizens with some effect. These data have even greater possibilities. The data on the numerical composition of households can also be fruitfully used, as I have tried to demonstrate in my analysis of the 1825 census of Radhvanaj. It should also be possible to use for sociological purposes the data processed and published in census reports. The main reason why sociologists have not found the census data useful is that they have not yet developed a conceptual framework within which such data could be fruitfully used.

What is really necessary is to collect detailed numerical data in micro-studies and to analyse them in such a way that the results are capable of being used in the analysis of numerical data collected in macro-studies. It is possible that a few carefully conducted micro-studies of this kind will lead to the formulation of numerical indices for correlations between social phenomena intensively observed in the field. For example, a particular ratio between simple and complex households may be an index of a certain type of developmental process of households. It may be possible to apply such indices to numerical data concerned with only a few easily observable features of the household and collected for a large sample. The ultimate aim should be to integrate the results of micro-studies such as those of villages, surveys such as those conducted by the Indian Statistical Institute, and the nationwide Census of India.

It is only the experience of handling numerical data in micro-studies that will enable us to see the national census data in a proper perspective and to use them effectively. It is also only when we have used the available census data constructively that we will be able to suggest improvements in the collection of such data. The census authorities will respond to our suggestions for improvement of census data only if we are in a position to convince them of the validity of our suggestions. It will be regrettable if we fail to develop the necessary expertise to use the huge machine of the Census of India as an aid in the study of the Indian family.

Joint Family as Joint-Property Group

Increasing emphasis is now being laid on the analysis of the situation in which the members of a defined genealogical unit live in separate households but are bound by a number of other activities of many kinds. I have not analysed in detail my data regarding this situation in Radhvanaj, nor have I given sufficient attention to it in the review of the literature, but certain points emerge clearly from both. (1) The existing analyses of inter-household kinship relations are as unsatisfactory as those of intra-household relations, but there is general agreement that a proper analysis of the situation is essential to the understanding of the changes in the Indian family in modern times. (2) The analysis of inter-household relations will have to be based on the foundation of the analysis of households. (3) The dichotomy of families into elementary and joint is as unhelpful in the analysis of inter-household relations as in that of the household. Some more suitable terms will have to be devised. (4) A consideration of inter-household relations within a defined genealogical unit poses the vexed problem of the distinction between "family" and "lineage." This in turn demands a more rigorous distinction between "household" and "family" than the one that I have made in this book, which has used the term "family" as a genealogical model (as a part of such terms as "elementary family" and "extended" or "joint family") and also as the idea of a field of social relations and activities (in such expressions as "family life," "family," "domestic family," and "study of the Indian family").

The fact that the members of a defined genealogical unit are bound by ownership and management of property, whether they live in the same household or not, is so important that a few sociologists, such as Bailey (1957, 1960), Madan (1962b, 1965), Mayer (1960), and Nicholas (1961), have suggested that the term "joint family" should be used only for the joint-property group. This suggestion may be examined here. First of all, it is necessary to decide whether the term should be used in its legal sense. As seen in Chapter 7, the legal term has a highly specialized meaning, and the *Mitaksara* and the *Dayabhaga* give different interpretations, which are different from the interpretation given in the income tax law, and all these may be different from the conceptions of the joint-property group in different sections of Hindu society. If a sociologist wants to study property relations in a society, then legal conceptions of these relations should be subjected to sociological analysis. If he accepts the framework of the legal joint family for the sociological analysis of property relations, he assumes a number of things before he begins the analysis. Even if the term is used to describe joint-property relations in custom and not in law, we cannot apply the dichotomy of elementary and joint family. For example, if joint-property rights exist between a man and his married son, we shall have to say that the father and son form a joint family within an elementary family. This would not only be clumsy but would also do violence to the word "family," reducing family relations to property relations. Madan emphasizes the dictionary meaning of "joint" in "joint family" but overlooks the meaning of "family" (1962a, p. 13). The "jointness" of "joint family" should not be considered to inhere only in joint-property relations. I suggest that the only way to remove the confusion regarding the term "joint family" is to use it in its strictly legal sense, in strictly legal contexts, and to devise some other terms for the sociological analysis of property relations.

The Joint Family and Perceptions of Educated Indians
The study of the Indian family has indeed progressed since it began with evolutionists such as Maine: crude evolutionist paradigms have been discarded and value judgements are being avoided; the Indian family system as a whole is no longer des-

cribed in terms of a large mono-type, multi-functional, three-or-four-generational group; and there is a growing realization that the elementary family is as much a part of the Indian family system as the joint family. Nevertheless, the dichotomy of elementary and joint family has continued to be the foundation of the description, analysis, and discussion of the Indian family. This is the last vestige of nineteenth-century evolutionism in the study of the Indian family, and I submit that it is necessary to get rid of it also.

One plausible argument for retaining "joint family" as a basic category in the study of the Indian family is that it is an integral part of the native categories of thought of the Indian people. But this argument needs to be carefully examined. The equivalence of "joint family" in all Indian languages is *samyukta kutumb* or *avibhakta kutumb* which occurs first in Yajnavalkya's legal text belonging to the third century A.D. and then in all subsequent texts of Classical Hindu Law (see Ghurye, 1955, p. 75). We have already seen that this term had a highly specialized meaning in Hindu Law, and that Hindu Law affected only a small section of Hindu society. The term must have been used and understood, therefore, only by this section of the society. During British rule the use of the term spread because of the spread of ideas of Hindu Law. Nevertheless, it is not as widely used as is generally believed. I have found it being used in villages in Gujarat only by those who have had experience of lawsuits or have received high school or college education.

The use of "joint family" as a more general term to describe the family as one of the social institutions of India is common only among the educated sections of the society; and their conception of "joint family" is the same as that of Indologists. It seems to me that this is due to the description of the Indian family according to the Indological view in the textbooks on such subjects as ancient Indian culture and civilization, civics, and social studies in high schools and colleges for over a century. The popular conception of the joint family owes its popularity not so much to its being a native category of thought but to its being popularized by Indologically oriented scholars, teachers, and textbook writers, and also to lawyers and the increasing popularity of lawsuits for partition of joint family property. Therefore, it is as unreal and vague as the Indological view of the Indian family. And because it is vague, it is necessary to be extremely careful in interpreting popular statements about the joint family. It seems to me useless to ask in a questionnaire or interview such questions as "Do you believe in the elementary or joint family?" or "Would you like to live in an elementary family or a joint family?"

It is significant that what has happened in the field of the family has also happened in the field of caste: the unrealistic popular conception of caste as *varna* is a result of the term being taken over by Indologists from classical literature and popularized by them through the educational system. These are only two of the many spheres in which the historian's, Indologist's, or lawyer's views on the nature of Indian society and culture have influenced the educated Indian's view of his own society.

The Study of Changes in the Household

We have seen how the basic assumptions about changes in the household pattern in India have begun to be questioned. On one side, our knowledge of the dynamics of the family at the present time drives us to question the assumption that there was just one uniform joint family in the Indian society in the past. The Indological literature does not provide the surest evidence of the kind of household pattern in the past. On the other side, the empirical evidence of the present situation shows that the expected changes have not come about.

It is not sufficient, however, to only question the prevalent assumptions; a more positive approach is called for. It is necessary, first of all, to construct a more realistic model of the household pattern in the past. We begin to get more certain information about the past with the beginning of censuses and surveys in the early nineteenth century. We have seen how the 1825 census of Radhvanaj shows that (1) the average size of the household was 4.54, (2) small and simple households were predominant, and even among the complex ones, the large majority were each composed of parents and one married son, and (3) the developmental process rarely went beyond the phase of co-residence of two or more married brothers. The census of a Maharashtra village of the same period, reported in Ghurye's *After a Century and a Quarter* (1960), shows an even smaller average size of the household — 4.26. Avalaskar (1966) has reported that in another Maharashtra village in the early nineteenth century the average number of persons per household was about 4, the nuclear family rather than the joint family was the rule, and there used to be a separation between brothers and division of their properties even while their father was alive and retained a separate share in the property. Shah, Shroff, and Shah (1963) have pointed out that the early nineteenth-century records of a number of villages and towns in Gujarat include censuses like that of Radhvanaj, and a recent publication of the Census of India (1961a) on population estimates for the decade 1820–1830 suggests that a considerable amount of census data on the household exist in several regions of India for this period. All these census data should be studied carefully to reconstruct a more reliable base line for the study of changes in the Indian family in modern times.

The censuses after the 1870 did not collect and record as much information on the household as did the earlier censuses. However, even the meagre information they provide is highly suggestive. We have already noted in Chapter 8 that according to these censuses the average size of the household was rather low, between 4.5 and 5, suggesting that most people in India lived in small and simple households. Orenstein (1961) has also shown that not only has the average size of the household not decreased from the 1871 to the 1951 census, there has been, on the contrary, a slight tendency toward increase. There are also probably more adults as well as more married and widowed

161

males per household, suggesting higher incidence of joint households, at the present time than in the past.

All the available evidence forces upon us the conclusion that there is no point in postulating a single line of change from joint- or extended-family household to the elementary-family household for the entire Indian society. There are many diverse social groups and there may therefore be many diverse lines of change. I suggest that it would be profitable to bring into the study of the household Srinivas' ideas on Sanskritization and Westernization (see Srinivas, 1962, pp. 8–11, 42–62; 1966, pp. 1–88). My analysis of the households in Radhvanaj as well as the review of the literature indicate that the principle of the residential unity of patrikin and their wives is weak among lower and less Sanskritized castes, and stronger among higher and more Sanskritized castes. I also get the impression from my limited reading of the literature on the so-called tribal or Adivasi groups that the principle is weaker among them than among the lower castes, just as they are less Sanskritized than the latter. On the other hand, the principle seems to be very weak in the Westernized section of the society, whose members have come mainly from the upper castes and urban areas. Although the tribal and the Westernized sections of the society seem to have the same degree of emphasis on the principle, it should not be forgotten that the institutional and ideological context in which it occurs is different in the two sections.

In this connection, it is worthwhile to recall the slight increase in the average size of the household indicated by Orenstein. It is possible that this increase is due to demographic factors. However, it seems worth inquiring whether the Sanskritization of lower castes and tribal groups that has been occurring on a massive scale has contributed anything to an overall greater emphasis on the principle of the residential unity of patrikin and their wives. The Westernization of higher castes must have contributed to a lesser emphasis on the principle, but the counteracting influence of Sanskritization might have led to an overall tendency in favour of greater emphasis on it.

Caste, Rural-Urban Community, and Household

As noted in Chapter 5, the historical data indicate that there was greater emphasis on the principle of the residential unity of patrikin and their wives in towns than in villages, since the higher and more Sanskritized castes formed a greater proportion of the population in towns than in villages. An examination of the empirical studies also shows that joint households are more common, and the limit of the extension of the principle of the residential unity of patrikin and their wives is wider, in small and traditional towns and in the traditional sections of large and modern cities than in the villages. This correlation between the household on the one hand and caste, Sanskritization, and rural-urban differences on the other is indeed broad, but I submit it removes a series of misconceptions about the household pattern in India and provides a more realistic framework for the study of interaction between it and the processes of industrialization, urbanization, and Westernization.

At the present time, there seem to be proportionally more simple households than complex ones in large towns and cities. It would be a mistake to regard *all* of these simple households as representing the modern ideal of the isolated conjugal family. It is necessary to consider several other possibilities also. First, a simple household in a town might represent a phase in the normal developmental process of households, in progression or in regression, in a caste group permanently settled in the town and laying strong emphasis on the principle of the residential unity of patrikin and their wives. Such simple households should not be confused with those guided by the modern ideal of independent residence. Second, a simple household in a town might have migrated into it from a village where its caste did not lay much emphasis on the principle of the residential unity of patrikin and their wives. This means that even if it had remained in the village it would have been a separate household in the normal course of development. A large proportion of the simple households of tribal and low-caste labourers found

163

in industrial centres today seem to belong to this category. They are not likely to be guided by the modern ideal of independent residence. Not only that but it is also necessary to consider the possibility of their acquiring greater emphasis on the norm of joint residence from the traditional urban society. Third, even if a simple household migrated to a town from a village or another town where its caste group laid strong emphasis on joint living, it might not have been guided in its action by the modern ideal of independent residence. It is possible that it might stay in the town for a short period, remaining linked with one or more households of near kin in the original village or town. Even if it came to the town with an intention to settle down permanently, it might remain linked for some time and become independent gradually. The phase of the developmental process during which it migrated is also important, as we have seen in Chapter 2. It might migrate during such a phase that the norm of residential unity is not violated.

Whatever the past background of a simple household migrating into a town, what is its process of development after it settles down in the town? Does it or does it not practise the traditional norms of residence? An adequate answer to this question will require observation over a long period of time. Otherwise our judgement is likely to be faulty. It seems that many of those who had migrated to towns during the earlier period of industrialization and urbanization have developed complex households and thus have joined the ranks of the permanently settled and traditional population of their respective towns. A large number of simple households in towns at the present moment, however, are of recent migrants. It is possible that they may follow the old pattern. However, if the tempo of industrialization increases, it may not give any opportunity to these as well as many other simple households to develop into complex ones. Sons and brothers may always be required to migrate out to seek employment, with the result that children grow up in milieus that are not likely to develop in them a regard for the norm of the co-residence of patrikin and their wives. They may not establish joint households even if they obtain suitable opportunities. The problem of the effect on household patterns as a consequence of migration into urban centres is thus far more complicated than it is usually believed to be.

Urbanization ought to include not only the migration of people to urban centres and the resultant changes in their style of life but also the diffusion of urban customs and institutions to rural areas. From the latter point of view, the inspiration for the increasing emphasis on the ideal of joint residence in rural areas seems to have been derived, to some extent at least, from their contact with small and traditional towns as well as the traditional sections of large cities. Contrary to the expectations roused by the familiar thesis, the urbanization of rural areas may not only not destroy jointness but in fact make it more popular.

With regard to inter-household family relationships, there is ample evidence to conclude that even those urban people who subscribe to the ideal of the simple and independent household are deeply involved in such relationships. In fact, frequently sons or brothers set up separate households in order to avoid the tensions of joint living and strengthen inter-household family ties.

Interpersonal Relations in the Family

Some studies on the Indian family are concerned only with the form or type of the family, and have nothing to say about behaviour or what is usually called interpersonal relations in the family (Mukherjee, 1959, 1962, 1965; Pakrasi, 1962). The majority of the writings, however, always include a description of behaviour, although only a few in reasonable detail (Dube, 1955; Gough, 1956; Madan, 1965; Mayer, 1960; Ross, 1961; Sarma, 1951; Srinivas, 1952a, 1952b). Taking all these writings together, we find three types of description of interpersonal relations, depending upon the level of abstraction: (1) description of the basic roles and relationships in the family, such as husband–wife, father–son, mother–son, father–daughter, mother–daughter, brother–sister, elder brother–younger brother, mother-in-law–daughter-in-law, and so on; (2) description of more general categories (i.e., each subsuming several basic roles and relationships), such as the Hindu widow, the Hindu woman, the aged, the youth, and so on; and (3) description of the general nature of interpersonal relations in the family, particularly of the personality traits and social values fostered in it. For example, whether the Indian family fosters individualism has always been a topic of discussion since Maine wrote about it in the middle of the nineteenth century. The preponderance of elementary-family households is itself considered a sign of the emergence of individualism.

I have not been able to give much attention to the descriptions of interpersonal relations in the review of the literature. I have also altogether excluded the psychological works on personality formation, child-rearing, and national character,[1] which always have something to say about interpersonal relations in the family. I have therefore not been able to evaluate my description of interpersonal relations in households in Radhvanaj in the perspective of the literature. However, I hope that my description will be useful in a comparative study of interpersonal relations, and that pending such a study it will not be out of place to point out a few implications of my description. First, interpersonal relations in the household have to be understood in the context of household forms. I have designed my analysis of the household forms in such a way that it is suited to an analysis of interpersonal relations. My contention that the classification of household compositions should take into account every member of the household is significant in this context. Equally significant are the implications of the situation in which the members of a defined genealogical unit live in two or more households but continue to be bound by a

---

[1] I have in mind particularly the works of psychologists and of anthropologists of the culture-personality school, such as Murphy (1953), Steed (1955), and Minturn and Hitchcock (1963).

number of other activities. It will readily be agreed that two given relatives behave in one way when they reside in a single household, and in another way when they reside in two different households. Furthermore, all relationships of a person with the members of his household as well as with members of related households are affected by the developmental process. In brief, general statements about each role and relationship in the family should take into account all the various situations in which the role is enacted. It will not be surprising if a number of notions about intra-family relations and their influence on personality traits of Indians, when examined from this angle, prove to be only superficial. It may also become necessary to revise ideas about the position of the Hindu woman in general and of the Hindu widow in particular, as well as about child-rearing and old age in Hindu society.

Economic Factors and the Family

How economic factors, such as property, occupation, and income, affect the Indian family has been a major problem of inquiry. I have not presented my village data on this problem because I have not so far been able to analyse them fully. Nor have I examined the literature on this point. I may, however, discuss the problem in a general way in the light of the foregoing analysis.

There is a widespread belief, particularly in the earlier literature, that the institution of joint household is found only among those who practise agriculture and allied occupations. In fact, however, it is found among people practising all kinds of occupations, in traditional as well as in modern India, in villages as well as in towns. A more significant problem in this connection is that of the effects of the increasing specialization and diversification of occupations on the household pattern in modern India. There is an increasing tendency for a son to take up a different occupation from that of his father, and for one brother to take up a different occupation from that of another. What is important is not only that the members of a family may belong to different occupational categories, but also that even within a single category they may be working separately from each other, with the result that they stay in two or more villages or towns.

Occupational diversification should not be thought of as necessarily resulting in the disintegration of joint households. In large towns and cities, occupational diversification in the household group frequently involves only the separation of places of work in different parts of the town, and many joint households are able to preserve their residential unity in spite of such separation. In villages on the rural-urban fringe, occupational diversification frequently involves only commuting for some of the members of the household group. More often, in villages as well as in towns, occupational diversification leads to migration, which obviously impairs the residential unity of the joint household. However, in this case also, as pointed out above, it is necessary to consider the possibility of the migrant household's being linked with the household of near kin in the original place of residence, and the process of development after the severance of the link. Rao (1968) has shown how the diverse economic pursuits tend to become complementary in maintaining joint households.

It is also necessary to observe the effects of occupational diversification on the household in the context of the established pattern of developmental process in a particular social group. The effects are likely to vary according to the emphasis placed by a group on the principle of the residential unity of patrikin and their wives. And within a particular group also, the effects would be different for different types of households. For example, the effects in the case of two or more brothers' practising different occupations would be different from those in the case of a father and an only son.

On the effects of wealth on the family, it is necessary to be clear about the precise sense in which the term "family" is used. If the family is considered to be a property-holding unit, there is considerable evidence to show that the incidence of joint families is greater in the wealthier sections of the society. It is also a matter of common observation that in traditional as well as in modern India the joint family is used as an instrument for getting more wealth.

How wealth affects the family as a residential unit is a more complicated problem. It is common to find in the wealthier sections of the society, households conforming to the traditional norm of joint residence as well as those conforming to the Western norm of independent residence. It may be argued, however, that there was a close relation between wealth and the household pattern in the past when there was no conflict between Indian and Western norms, and that such correlation continues to operate in the traditional sections of the society at the present time.

It is a matter of common observation that in the traditional sections of Indian society, in villages as well as towns, many joint households break up even if all the constituents of the household follow the same occupation and are wealthy. I observed in Radhvanaj how two sons of a wealthy and powerful Rajput landlord established two separate households in the village even though there were two other sons who were young and unmarried. There were also several other cases of such separation in the village. Cohn has also reported that "some of the wealthiest Chamar families do not have joint households" (1961, p. 1055).

Material interests do not seem to be a sufficient condition for maintenance of harmony in the home. Are they, however, a necessary condition? In other words, is there a certain subsistence level necessary for the existence of a joint household? Or to use Stenning's term (1958), are there any economic conditions of "viability" of a joint household? Usually there are more persons, especially more adults, in a joint household than in a simple one, and the former would need more income than the latter. It may be argued, therefore, that joint households are found only where there is more wealth. This appears to be a plausible argument. However, there are two important objections against its ready acceptance. First, it would be impossible to establish objectively a minimum standard of living for a joint household, primarily because it is necessary to take into account the preparedness of the members of a joint household to undergo economic hardships for the sake of living together. Second, a joint household as a consumption unit has many economies of scale. I have found villagers themselves pointing out the economic advantages of joint, and disadvantages of separate, households. The point is that in most cases the joint household permits a higher standard of living at a lower level of income, and that joint households can and do exist at the lowest level of subsistence.

Thus the real problem is not that joint households do or do not exist in a certain economic class but that their incidence seems to differ in different economic classes. In particular, one gets the impression that in traditional Indian society there has been a greater incidence of joint households in the wealthier classes than among the poor. Sometimes it is even argued that the greater emphasis on joint residence in higher castes is due to their being richer than the lower castes, and not due to their higher ritual status or higher degree of Sanskritization.

While the impression that there is a greater incidence of joint households among the wealthy seems to be borne out by the facts, it is not clear exactly how wealth brings this about. In other words, it is not clear exactly how wealth affects the composition and working of households. We can know this only if we know how wealth affects the several basic factors that have been identified as affecting the developmental process of households.

First, we should inquire if there is a higher frequency of migrations (permanent and not seasonal) among the poor than among the rich in traditional sections of Indian society. It is likely that poverty forces people to migrate in search of livelihood and therefore reduces the chances of formation of complex households.

Second, it is possible that poverty affects longevity adversely. This would reduce the extent of the developmental process of households among poor people — it would cut short progression and hasten regression.

Third, we should inquire if wealth affects the expected norms of household formation. I have frequently observed that "wealthy people" are expected to practise the principle of the residential unity of patrikin and their wives to a greater extent than the others. What is important here is not any specific amount of wealth — people with the same amount of wealth do not always share the same norms of household formation — but the social evaluation of wealth in different sections of the society. For example, if a leather worker and his sons are successful in acquiring more wealth than their local caste-fellows, they would be expected to conduct their home affairs in such a way that they maintain residential unity. Similarly, among businessmen in a town, who have on the whole a higher standard of living than leather workers in a village, a very wealthy businessman and his sons would be particularly expected to maintain residential unity. This relation between wealth and the norm of residential unity seems to form part of a more general phenomenon: wealth confers a certain social status; in traditional Hindu society a high degree of Sanskritization is essential for gaining high social status; and a high degree of emphasis on the norm of residential unity is one of the marks of Sanskritization. I would hasten to add, however, that the observance of many Sanskritic norms, including that of residential unity, is not always dependent on wealth and power. For example, I have found many poor Brahmans maintaining a high degree of residential jointness.

Finally, it is necessary to inquire if wealth affects the pattern of interpersonal relations in the household. We have already seen what sort of interpersonal relations are found in different types of complex households and how they are related to the roles played by the members of the household. Would the enactment of these roles differ from one economic class to another? Take, for example, the household of a man, his wife and

171

their only son and his wife. Would the mother-in-law and daughter-in-law quarrel more if the household were poor than if it were rich? Similarly, would there be more quarrels between the wives of brothers in a poor household than in a rich one?

Only systematic investigations on the questions raised above can make clear the effects of wealth on household pattern. It is possible that wealth has a considerable effect on some of the basic factors in the developmental process, such as demography and migrations, while others are affected only minimally or not at all. We should not be surprised if empirical investigations show that, taking all these basic factors into account, wealth has a minor role compared to that of caste, tribe, and Sanskritization, which, as I have indicated, greatly influence the norms of household formation.

The Threshold of the Study of the Indian Family

In the last four sections a few problems in the study of the Indian family were discussed within the framework of the dichotomy of simple and complex household even though it was pointed out earlier that this dichotomy was not meaningful. This was inevitable, because in the literature on the Indian family almost every problem is posed and discussed within the framework of the dichotomy of elementary and joint family, and the dichotomy of simple and complex household was essential to maintain continuity of discussion. It must have been noted, however, that this discussion did not take us very far in the understanding of the Indian family. I leave out for this reason the discussion of several other problems, such as those of relation between the family on the one hand and religion, education, ideology, social security, neighbourhood, and housing on the other.

It is necessary to pose the problems in the study of the household dimension of the Indian family differently — in terms of the developmental process, the principle of residential unity of patrikin and their wives, the extent of observance of the principle and of the various norms subsumed under it, the pattern

172

of interpersonal relations in the various types of households, and a real rather than hypothetical view of the past. The problem of inter-household relationships also needs a thorough re-examination.

Not only should the problems be posed differently, they should also be studied in different sections of society in different regions of the country, so that it may become possible to evolve an all-India picture. It is also necessary to employ a variety of methods and techniques of investigation, although a concentration on micro-studies and participant observation for some time to come is likely to help lay a more solid foundation for the future.

When we think of past achievements and future tasks it looks as though we are only on the threshold of the study of the Indian family.

Annotated Bibliography

Annotations have been provided mainly for those items which form part of the discussion of the empirical studies of the Indian family in Chapters 8 and 9.

AGARWALA, B. R. "In a Mobile Commercial Community," *in* "Symposium on Caste and Joint Family," *Sociological Bulletin*, IV (1955), 138–145.

This is a brief and general description of the large and multi-functional joint family in the well-known merchant caste of the Marwadis. It does not deal with the household dimension at all. The author states, "I do not regard it as essential that in a joint family all the members should stay at one and only one place and eat in one kitchen" (p. 142). They live together and take meals at one place only when they are at their native place (p. 141). They "perform religious and family rites at one place and collectively, are under the authority of the elder in matters of family and religion, joint investment of capital, joint enjoy-ment of profits, and of incurring birth, marriage and death expenses from the joint funds" (pp. 140–141). Such a family includes "direct descendants" and "cousins, grand cousins, and relations up to second and third degree. In many families not only are there lineal descendants but also sons-in-law, brothers-in-law and maternal relations" (p. 141). Many of these relatives would not fit into the definition of the joint family as a patri-lineal and patrilocal unit, and it is not possible to get a precise idea of the composition of the patrilineal and patrilocal unit, because of the use of such imprecise terms as cousins, grand cousins, and relations up to second or third degrees. The author seems to have in mind the three-or-four-generation formula of law and Indology.

AIYAPPAN, A. "In Tamil Nadu," *in* "Symposium on Caste and Joint Family," *Sociological Bulletin*, IV (1955), 117–122.
   This is a general discussion of caste and family in India, advocating quantified studies.

ARID ZONE STUDIES : A. B. Bose, "The Size and Composition of Households in Dispersed Dwellings," *Journal of Family Welfare*, X–1 (1963a), 24–31; A. B. Bose, S. P. Malhotra, and L. P. Bharara, "Socio-economic Differences in Dispersed Dwelling and Compact Settlement Types in Arid Regions," *Man in India*, 43 (1963b), 119–130; A. B. Bose and P. C. Saxena, "Composition of Rural Households in Rajasthan," *Indian Journal of Social Research*, (1964a), 299–308; S. P. Malhotra and M. L. Sen, "A Comparative Study of the Socio-economic Characteristics of Nuclear and Joint Households," *Journal of Family Welfare*, XI–2 (1964b), 21–32; A. B. Bose and P. C. Saxena, "Composition and Size of Rural Joint Households," *Indian Journal of Social Research*, (1965a), 29–40; A. B. Bose and P. C. Saxena, "Some Characteristics of Nuclear Households," *Man in India*, 45 (1965b), 195–200.
   A. B. Bose and his colleagues at the Arid Zone Research Institute, Jodhpur, have presented in these papers the data on the household collected during several surveys in southwestern Rajasthan. The 1963a and 1963b papers are concerned with a village with 405 households, 207 of which live in houses forming a compact cluster, and 198 in houses dispersed all around. A random sample of 100 households was drawn from each group for investigation. The 1963b paper provides a comparative view while the 1963a paper deals only with the dispersed dwellings. The nuclear households form 45 and 42 per cent in the compact and the dispersed dwellings respectively, and the joint house-

ho!ds 55 and 58 per cent respectively. The terms "nuclear" and "joint" are not defined, but seem to be equivalent to "simple" and "complex" households respectively. The percentages of households of the two types seem to be consistent with the figures for the average size of the household — 7.00 and 6.62 for the compact and the dispersed dwellings respectively — which are slightly higher than the all-India figures. The data about the kinship composition of the household is presented in the same way as in the reports of the 1951 census, and therefore, not useful sociologically.

The 1964a, 1965a, and 1965b papers report the data of a survey in Jalor district. At first forty-one villages were selected, one in fifteen in each Community Development Block, by systematic sampling, and then twenty per cent of all households in each village by simple random sampling, making a total sample of 1218 households. 46.5 per cent of these households were joint and 53.5 per cent nuclear.

The 1964b paper reports the findings of a survey in Barmer district. At first one in fifteen villages in each of five Panchayat Samiti Areas in the district was selected by systematic sampling, and then twenty per cent of all households in each village by simple random sampling, making a total sample of 796 households. 48.24 per cent of them were joint and 51.76 per cent nuclear. The average size of the household was 6.21, which seems consistent with the figures for joint and nuclear households.

All the papers deal mainly with demographic and economic characteristics of households. None provides sufficient information about the nature of sampling procedure, which makes critical evaluation of data impossible.

AVALASKAR, S. V. "Some Notes on the Social Life in Nagaon in the Early 19th Century", *Indian Economic and Social History Review,* III (1966), 169–173.

This provides information from a Marathi book on a predominantly Brahman village in Kolaba district in coastal Maharashtra. The book is based mainly on Marathi records of 1760–

1841 A.D., which include records of a census of population in 1840–1841 and of landholdings and land tax. They show that "the nuclear family rather than the joint family was the rule. The average number of persons per house was about four. [There was] separation of brothers and division of their properties even while their father was alive and did retain a separate share in the division" (p. 171).

BAILEY, F. G. *Caste and the Economic Frontier* (Manchester: Manchester University Press, 1957) ; "The Joint Family in India: A Framework for Discussion," *The Economic Weekly,* XII (1960), 345–352.

In *Caste and the Economic Frontier,* Bailey has tried to show that the joint-family system in Bisipara, the village of his study, has broken down under the impact of modern economic change, but it should be noted that throughout the book he uses the term "joint family" for the property-holding group and not for the household group.

It is quite clear from the description of the process of partition of estates that if a man has only one son there is no likelihood of partition (pp. 86, 90, 91). Let us believe that the partition of property between a man and his only son has never taken place in Bisipara, although it is not entirely unknown in Hindu society. Bailey does not refer to the situation in which the parents and their only son live in separate households but own and manage property jointly. He does refer, however, to the separation of a married son from his parental household because of tensions between mother-in-law and daughter-in-law, but he does not tell us whether the separation would take place if the son were the only son of his parents. The father and son may also live in two different places because of their jobs in different places, but they may remain joint in property, earnings, expenses, and so forth. It is not clear whether Bailey would use the term "joint family" for the joint-property unit of parents and their only son living in two separate households, or for a group of a man and his married son living in a single household as well as managing property jointly. It is also not clear whether Bailey would apply his ideas about the causes of the break-up of joint family — divergent interests and disparate incomes — to the group of parents and their only son.

The description of the process of partition of the property-holding group on pp. 87–89 applies only to the group of parents and a plurality of sons: "When the eldest son marries and brings a wife to his father's house ... the father, mother, son and his wife form one household, both as producers and consumers. Some households go on like this for quite a long time, but most seem to break up within six months. The trouble starts within the kitchen and the girl demands a separate cooking place. Usually she gets her own share of the harvest as well as her own fire. They [the father and the eldest son] are still working the land in common under the management of the father. But when the harvest is gathered and thrashed, the grain is divided between the kitchens of the mother-in-law and daughter-in-law." This means the father and the son now form a joint-property group even though they live in separate households. The eldest son, however, soon demands his share of the fields, and an anticipatary division of property is made. That is, as Bailey states, "The size of the share will depend on the number of sons who will inherit and it is usual for the father to take the opportunity to settle once for all which field will go to which son and which he will retain for himself and his wife. It is usual for the father to allow for the expenses of marrying off daughters in the share which he keeps for himself, and to divide the brass vessels and jewellery into dowry-lots. He usually retains the management of the land of the unmarried sons."

Bailey does not go further, but let us follow his logic. When one of the unmarried sons marries and brings his wife to his father's house, a joint household and property-holding unit will come into existence. This son will also secede. If there is a third son, the process will be repeated. What happens to the parents when the last son is married? Does he also secede, leaving the parents alone? Or do the parents live with one of the sons? If the latter happens, a joint household and property-holding group continues to exist. At any one point of time, therefore, there would be a fairly large number of joint-property groups composed of parents and one married son. Furthermore, as Bailey himself tells us, if the land is divided at the father's death and the younger sons are unmarried, then a married brother will manage the estate. Strictly speaking, this is also a joint-property unit and therefore a joint family. The point is that Bailey seems to consider only that property-holding group a joint family which is composed of two or more married brothers. This can hardly be considered the proper definition of the joint family. It is also noteworthy that in the analysis of this property-holding group only landed property is taken into account, but joint families exist among non-landowning groups also, and it is doubtful if Bailey's ideas about the breakdown of the joint family would apply to these groups. Finally, his analysis of changes in the property group rests on doubtful assumptions about the past.

"The Joint Family in India: A Framework for Discussion" is a methodological paper wherein Bailey has asserted that "there is only one definitive activity of the joint family: common ownership of property (for the coparceners) and a right to maintenance from common property (for the whole joint family)." He clarifies: "Living under the same roof, eating from the same hearth, or practising common rituals are activities in which a joint family may indulge, but we will not deny the name 'joint family' to groups which do not have these latter activities in common. On the other hand we cannot apply the term 'joint family' and still less the term 'coparcenary' to those who have no common property" (p. 345). All this sounds like the provisions of Hindu Law, but actually Bailey is interested in making a sociological study of the joint-property group within the general framework of S. F. Nadel's ideas on social equilibrium (see p. 347). He takes into account kinship behaviour, laws, morals, and so forth, but views them as only helping or obstructing the maintenance of equilibrium of the joint-property group. We may say the study of the joint-property group is Bailey's central interest, but his insistence on the common ownership of property and the right to maintenance from common property as *the only definitive activities* of the joint family narrows drastically the scope of joint-family activities. He seems to admit this in a sentence on p. 349: "I have taken a narrow definition on the criteria of recruitment in two ways and activities concerning property."

Concerning the criteria of recruitment, Bailey maintains that a *coparcenary* composed of males of common descent becomes a *joint family* when we take into account the wives of the coparceners. He admits that "these definitions do not deal very happily with the daughters of the coparceners," but he includes them as members of the joint family until they marry, because they have "defined claims on the joint family property" [of maintenance and marriage expenses?] and "may opt to return to it and in certain circumstances their children may inherit joint property" (p. 347). These criteria are almost the same as those given in Hindu Law, but Bailey does not provide any precise definition of the number of patrilineal descendants to be included in the coparcenary. He refers to the lineage but does not say where the joint family ends and the lineage begins. He frequently mentions what he calls the "complete" joint family, but does not provide its definition. The "overcomplete" families are "those which include such persons as widowed sisters returned to their natal homes, or uterine dependents" (p. 347). This does not give us any idea of the extension of patrilineal descent in the formation of the coparcenary.

Bailey suggests that in the study of the joint family "the first task would be to collect the 'incomplete' forms of joint family, *starting from nuclear family* and building up towards what we *assume* to be the norm. These would then be arranged in a sequence and the steps from one to the other would have to be described" (p. 349, italics mine). He also considers "the division into nuclear families" an important characteristic of the joint family (p. 347). Madan has rightly pointed out two important inconsistencies in Bailey's formulation: (1) "If coparcenary rights exist between a man and his unmarried sons, is that nuclear family a joint family or not?" (2) "Why is the joint family to be conceived of as a group divided into nuclear families only? Is there a reason as to why smaller joint families cannot exist within larger ones?" (1962b, p. 11). Moreover, how do we decide the norm? Should the *assumption* regarding the norm be arbitrary? If the legal norm is assumed, then there is no problem of definition. But if we insist on defining the customary norm, it does not seem to me to be an easy task. Finally, I wish Bailey had provided a few examples of "incomplete" forms and indicated the method of arranging them in a sequence. I raise this question because the way in which he exemplifies his general ideas in this paper makes me suspect that he has in view the same kind of analysis of the joint family as that in his Bisipara book. We have already seen the limitations of that analysis.

Bott, Elizabeth. *Family and Social Network* (London: Tavistock Pulications, 1957).

Carstairs, G. Morris. *The Twice-Born: A Study of a Community of High-Caste Hindus* (Bloomington: Indiana University Press, 1957).

Census of India, 1911a, I (India), I (Report); 1911b, V (Bengal, Bihar, Orissa, Sikkim), I (Report); 1911c, X (Central Provinces), I (Report); 1911d, XII (Madras), I (Report); 1911e, XIV (Punjab), I (Report); 1911f, XV (United Provinces), I (Report); 1921a, I (India), I (Report); 1921b, III (Assam), I (Report); 1921c, VIII (Bombay), I (Report); 1921d, XV (Punjab, Delhi), I (Report); 1921e, XVI (United Provinces), I (Report); 1921f, XVII (Baroda), I (Report); 1931a, I (India), I (Report); 1931b, V (Bengal, Sikkim), I (Report); 1931c, VII (Bihar, Orissa), I (Report); 1931d, VIII (Bombay), I (Report); 1931e, XIX (Baroda), I (Report); 1931f, XXV (Mysore), I (Report); 1951a, I (India), I-A (Report); 1951b, IV (Bombay, Saurashtra, Kutch), I (Report and Subsidiary Tables); 1951c, Paper I, *Characteristics of Family Households, West Bengal;* 1961a, *Report on the Population Estimates of India* 1820–30; 1961b, I (India), II–c (i) (Social and Cultural Tables).

COHN, BERNARD S. "Chamar Family in a North Indian Village: A Structural Contingent," *The Economic Weekly*, XIII (1961), 1051–1055.

In the beginning of this paper Cohn states Murdock's definitions of nuclear and extended families with regard to their composition, and Karve's definition of joint family with regard to its functional characteristics, rejecting implicitly her definition of its composition (see pp. 247 and 219–220 for Murdock's and Karve's definitions respectively). He then classifies extended families into two sub-types, *stable* and *unstable,* and calls the *stable* one the *joint family* (p. 1051). This means he does not consider the terms "joint family" and "extended family" synonymous. He states further that the ideal type of household among the Chamars "consists of three generations in which grandfather, his sons, and their wives and families lived in one house and ate from the same *chula*" (p. 1052). The meaning of "families" in this statement is not clear; it does not indicate whether the grandchildren's generation includes married grandsons or not, but I guess it includes only unmarried grandsons.

In Table 1 Cohn classifies 80 out of 122 households of the Chamars in the village as nuclear and 42 as extended. The 80 nuclear households, however, include 8 each composed of "a single aged adult," and 72 each composed of "man, wife and unmarried offspring," or "woman and unmarried offspring." In his discussion, however, Cohn does not use this distinction between the complete nuclear family and two types of the incomplete nuclear family.

Four out of 42 extended families are each composed of a man, wife, daughters, daughters' husbands and offspring — obvious cases of the custom of *ghar-jamai*. 24 households are each composed of "man, wife, sons, sons' wives and offspring," and 14, of "brothers, wives and offspring." The former are simply extended and the latter both extended and joint. Cohn explains, "Only 14 approximate the cultural ideal type of a joint family in that there were either three generations living together, or if the grand-parental generation had died off, the brothers were over the age of twenty." (There is a discrepancy between this statement and the composition of the 14 households mentioned in Table 1.) "Many of those families classified as extended predictably were going to break apart within a few years. In many of the cases there were several sons, one or two of whom may have been married and may have had infant offspring, giving three generations; but when the sons got older, usually above the age of twenty, the households would break apart into their constituent nuclear components" (p. 1052). Cohn describes at some length the factors responsible for this break-up or "which make the achievement of the ideal joint family difficult." These are (1) low life expectancy, (2) low level of subsistence, (3) frequent migrations in search of livelihood from one village to another village and to cities and towns, and (4) quarrels between wives and sons and between mother-in-law and daughter-in-law. What Cohn really wants to convey, it seems to me, is that there is a widespread tendency among the Chamars towards the break-up of households of parents and married sons, either because of premature death of parents or because of tensions and migrations during the lifetime of parents. With regard to the households of brothers, wives, and offspring, the married brothers must have lived together during the lifetime of their parents, they have continued to live together after the death of their parents, and their married sons also live with them. This seems to me to be the reason why Cohn has classified these households as both extended and joint families, and the households of the other types as simply extended, the implication being that the former are *stable* and the latter *unstable*.

If the above inferences are legitimate, then several statements at the end of the paper seem to be questionable. All the 42 extended families are referred to as joint-family households (p. 1055). We further read, "If a man leaves his family behind while he goes to work in the city, he usually leaves his family *with his parents or with his brother*. For the period of the man's absence, there is a joint family since the money remitted from the city goes into common fund and what land the man may have is used jointly. When the man returns, however, he may set up an independent household, and he will then not share the money he brings. I call this type of joint family an *unstable joint family:* one which has been set up to meet a particular economic situation" (italics mine). It is not clear whether the phrase "unstable joint family" shows a further differentiation of the joint family (stable extended family) composed of brothers, wives, and children, or an inconsistent application of the terms "stable extended family" and "unstable extended family" as they are defined in the beginning of the paper. It is also not clear which of the three sub-types of extended family comes into existence temporarily when a man leaves his family with his parents or with his brother.

Leaving these terminological difficulties aside, Cohn's paper is valuable for the demonstration of his central point that "the type of family is not a fixed entity but rather a structural contingent," a result of the operation of a combination of factors. He discusses mainly four factors (1) life expectancy (i.e., demography), (2) economy, (3) interpersonal relations in the family, and (4) migration, but he also suggests several other factors such as Sanskritization, tradition of living in joint-family households, urban employment, and literacy. His observations on the economic factors are particularly significant: "A joint-family household requires something above a bare minimum subsistence for its continuation" (p. 1053), and "It is not only land or property which tends to bring about joint-family households among Chamars; rather a combination of factors may be involved. Land is important, but not sufficient; some of the wealthiest Chamar families do not have joint-family households" (p. 1055).

CONKLIN, GEORGE H. "The Family Formation Process in India: An Overview," *Journal of Family Welfare,* XIV (1968), 28–37; "Social Change and the Joint Family: the Causes of Research Biases," *Economic and Political Weekly,* IV (1969), 1445–1448.

The first paper is concerned with the household, although the word family is also used as its synonym frequently. The focus is on the process of family formation. It is considered to be dependent on (1) the family cycle, that is, the cycle of births, marriages, and deaths, and (2) the social customs and the norms governing the family. "The lineal joint family consisting of a father and his married sons, with scattering of brother-brother joint households" is considered to be the traditional norm, and the life cycle is considered to make norm-fulfilment difficult and to lead to a large number of non-normative households (p. 29). It is rightly argued that joint households would constitute only a minority of households at any one time, and the presence of many nuclear households cannot be attributed to a breakdown of traditional patterns. This argument is supported mainly by data collected by Allen Grimshaw on a sample of households in Poona. No attention is paid, however, to partitions, which signify non-fulfilment of norms owing to factors other than the family cycle.

The households are classified into four types defined as follows (p. 31): (1) *nuclear*: father, mother, their unmarried children, and no other relative; (2) *transitional*: father, mother, children, plus assorted single relatives, such as father's mother; (3) *joint*: two or more related couples, including children and other added related persons; and (4) *sub-nuclear*: uni-member families, and those nuclear families who lack one parent. Of the 800 households of the sample the nuclear constitute 43.4 per cent, the transitional 23.5, the joint 18.5, and the sub-nuclear 14.6 per cent.

This typology has two major limitations: (1) it is not clear in which type would a married couple without children be included, and (2) the phrase "other related persons" in the joint type lacks precision. What is even more important, however, is that although the types sub-nuclear and transitional have been formulated the general discussion of the Indian family vis-a-vis the American family is carried on in terms of only the nuclear and the joint types. While the transitional type should not be included in the nuclear in the American context, it should not be excluded from the joint in the Indian context.

The transitional and the joint types together account for 42 per cent and the nuclear and the sub-nuclear together 58 per cent. This supports my contention that the complex households form a relatively higher proportion in older towns (of which Poona is one) than in villages.

The second paper is an excellent discussion of three important points. (1) Scholars approach the study of the Indian family with a bias that economic development in traditional societies would cause a change from the joint family of the East to the nuclear family of the West. They find a perfect fit in the statistical preponderance of the nuclear families at the present time. "Scholars too often assumed what they set out to prove... The actual practice of today is being compared to a very idealised pattern of the past, and the necessary differences interpreted as a change over time" (p. 1447). (2) The people, particularly in the villages, also idealise the past. They believe in the "good old times" when the joint family was the rule; and its decline is recent. (3) Both of these biases have led the scholars to neglect the influence of demography on the observance of family norms.

In this paper also, while the role of demography is emphasised, that of partitions is neglected.

DAVIS, KINGSLEY. "Changing Modes of Marriage: Contemporary Family Types," *in* H. Becker and R. Hill (eds.), *Marriage and the Family* (New York: D. C. Heath, 1942); *Human Society* (New York: Macmillan, 1948).

The paper in the Becker and Hill volume is one of the earliest attempts by a professional sociologist to view the Indian family and marriage in a cross-cultural perspective on the basis of available literature. It describes essentially the "classical" form of each family system and attempts to indicate briefly the direction of change. Each system is viewed as moving toward a standard Western type, "a part of highly transmissible culture which Americans and Englishmen diffuse wherever they go" (p. 92). Davis's general approach is evolutionist and ethnocentric. In the specific case of India, the conceptual framework is the same as that of Maine's and O'Malley's, and the sources of information are hardly any different from O'Malley's (see Chapter 8 for my discussion of Maine and O'Malley), but it shows the continuing interest in the Indian family for cross-cultural studies.

The section on the Hindu family in *Human Society*, a very widely used textbook in sociology, is essentially the same as in the preceding paper (pp. 418–422).

DERRETT, J. DUNCAN M. "Law and the Predicament of the Hindu Family," *The Economic Weekly*, XII (1960), 305–311; "The Administration of Hindu Law by the British," *Comparative Studies in Society and History*, IV (1961), 10–52; "The History of the Juridical Framework of the Joint Hindu Family," *Contributions to Indian Sociology*, VI (1962), 17–47; *Introduction to Modern Hindu Law* (Bombay: Oxford University Press, 1963).

DESAI, I. P. *High School Students in Poona* (Poona: Deccan College, 1953); "Caste and Family," *The Economic Weekly*, VI (1954), 249–254; "An Analysis" *in* "Symposium on Caste and Joint Family," *Sociological Bulletin*, IV (1955), 97–117; "The Joint Family in India: An Analysis," *Sociological Bulletin*, V (1956), 146–156; *Some Aspects of Family in Mahuva* (Bombay: Asia Publishing House, 1964a); *The Patterns of Migration and Occupation in a South Gujarat Village* (Poona: Deccan College, 1964b).

I. P. Desai has been studying the family in India for a number of years. He asked a few searching questions in the questionnaire he used for his study of the high school students of Poona. His review of Murphy's book *In the Minds of Men* (1953) was virtually a general article on "Caste and Family." He presented his thoughts in a comprehensive manner, however, first in his paper "An Analysis" in the "Symposium on Caste and Joint Family." In the first half of this paper he examines at some length the views expressed and the data presented in some of the reports on the 1951 Census of India. In the course of this examination he raises the question of definition of terms. His basic stand is that the family is different from the household — a distinction he follows in substance but not always in language. In the census reports the high proportion of households of small size is taken to be an indicator of a trend toward the break-up of the traditional joint family as a residential group (see pp. 133–138 for my discussion of the census reports). Desai argues that is is not an indicator of the break-up of the joint-family system as such, because a household composed of a nuclear family continues to be a part of a joint family for a number of other functions. This is a valid argument in itself, but Desai criticises the census officials for a proposition that they have not in fact made. They speak of the break-up of the joint family in the sense of the household group, but he presumes they speak of the break-up of the entire joint-family system. As far as households are concerned, he thinks on the basis of Kapadia's *Hindu Kinship* (1947) that the classical joint household was composed of more than three generations (pp. 110–111) but that it has contracted to the household of three generations (pp. 108, 111) and has not disintegrated as the census officials and others believe. While census officials assert that joint households are not common, Desai asserts that nuclear households are not common. He advances four major arguments against them. (1) The kinship composition of the household cannot be inferred from its numerical composition (pp. 101, 103, 107). (2) The total number of persons living in households of the joint-family type is a better index of the strength of the joint family than the total number of households of the same type, because the former indicates the influence of the household group on the individual (pp. 101, 103). (3) If a household is composed of a nuclear family plus any dependent, it should be considered a joint family. The data on dependents provided by the census itself suggest wider prevalence of the joint household (pp. 100–101, 105–107). (4) Nuclear households grow into joint households and therefore the higher proportion of nuclear households is not an indication of the break-up of the joint household. On the whole, Desai concludes, "the census authorities do not have basis in their own data for making the statement regarding the prevalence of the joint family" (p. 108). There is a great deal of validity in all four arguments, except

189

that the census data on the numerical size of households are not as useless as Desai suggests.

In the latter half of the paper Desai discusses in a general way the nature of the joint family found at the present time and the changes that have taken place in what he considers to be the classical joint family. He raises more questions than he answers. The discussion suffers also from two basic weaknesses: first, imprecise use of the term "generation," and second, uncritical reliance on Kapadia's *Hindu Kinship* (1947) for knowledge about the classical family. The major conclusion of the discussion is the necessity to distinguish between the household group and the functional group.

The theme of Desai's next paper, "The Joint Family in India: An Analysis," is the same as that of the preceding one — to show that the household group is different from the functional group and that the kinship composition of the household cannot be inferred from its numerical composition — but he now makes these points on the basis of the preliminary results of his own investigation in Mahuva, a small town in Saurashtra (a part of Gujarat). He provides here his own definition of the nuclear family: "We can call a household a nuclear family if it is composed of a group of parents and their unmarried children or of the husband, wife and unmarried children, not related to their other kin through or by property or income or the rights and obligations pertaining to them and as are expected of those related by kinship" (p. 148). This means that, according to Desai, a household which is composed of a nuclear family but is related to other households in the specified ways is not a nuclear family — a confusing phraseology. Another special feature of this paper is the presentation of no less than twenty-eight types and sub-types of family and their correlation with eleven household types. I need not comment upon this typology, because it was published as an agenda for discussion and a new typology was evolved for the final report. I shall rest content with only one general observation: Desai's "joint family" includes, consistent with its general definition, all persons not included in "elementary family."

In the final report, *Some Aspects of Family in Mahuva,* the most crucial concepts are "jointness" and "nuclearity," which are frequently described as abstractions and cultural objects, the former a part of the ancient heritage of India, and the latter a borrowing from the West. While nuclearity is represented by the household composed of a man, his wife, and unmarried children *and* not related in any way with any kinsmen living in other households (pp. 30–34, 157), jointness is represented by joint activities. The primary aim of the book is to present an analysis of jointness in Mahuva.

In this book also Desai frequently emphasises the necessity to distinguish between the household and the family, and follows the distinction in substance though not always in language. We frequently find such confusing statements as "Nuclear families are really joint families" (pp. 34, 42–43). I shall soon indicate the source of this confusion.

Desai took a sample of 423 households in Mahuva and concentrated his investigation on the relations of each household with other households in the joint-family setting. He has formulated two schemes of classification of the sample households. Classification I is based on kinship relationships among members of the household, and Classification II, on relations of one household with other households.

In Classification I there are four major types (see pp. 34–35, 41–44, 151–156). Desai states repeatedly that this typology is based on the generation principle. Types I, II, III, and IV are constituted of one-generation, two-generation, three-generation, and four- or more-than-four-generation households, respectively. He also mentions the difficulties he experienced in applying the principle and makes a number of qualifications to it while fitting the households of various compositions into the four types. He has devised two sub-types in Type I as well as in Type II. Type I-a includes husband-wife households, and Type I-b, uni-member households. Type II-a includes households composed of a male Ego, his wife, and unmarried children, or married sons without children, or both. Type II-b includes households of the above-mentioned relatives *plus* other relatives who do not add to the generation depth (these latter include mostly relatives on the side of Ego's sister, mother, and wife). After classifying 423 households of the sample into these six types, Desai tries to fit them into the usual dichotomy of nuclear and joint family (see pp. 41–44). The households of Types I-a, I-b, II-a, and II-b are nuclear and those of Types III and IV are joint. He is aware, however, of the difficulties implicit in his classification. First, the households of II-b are nuclear according to the typology, but "really speaking, they are joint." Second, the households of II-a include some ˉomposed only of the nuclear family *plus* one married son without children, and these are really joint families. Thus, according to the typology the nuclear households constitute 61 per cent of the sample, but really speaking they are only 42 per cent — almost complete reversal of the percentage. It is difficult to understand why Desai remains faithful to his typology even though he is fully aware of its inadequacies. He states, "The Type II-b is not joint *because of the criterion of generation,* but they are, really speaking, joint households. But we have put them in the category of nuclear *for the sake of logical consistency*" (p. 35, italics mine). The preference for a logical consistency that grossly distorts social reality is difficult to understand. In effect, he is trying to defend his typology although it is logically inconsistent with the generation principle which, in fact, provides the basis of his typology.

As Classification II is meant to deal with inter-household relations I shall not examine it here in detail, but I shall make two general comments. (1) In this classification the households are first classified into nuclear and joint according to their internal composition. Nuclear households are then classified into three types. Type I includes those nuclear households which are also nuclear families, that is, those having no joint activities whatever with other households. Types II and III include those nuclear households which are joint families, that is, those having joint activities with other households; the two types are distinguished on the basis of the nature of joint activities. All joint households are considered joint families on account of their internal composition, irrespective of whether they have joint activities with other households. They are classified into two types (IV and V) on the basis of their internal composition, and the two together account for 51 per cent of the sample households (see Table 10). The point is that Classification II is not based entirely on relations of one household with other households. This is a serious limitation of Desai's analysis of inter-household relations. (2) It is important to note that the unit of observation in Desai's investigation is the household. When he considers joint family activities he considers the joint activities of each sample household with one or more other households outside the sample, and not of the entire group of two or more households involved in criss-cross activities. This is another serious limitation of Desai's study of inter-household relations. It seems to me that the failure to take note of this situation is one of the sources of terminological confusion in his book. When he states that a nuclear family is really a joint family, what he means is that a nuclear household is *joint with* other household(s), and not that it is *joint in itself*.

In Part I of the book there is a chapter on the household, and the other chapters deal with the nature of Mahuva town and the approach to the study of the Indian family, while the whole of Part II deals with inter-household relations. The major part of the book is thus concerned with inter-household relations. However, Desai recognizes the necessity for intensive study of the internal nature of the household, not only for its own sake but also for the sake of a proper understanding of inter-household relations. He considers a study of the household to be the starting point of the study of the family (pp. 25–26, 60–62). At an early stage in the book (p. 27) he mentions what he calls "the very relationship of living together," and explains it in a footnote: "It is not considered right for the son to separate away from the parents. But it is considered more normal for the brothers to separate, though living together may be appreciated. Among the relatives other than these, the type and distance between them enters into the expectations about living together. Uncle and nephew could expect of each other that the one should keep the other with him. But as distance increases this expectation becomes less srong." Desai is actually mentioning here the hierarchy of norms governing the formation of households. Unfortunately he has decided not to consider it any further in his analysis.

In the chapter on the household Desai deals first with the classification of households as discussed above. He then considers the developmental cycle of households (although he does not use this phrase), and points out that separation of nuclear households from joint households used to occur in the past as at the present, but he conceives of only two phases of development, nuclear and joint. He then deals with the causes of separation of nuclear households from joint households. He reports in Tables 6 and 7 the answers regarding causes given by heads of nuclear households, and classifies the causes into "natural to joint living" and "circumstantial and/or temporary." The formulation of the tables, the classification of causes, and their interpretation are all unsatisfactory. I shall consider here only a few important points. One major cause of separation is migration for the sake of occupation, either of the head of the nuclear household into Mahuva or of his close kin from Mahuva. Another cause is the death of certain members of the household. The third cause is rivalry, competition, "heart-burning," disputes, quarrels, and so on. The description of the various kinship situations in which quarrels lead nuclear families to set up separate households suggests that there is an interrelation between kinship situations or norms concerning the formation of households on one side and quarrels and separation on the other. Desai does not examine this interrelation, but it is clear that in certain situations the society permits individuals to establish separate households if they wish to. Table 7 contains evidence for something even more radical: 16 per cent of the households were "separated after marriage as a matter of course." We also read on p. 79 about the Harijans: "As a custom, separation after marriage is more common among them than among others." This means that something very nearly approaching neolocality is widely practised in at least one caste in Mahuva. This fact contradicts the view that the concept of the nuclear household is alien to India. Nor is Desai correct in asserting that the joint family (of his definition) is non-existent in the West.

I have already shown the shortcomings of the figures for different types of households presented by Desai. Despite these shortcomings it is clear that in Mahuva the proportion of joint households is much larger than that of nuclear households. And among the joint households there is a larger proportion of joint households with greater genealogical depth. Six per cent of the sample households are composed of four or more than four generations. The biggest household consists of twenty-seven persons, and there are instances of still larger households outside the sample (p. 42). We are further informed that there is a higher degree of jointness among the long-established population of the town than among the recent immigrants (pp. 115–123).

Desai explains these facts as follows: "The belief that the nuclear type of family is consistent with urban area may not be true. Or the urban area we have investigated is not urban. If we think of Mahuva in terms of its social structure and functional systems, Mahuva is not very much different from the surrounding rural areas. It is a rural town. The population can be characterised as urban-dwelling ruralites" (p. 124; see also p. 111). Desai is puzzled here because he makes, implicitly, the common assumption that the joint family is a characteristic of only villages and not of towns. The solution of the puzzle seems to me to lie in the correlation between caste, village/town, and household I have suggested in Chapter 5. (Note that Mahuva and Radhvanaj are in the same culture area.) In other words, the explanation of the strong emphasis on the joint family in Mahuva lies in the fact, described by Desai himself, that Mahuva is an old town with a high proportion of the population of higher castes (pp. 5–22, 74–80).

Part II deals with the relation between jointness and other social groups and institutions, such as religion, caste, occupation, education, urbanization, and kinship obligations. This is indeed an important contribution to the study of interhousehold relations, but I do not discuss it here in detail, for it says very little on the nature of life within the household. It is sufficient to remark that the analysis of each social group or institution has suffered because of, first, the use of the two schemes of classification of households, and second, a failure to see each group or institution in a proper structural setting (see, for example, my comments on rural-urban differences in the preceding paragraph).

DESAI, N. C. *Report on the Hindu Joint Family: Its Economic and Social Aspects* (Baroda: Baroda State Press, 1936).

This is perhaps the first full-length general book, though a neglected one, on the Hindu family. Its first chapter deals with definitions and theories of evolution of the joint family; the second, with the role of the joint family in the economic life of a rural population; the third, with the role of the joint family in the economic life of an urban population; the fourth, with the legal aspects of the joint family; and the fifth, with its social aspect. Desai used his personal observations as well as the published material about the Hindu family in census reports, reports of socio-economic surveys, reports of government committees, historical and legal works, novels and biographies, and other works. What is more noteworthy, however, is that the treatment of the subject is mostly "social structural," although Desai had not studied sociology and the structural approach was not fashionable in those days. For example, the book deals with the family in rural and urban areas and among various social and economic groups and classes within each of the two areas. Desai's book is in many ways better than the contemporary works of O'Malley, but while the latter has received much attention, the former was completely neglected, presumably because of poor publicity. It came to the attention of sociologists after the establishment of the Department of Sociology in the University of Baroda in 1951.

DUBE, S. C. *Indian Village* (London: Routledge & Kegan Paul, 1955).

In the chapter on the family in this monograph on a village in Telengana, Dube first describes the composition of households in terms of the elementary and joint family. He defines an "ideal" joint family as a five-generation unit, composed of Ego, his wife, his parents and paternal grandparents, his brothers and their wives and children, his sons and their wives and children, and his unmarried sisters and daughters (p. 133). He further mentions a family type in which "all nuclear families of three generations share a common house." If the great-grandchildren were included, this would be a four-generation family. Dube considers households of both the four-generation and the five-generation types almost impossible to find in villages in Telangana, though they are found in small number in towns and cities. He mentions joint families found in actual practice in rural areas as belonging to two well-known types — one composed of parents and their married sons and their wives and children, and the other composed of brothers and their wives and children. Joint families of even these two types are not common, because it is common for sons to separate from their parents within a few years of their marriage (p. 133). Dube's vivid description of the web of family ties applies mostly to these two types of joint family and to its antithesis, the elementary family.

Dube does not make it clear whether all the married sons leave their parents, or whether at least one of the sons remains with them to look after them in their old age. He also does not tell us whether an only son separates from his parents to establish a separate household. On the other hand, he refers to old parents living with their son's elementary family, and to their returning to live with thir son (p. 135). He also describes the relation between sons and aged parents: "At this stage the old people are expected not to interfere with the domestic management of the household, and as a price for this non-interference the sons and their wives are enjoined by tradition to forget all disputes and dissensions and 'give as much comfort to the old

people in their last days' as they possibly can" (pp. 152–153).
All this shows that some, if not many, old parents do live with
a married son, but it is not clear whether Dube would use the
term "joint family" for a household composed of one or both
parents and one married son.

Dube shows that after separation the seceding family and the
main family take an interest in each other's affairs and problems
and participate in common ceremonies, feasts, festivals, and
rites of passage (p. 134). He does not refer, however, to the
situation in which a man may live in a separate household and
own property and participate in occupational activities jointly
with his parents or brothers. Should we assume that in this
Telengana village this situation is totally absent?

Dube then shows how a local word equivalent to "family" is
used to denote three different social units. First, it denotes "the
elementary family or the 'house'" (p. 134). Its composition is
stated as follows: "In many cases it consists only of the husband
and wife, their sons and unmarried daughters. In others one or
both parents, unmarried brothers and unmarried sisters may
also belong to this unit" (p. 135). The former undoubtedly
denotes an elementary family, but the latter denotes a unit wider
than an elementary family. The classification of both as elementary family is an illustration of inconsistent application of the
dichotomy of elementary and joint family.

The second social unit denoted by "family" is "extended
family or allied families," and the third is "a still larger group
comprising the near-kin on the paternal side" (pp. 134–135).
The composition of these units is shown in a diagram, a full
discussion of which would require much space and is also outside the scope of this book. However, it may be stated briefly
that the "extended family" is a unit composed of a man, his
wife, and all of his male patrilineal descendants and some of
his female patrilineal descendants for four generations (a four-
generation group, excluding the common ancestor's generation)
and wives of some male descendants. The members of the extended family meet on ceremonial and ritual occasions, consult
one another on important social, economic, and political

problems, and are expected to be a united group. The wider group of near-kin is, roughly speaking, a five-generation group (excluding the common ancestor's generation). Its functions are not described, and it is not related to the *vamsham* or lineage described on pp. 42–43.

DUMONT, LOUIS. "Marriage in India: the Present State of the Question," *Contributions to Indian Sociology*, V (1961), 75–95.

DUMONT, LOUIS, and POCOCK, DAVID F. "Kinship," *Contributions to Indian Sociology*, I (1957), 43–64.

EPSTEIN, T. SCARLETT. *Economic Development and Social Change in South India* (Manchester: University Press, 1962).

This study of economic development and social change in Wangala and Dalena, a wet and a dry village respectively in Mysore, includes a study of the relation between economic development and the family. Wangala has 958 people residing in 192 households and Dalena 707 people residing in 153 households. The average size of the household is thus 4.0 and 4.6 respectively, which reflects the predominance of "small" households as in the rest of the country.

Epstein provides very little information on the kinship composition of households. She states only that "most households in Wangala are composed only of elementary families: only 10 per cent of the total 192 households contain more than the members of the elementary family and an occasional grandparent" (p. 176), and "only about 8 per cent of all Dalena households still live as joint households" (p. 306). The relative importance of the elementary family indicated by these figures conforms to the all-India picture.

Epstein does not provide definitions of the elementary and the joint family, but it may be assumed that she has followed the usual definitions. Another and even more serious problem in following Epstein's analysis of her data on the household and family is that she confuses between the family as the household unit and the family as the property-holding unit. She repeatedly asserts that "joint families can exist only on the basis

199

of jointly owned estates" (pp. 176, 306). This assertion, however, does not apply to the joint family as the household unit: there are several types of joint or complex households which are not joint-property units. And a single joint-property unit could be divided into several household units. Epstein believes that "economic development will almost invariably result in the breaking up of joint family ties" (p. 322). "A cyclical process of the periodic break-up of joint families and the emergence of new ones, has given way to a process of change in which joint families break up under the impact of economic change and no new ones emerge" (p. 177). Epstein tries to support this view by certain ideas about the past. She states, "In the course of collecting genealogies [in Wangala], I found ample evidence of the predominance of the joint family among Peasants and Functionaries, but none among Untouchables" (p. 176). It is possible that genealogies provide information about ownership of property, but I doubt they provide accurate information about the composition of households in the past. As a matter of fact, Epstein got information only about land: "Peasants had such [joint] estates, whereas Untouchables had only small land grants from Government" (p. 176). In Dalena also, "Peasants used to have joint estates and therefore had joint families" (p. 306). This cannot be considered evidence about the nature of the household in the past. In particular, her idea that in the family system in India the egalitarian principle operated in the past, and the individual initiative and competitive attitudes have arisen only in recent time because of economic development, is one of the facile assumptions usually found in the study of the Indian family over a long period of time.

Epstein's hypothesis regarding the breakdown of the joint family as the joint-property unit is also far from convincing. She describes at some length the high frequency of adoptions of sons in Wangala — 10 per cent of the total male Peasants at the time of her census were adopted (pp. 178–179). This shows that the jointness between father and son is still as strong as before. On jointness between brothers, it would be necessary to have more convincing evidence to believe that it was very strong among Peasants in the past. Epstein also seems to be ignoring the shrewdness of the Mysore peasant when she considers the formality of transfer of land-title required for obtaining sugar cane contracts as encouraging real partition of family property (pp. 58–59).

EVANS-PRITCHARD, E. E. *Social Anthropology* (London: Cohen & West, 1951).

FORTES, MEYER. "Time and Social Structure: An Ashanti Case Study," *in* Meyer Fortes (ed.), *Social Structure: Studies Presented to A. R. Radcliffe-Brown* (Oxford: Clarendon Press, 1949), 54–84; "Introduction," *in* Goody (ed.), 1958, pp. 1–14.

GHURYE, G. S. "Dual Organization in India," *Journal of Royal Anthropological Institute,* LIII (1923), 79–91; "Some Kinship Usages in Indo–Aryan Literature," *Journal of Anthropological Society of Bombay,* New Series, I (1946), 1–80; *Family and Kin in Indo-European Culture* (Bombay: Oxford University Press, 1955); *After a Century and a Quarter: Lonikand Then and Now* (Bombay: Popular Book Depot, 1960).

After a Century and a Quarter: Lonikand Then and Now is a description of a village near Poona at two points of time, 1819 and 1954–1958. The account of 1819 is based on an article published in *Transactions of the Literary Society of Bombay* in 1823, on a survey of Lonikand carried out by Surgeon Coats in 1819. This was roughly the same period in which Radhvanaj was surveyed. With regard to the famliy in Lonikand in 1819, Ghurye presents one table on p. 13. According to it, the village had a total population of 565 persons. Eleven of them were hired servants without any household of their own. The remaining 554 persons were divided into 130 families (=households). The average size of a household was thus 4.26, only a little less than the average for Radhvanaj for the same period (4.54), which supports my contention that most of the Indian villagers lived in small and simple households in the past.

Ghurye's account of the present-day village is based on field data collected by his two research assistants. The village has a total population of 1,404 divided into 306 families or households (p. 14). The average size of a household is 4.58, only a little less than that of present-day Radhvanaj (4.61). The average size of the household has thus increased since the early nineteenth century both in Radhvanaj and in Lonikand. Ghurye, following a remark by Coats, attributes the increase to an increase in the average number of children per household (p. 14). This comparison between the past and the present size of the household is the only significant contribution this book makes to the study of the Indian family.

I would not have pointed out the negative features of Ghurye's work but for the prominent position his writing holds in the literature on the Indian family. He states, "On a prepared plan, [the research assistant] sorted out the number of the present families according to their caste, and out of them he took at random a 20 per cent sample, that is, one in five" (p. 70). Ghurye does not reveal to us his "prepared plan," but it is clear that the 48 families included in the detailed study form only 16.5 per cent and not 20 per cent of 306 families. It is likely that the sample is taken only from 207 families shown as house-owners in the *panchayat* records (p. 14), but then the percentage would be 23 and not 20. Moreover, two families are added in the descriptive account (p. 70), for reasons which are not stated. The 50 families have a total number of 470 persons, giving an average of 9.52 persons per family (p. 71), which is much higher than the average (4.58) for all the families in the village. All in all, the sample is not a fair representation of the village families. Finally, the major part of the two chapters on domestic life is devoted to a description of the kinship composition, occupation, and property of one sample family after another, but there is no sociological analysis, except that a few typological labels — "aberrant," "nuclear," "otherwise nuclear," "extended," and "joint" — have been used for the families. And these labels are used not only confusedly but also casually.

GLUCKMAN, MAX. *The Judicial Process among the Barotse of Northern Rhodesia* (Manchester: Manchester University Press, 1955).

GOODE, WILLIAM J. *World Revolution and Family Patterns* (New York: Free Press, 1963).

In this global study, Goode holds that in every society the forces of industrialization and urbanization are bringing about a change in family patterns in the *direction* of the conjugal family pattern — that is, toward fewer kinship ties with distant relations and greater emphasis on the "nuclear" family unit of couple and children (p. 1). This means the change would occur both in the household as well as in extra-household relationships.

The chapter on India discusses several problems connected with marriage and the family, including fertility, contraception, and infanticide. Only the discussion of the joint family is relevant here. Goode arrives at four conclusions in this regard. (1) The census data and the family cycle indicate that, at any given time, most Indian households are not joint in composition, and most were not joint in the past either (pp. 238–240, 243–244). (2) It is difficult to assess the prevalence of the multifunctional joint family because of the multiplicity of definitions of its composition. Compared to the traditional ideal structure, however, present data do not show the continuation of the complete joint family (pp. 240–243). (3) The studies of attitudes show that there is yet no firm and active set of values asserting that the joint family should no longer exist (pp. 244–246). (4) The attitudes are more in favour of the lineal than the collateral joint family (pp. 246–247).

The first conclusion does not indicate any change in the household in any direction; the validity of the second depends upon correctness of the assumption about the past; the third does not indicate any change toward the conjugal family; and the fourth only reflects the long-established difference between the lineal and the collateral joint family rather than any change. Nevertheless, Goode asserts his faith in the end: "Although the changes are not as yet great, the direction of change is clear," that is toward the conjugal family (p. 247).

GOODY, JACK (ed.). *The Development Cycle in Domestic Groups* (Cambridge: Cambridge University Press, 1958).

GORE, M. S. *Urbanization and Family Change* (Bombay: Popular Prakashan, 1968).

Gore tests here the well known hypothesis that the joint family system, a characteristic of the rural society, changes into the elementary family system due to industrialization and urbanization. He took samples of families (= households) from three different kinds of communities, representing three stages of urbanization, in the Delhi region: (1) the city of Delhi, (2) villages on the fringe of Delhi, and (3) villages away from Delhi. To control the complicating variable of caste, he selected only one caste, namely, the well-known merchant caste of Aggarwals. He took his samples of families according to fixed quotas: an almost equal number of families, 200 and 199, from the rural and the urban communities respectively; equal division of the 200 rural families between the fringe and the distant villages; and almost equal division of the quota of families for each of the three kinds of communities into nuclear and joint families. Thus, 48 nuclear and 52 joint families were taken from the distant villages, 49 nuclear and 51 joint from the fringe villages, and 98 nuclear and 101 joint from the city, making a total of 399 families. Information about life in these families was gathered through a structured questionnaire administered to two or more respondents from each family. The total number of respondents was 1,176.

As most of the 399 families practised traditional trade and commerce and included very few college-educated members, an additional sample of 100 families with members educated in colleges and employed in modern urban occupations was taken at a later stage in the enquiry. The questionnaire was administered to only one member (the eldest male) in each of these families due to shortage of time.

A number of arbitrary decisions were taken in selecting the sample villages, the sample families from the villages and the city, and the respondents from the families. As Gore frequently clarifies, no attempt was made to randomize the sample at any stage, and therefore no firm conclusions could emerge from the quantitative data.

The term "family" is used for "a residential unit consisting of at least one married couple" (pp. 86–87). This rules out several types of the incomplete nuclear families. The term "nuclear family" is used not only for the unit of husband, wife, and their children, but also for wider units which include besides these persons certain dependents, such as the husband's widowed mother, and his unmarried brother, or sister, or both (p. 87, 94). The joint families are classified into two well known types, the filial or lineal and the fraternal (pp. 4–6, 87, 94). Gore thus takes into account only the ideal-typical nuclear and joint families. Basically, he looks upon the joint family as "a group consisting of adult male coparceners and their dependents" (p. 6) — the Indological-cum-legal notion, which is the source of the ideal-typical construct of the joint family as well as of the inconsistencies in terminology and typology. Gore is aware that the dichotomy of nuclear and joint family is crude, arbitrary, and unsatisfactory, but has used it as "the only simple and quick mode of distinguishing between families" (p. 80, n.; see also p. 229).

The developmental process of the household is taken into account, but it is viewed mainly as a cycle with only two phases, the joint and the nuclear family (pp. 1, 21–22, 37–38). The household is distinguished from the family, but the distinction is not followed up in analysis and discussion, except to show that nuclear households are always involved in joint family relationships (pp. 36–37, 99–110).

Gore describes at length what he considers to be the requirements of the ideal-typical joint family. In brief they are four: (1) ensuring a community of material interests and outlook among adult males, (2) ensuring the assimilation of women who come as strangers into the kinship group, (3) minimizing the conjugal bond, and (4) allocating the leadership status to one among the many adults in the family (pp. 2–27, 223). The requirements of the ideal-typical nuclear family are: (1) full acceptance of the conjugal tie as the primary relationship in the family, (2) full and exclusive acceptance of the goal of 'companionship' between husband and wife, and (3) the limitation of circle of relatives, whether of the husband or of the wife, who may normally be helped (p. 36). Gore points out the economic, political, and social institutions and values of the traditional Indian society that he thinks support the ideal-typical joint family, and of the industrial-urban society that he thinks support the ideal-typical nuclear family (pp. 27–36, 43–50). He clarifies that his ideal-typical descriptions are not likely to always conform to reality. The gap between the two, however, seems much greater than that he would have in mind.

Noting that urban communities have existed in India and that their social system has included the joint family for many centuries, Gore disentangles urbanization from industrialization. According to him, industrialization in India is in an early stage, and there is therefore likelihood of only a limited change in the joint family. He points out, however, two other factors, namely, higher education and modern professions and bureaucratic occupations, which encourage liberal ideas and consequently family change. Neither of these factors, nor industrial occupations, were found to an appreciable extent in the main sample of 399 families, and it would not therefore show an appreciable change in the joint family. This was realized at a later stage in the inquiry, whereupon the additional sample of 100 families with college education and modern occupations was taken.

The questionnaires provided data mainly on attitudes, values, and perceptions concerning choice of family type, difficulties experienced in joint family life, authority and freedom in the family, the role of women, husband-wife and mother-son relationships, and various aspects of marriage. In the analysis and discussion of the data, Gore has tried to be as close to the data as possible, avoiding hasty conclusions. In the process, he provides deep insights into family life. It is clear, however, that he is handicapped by his sample, the terminology and typology, the ideal-typical constructs, and the shortcomings of the questionnaire method.

Gore arrives at two conclusions: (1) the sample as a whole still largely conforms to the pattern of joint family living, and (2) the additional sample indicates a change in the direction of the nuclear family in some attitudes and perceptions. On the whole, the inquiry shows "a limited change," the general discussion of which is the most illuminating part of the book (pp. 232–236).

GOUGH, E. KATHLEEN. "Brahman Kinship in a Tamil Village," *American Anthropologist,* LVIII (1956), 826–853.

Gough states: "The traditional Brahman *dwelling group* is patrilineal, patrilocal extended family *with joint ownership of land.* In Kumbapettai [the village of this study] today, however, the departure of some men to urban work has tended to upset this traditional residential pattern" (pp. 831–832, italics mine). She does not state the kinship composition of the traditional group as such; but she defines two types of extended family: (1) complete extended family, composed of "an older married couple and one or more married sons," and (2) incomplete extended family, composed of "a married couple with unmarried children and with some bereaved person of the husband's parental generation such as a widowed mother, a widowed father, or a widowed sister" (p. 832). These are very broad types. Moreover, according to the definition of the traditional family mentioned above, the extended families of both the types would be dwelling groups as well as property-holding groups, which rules out the possibility of their being, in the past, separate in dwelling but joint with regard to property.

Kumbapettai has forty-eight houses belonging to Brahmans. Six of them lie permanently empty and derelict; their owners have moved to towns, sold their village land, and ceased to be members of the village (p. 833). Of six of the remaining forty-two houses, each is owned by an extended family, all its members are absent in the town, their village land is managed by an affine who retains a portion of the crop, while the members return to the village for vacations, harvests, festivals, rites, ceremonies, and so forth (pp. 832–833). These families are thus similar to what I have called "independent emigrant" households.

Of the remaining thirty-six houses, thirty are owned by extended families falling into two main categories. (1) Five families do not own any land in the village and depend entirely on salaries of junior members. Generally the young men are absent in the town, while aged parents or a widowed mother or young children live in the village house (p. 833). The village households are incomplete elementary families, but the composite units of the village and the town sections together constitute extended families. (2) Twenty-five families depend wholly or partly on land (p. 832). In the case of those depending wholly on land, all the members of each family reside in a single house in the village. In the case of those depending only partially on land, a few members of each family reside in the village house and the others reside in the town, the two sections constituting an integrated group in many respects, including ownership of land. In some of these cases the village section is a complete or an incomplete elementary family, and its jointness with a town section makes it an extended family, while in other cases the village section seems to be an extended family in itself.

Finally, six houses are both owned and occupied by complete or incomplete elementary families, all of whom own land in the village but whose close patrilineal kin have either died or have sold their shares of land and moved to the town (p. 833).

If we leave out the six households which have ceased to be members of Kumbapettai there remain thirty-six extended families (complete and incomplete, dispersed and unitary) and six elementary families (complete and incomplete). However, if only the permanent residents of Kumbapettai are considered, there are fifteen extended families (seven complete and eight incomplete) and twenty-one elementary families. From these figures Gough concludes, "In Kumbapettai as perhaps everywhere in India, under the impact of change from a feudal to a mercantile economic system, the patrilocal extended family is disintegrating as a permanent residential unit" (p. 832). She makes it quite clear that her conclusion applies only to the dwelling group and not to what she calls the "economic and social unit."

How far is this conclusion regarding the dwelling group valid? If we go by the definition of the complete extended family, it seems the maximum extent of the developmental process of the household in the past among Kumbapettai Brahmans was the same as in Radhvanaj, that is, co-residence of two or more married brothers during the lifetime of parents. But what about the frequency of such households? Were there no partitions of households during the lifetime of parents? It is very possible that there were very few such partitions, or none at all, because Kumbapettai Brahmans seem to have had a high degree of Sanskritization and a preference for cross-cousin and uncle-niece marriages. If this was the case, then the conclusion regarding disintegration of the traditional dwelling group would be largely valid. I cannot help feeling, however, that Gough has assumed, like many others, that the traditional group was a large and complex extended family. An analysis of the households unaffected by migration, and a little probing in the past, might have revealed at least a few partitions during the lifetime of parents. In any case, the traditional emphasis on co-residence of parents and married sons during the lifetime of parents is reflected in the present strong emphasis on integration of the village and the town sections of the extended family. (How many of these extended families are really integrated is not clear from Gough's paper). The most striking feature of the traditional dwelling group among Kumbapettai Brahmans is that its generation depth was less than that of the group of Indological literature.

After considering the composition of the dwelling group, Gough describes interpersonal relations in the elementary family. It seems this description is intended to apply to the period when the traditional extended family had not disintegrated. It deals mostly with father-son, brother-brother, and husband-wife relationships, and takes into account mostly the ideal or expected modes of behaviour. Frequently, the source of Gough's information for the deepest experience in the home seems to be only myths, legends, folk tales, proverbs, and public rituals and ceremonies.

She describes the relations between brothers as "covertly hostile to each other, so that the sibling group as a whole seldom acts as an organised, solidary unit" (p. 840). If Kumbapettai Brahmans had a strong emphasis on co-residence of parents and all the married sons, Gough's description of parent-son relationship would apply only to a very limited situation. Her general conclusion is that parent-son relationship is "a unique and sacred bond" (p. 839). If, as I have suspected, one of the sons sets up a separate household during the lifetime of the parents, the father-son bond is not as strong as Gough describes. Even if all the sons remain in the father's household, the existence of covert hostility between sons would affect the father-son relationship, which would not be identical for all the sons.

Gough ends her paper with a summary description of contrasts between Brahman and non-Brahman kinship. She mentions that among lower castes a man's sons, once married, move into separate houses (p. 846). This is in line with what we know about lower castes in other parts of India, but I do not think joint- or extended-family households would be totally absent among lower castes.

GOULD, HAROLD A. "Time Dimension and Structural Change in an Indian Kinship System: A Problem of Conceptual Refinement," *in* Milton Singer and Bernard S. Cohn (eds.), *Structure and Change in Indian Society* (New York: Wenner-Gren Foundation for Anthropological Research, 1968), pp. 413–421.

After a general discussion of the problem of the developmental cycle of the family in India, mainly on the line charted by Fortes and his associates, Gould posits the developmental cycle of the North Indian family. It consists of three phases. In phase 1, daughters of a married couple go to their husbands' homes and the sons' wives come in, making a joint family of parents and married sons. This phase has two subphases. Subphase A begins with the departure of a daughter and the simultaneous entry of a daughter-in-law, and ends when fifty per cent of the daughters have left and fifty per cent of the daughters-in-law have come in. Where subphase A ends subphase B begins, and it ends when all daughters have been replaced by daughters-in-law. This phase represents the maximal development of the father-son joint family. Phase 2 is marked by the father's death and the emergence of a fraternal joint family. In phase 3 the fraternal joint family is partitioned, leading to the establishment of nuclear families. They "then set about repeating the developmental cycle. [They] are mere milestones on the circular pathway" (p. 418). This phase has two subphases. In subphase A the first marital ceremony of a child of the newly formed nuclear unit takes place, and in subphase B the newly married couple begin to cohabit. "The developmental cycle has been completed; phase 1 has once more been reached" (p. 419).

It is clear from the above that (1) Gould conceives of the developmental process as cyclical; (2) there is only one cycle; (3) the cycle is viewed within the dichotomy of the "real" joint families and the nuclear family; and (4) it does not take care of a number of important possible developments, such as parents' having only one son or no son, unequal number of sons and daughters, and differences in their ages.

GULATI, I. S., and GULATI, K. S. *The Undivided Hindu Family*: *Its Tax Privileges* (Bombay: Asia Publishing House, 1962).

KANE, P. V. *History of Dharmasastra,* Vol. III (Poona: Bhandarkar Oriental Research Institute, 1946).

KAPADIA, K. M. *Hindu Kinship* (Bombay: Popular Book Depot, 1947); "Changing Patterns of Hindu Marriage and Family — I" *Sociological Bulletin*, III (1954a), 61–87; "Changing Patterns of Hindu Marriage and Family — II," *Sociological Bulletin* III (1954b), 131–157; "Changing Patterns of Hindu Marriage and Family — III," *Sociological Bulletin,* IV (1955a), 161–192; *Marriage and Family in India* (Bombay: Oxford University Press, 1955b); "Rural Family Patterns: A Study in Urban-Rural Relations," *Sociological Bulletin*, V (1956), 111–126; "The Family in Transition," *Sociological Bulletin,* VIII (1959), 68–99.

Hindu Kinship is a sociological work based on Indological sources and includes a description of the classical joint family.

In the long paper "Changing Patterns of Hindu Marriage and Family" Kapadia reports the results of a questionnaire he issued to 513 teachers in high schools in Bombay city (279 Gujarati, 187 Maharashtrian, and 47 Kannadiga). In the first two parts he reports the analysis of answers to his questions on the teachers' attitudes regarding the age of girls at marriage, selection in marriage, inter-caste marriage, and status of women. The third part is devoted to the joint family. Here he deals first with the attitudinal aspect and then with the structural aspect of the problem. With regard to the attitudinal aspect, Kapadia himself is not happy with the kind of response he received from the teachers — all of them did not reply to all of his questions in all the details. He is also doubtful about the validity of the conclusions to be drawn from the replies. I am even more doubtful and therefore shall not comment upon the attitudinal aspect of his investigation. With regard to the structural aspect, he considers that the addition of any person to a nuclear family results in its becoming a joint family. He also distinguishes between a family that is residentially as well as functionally joint and a family that is functionally joint but residentially separate.

Most of Kapadia's data are confined to the residential family. Of 513 teachers, only 219 (42 per cent) live in elementary families (p. 160). Of the 294 teachers (67 per cent) who live in joint families, only 185 gave detailed information about the kinship composition of their families (pp. 181–186). Of these 185 families, as many as 80 are composed of two or more married brothers with or without their parent(s) and brother(s) or sister(s), or both, and 27 are composed of two or more married brothers, their married sons, and sons' unmarried children, with or without the brothers' parent(s). 73 of the remaining families each include one married man and his parent(s) and brother(s) or sister(s), or both. Along with the high degree of jointness in the residential group, Kapadia finds a high degree of jointness outside the residential group (pp. 180–181), and an overwhelming opinion in favour of the joint family (p. 163). He also finds the same structural and attitudinal position in Merchant's investigation among youths in Poona city (p. 164).

Kapadia contrasts this situation among the urban and educated Gujaratis, Maharashtrians, and Kannadigas of Bombay with the situation that he finds in some villages in South Gujarat from a preliminary analysis of the data provided by the National Register of Citizens of 1951. Of 1,639 families (=households) in fifteen villages, he first leaves out 1,159 families belonging to tribal groups, untouchables, and a few other very low castes (p. 164). He does not mention the reason for omitting them, but it is perhaps because the joint family is very weak among them. Even among the remaining 840 families of higher, middle, and some lower castes, 215 (44 per cent) are nuclear. And of 230 joint families, the numerical and kinship composition of which is analysed in Tables 30 and 31, a large proportion have a weak emphasis on the joint family. If the 1,159 families of tribal and low caste groups had been included in the analysis, it would have shown a much weaker overall emphasis on the joint family in villages.

Kapadia frankly admits his inability to explain this contrast between the rural and the urban patterns: "The existing pattern of family in Gujarat is much different from the impression one gains from the attitudinal study. It is difficult to account

213

for this disparity. ... I am not quite confident how far this analysis based on the opinions of the teachers reflects the reality of the situation. My analysis of the contemporary patterns in rural Gujarat does not bear out the conclusions arrived at on the basis of the schedules" (pp. 165, 188). I suggest that Kapadia is puzzled because he assumes implicitly that a strong emphasis on the joint family is a characteristic of traditional India, or that the classical joint family has survived in villages. The explanation for the strength of the joint family among the teachers in Bombay seems to lie in the fact that they belong to higher castes (1954a, p. 63) and in the possibility that they may have migrated to Bombay from smaller towns in Gujarat, Maharashtra, and Karnatak and continued to live in the traditional sector of Bombay.

In "Rural Family Patterns: A Study in Urban-Rural Relations" Kapadia has presented an analysis of the National Register data on households in a small town, Navsari, and in fifteen villages around Navsari, in South Gujarat. The villages are the same as those considered in the previous paper. They are selected in such a way that five of them are within the range of one to three miles from Navsari, seven are within the range of four to nine miles, and three are within the range of ten to thirteen miles. The first three are under the impact of the town and are therefore called "impact villages."

The fifteen villages have a total of 8,260 families (=households). Kapadia has excluded from them 3,003 (36.2 per cent) families of tribal, untouchable, and non-Hindu groups, as in the previous analysis. Here also he does not mention the reason for their exclusion, but the most probable reason is that these groups have a very weak emphasis on the joint family. From the remaining 5,263 families of higher and middle castes, Kapadia has taken a sample of 1,099 (20.9 per cent) families for analysis. As for Navsari, out of its twelve wards, only six — where higher incidence of castes included in the village sample was traceable — were selected. From these six wards 246 families were selected by a procedure that is not clearly stated in the paper. They were selected "after elimination and necessary discrimination" (p. 113), which means the families belonging to the same castes as those selected for the village sample were selected. They were also selected "proportionately from each ward," but the proportion for each ward is not mentioned. The analysis is confined to higher and middle castes in the villages as well as in the town.

After a classification of the families on the basis of their numerical size and of their being nuclear or joint, Kapadia concludes: "First, not only the total complement of the joint family is higher in the town but even its size is larger there than in the rural area. The latter fact reinforces the validity of the former. . . . Secondly, both in the strength as well as in the structure, the impact villages stand midway between the village and the town, substantiating thereby the act of impact" (p. 119).

Kapadia has thus found once again that the general assumption that people in cities and towns live in nuclear families does not hold good. He would have found much weaker emphasis on the joint family in the villages if he had not excluded the tribal and untouchable castes from his analysis. He still thinks that "it would not be proper to generalise anyway on the basis of such a small sample" (p. 115). But he is not prepared to consider his facts "accidental" (p. 119); he seeks to find an explanation for them. He inquires if caste has any relevance, but this part of the analysis suffers from one basic weakness. It lies in the classification of the castes in the sample into nine categories in Table 1–5. Some classification is certainly necessary, but Kapadia's classification seems to lack any system. His analysis would have gained in perspective if he had not excluded the tribal and untouchable groups. Nevertheless, the results of his analysis are noteworthy. First, the conclusion that the joint family cannot be considered a necessary concomitant of the agricultural economy (pp. 114, 124) is well founded. Second, in the town as well as in the villages different castes have each a different incidence of joint families, and higher castes have on the whole a higher incidence of joint families, but there are also differences between the rural and the urban sections within the same caste. The overall higher incidence of joint families in the town is reflected in the higher incidence of joint families in most of the castes, but one or two have a lower incidence in the town than in the villages. Therefore, Kapadia concludes, "Caste cannot precisely be said to be the demarcating line in the family pattern, though it would not be at the same time justifiable to rule out altogether its role in the understanding of the family pattern" (p. 120). Kapadia does not push his analysis further (though he suggests that the economic factor is important), but it seems to me from his data, admittedly meagre, that the long-established population of the town has a stronger emphasis on the joint family than have recent immigrants.

The section of the paper dealing with the kinship composition of joint families (pp. 120–125) is poor. The data for all the villages included in his study are not analysed, the procedure for the selection of 230 joint families for analysis is not mentioned, and there is no analysis on the basis of caste. But the point that the joint family is stronger in the town than in the villages is repeated.

In "The Family in Transition" Kapadia considers changes in the structure of the family and in the nature of interpersonal relations in the family on the basis of a questionnaire issued to students of matric and pre-matric classes in high schools in Navsari and surrounding seven villages. The paper has several shortcomings, but I shall mention only two. First, Kapadia follows uncritically I. P. Desai's typology, which is based on the generation principle and formulated for an analysis of inter-household relations (see pp. 190–193 for my discussion of this typology). It leads Kapadia to consider even the family composed of a man, his wife, his unmarried children, his married son and son's wife, as a nuclear family (pp. 74, 76). Second, on the basis of his questionnaire, Kapadia finds that there are more nuclear than joint families in the town, and on the basis of these figures he makes general remarks about the rural and the urban family (pp. 76–81). He does not pause to ask how his earlier findings about the same area are reversed. He also ignores the fact that many nuclear families would not have children studying in matric and pre-matric classes, and therefore would not be represented in his sample. Similarly, the caste composition of the sample would also affect its family composition.

Marriage and Family in India, first published in 1955 and then revised in 1958 and 1965, includes three chapters on the joint family: on the classical (patrilineal) family, on the matrilineal family, and on recent changes in both. The portions dealing with the matrilineal family are out of tune with modern research on the subject, the portion on the classical family is mainly a repetition of parts of *Hindu Kinship,* and the portion on changes in the classical family merely summarises his and others' work on the subject.

KAPOOR, SAROJ. "Family and Kinship Groups among the Khatris in Delhi," *Sociological Bulletin,* XIV (1965), pp. 54–63.

This paper is based on a study of 135 households of Khatris, a highly Sanskritized caste of wealthy businessmen, living for many generations in a compact neighbourhood in the older sector of metropolitan Delhi. Although Kapoor gives the total number of households as 136, with ten compositional types (p. 56), she defines only nine types, and the frequencies of households of these types make a total of 135. Type I is composed of one generation, Types II and IIa of two, types III and IIIa of three, and Types IV and IVa of four. Types V and VI are not based on the generation principle. As usual, in each type based on the generation principle several different types of households are lumped together. It is clear, however, that the households of Types III, IIIa, IV, IVa, V, and VI, totalling 58, are all complex. Similarly, the fourteen households of Type I, composed of the husband-wife couple, or a widow, or two widowed sisters, are simple. Type II includes one or both of the parents and unmarried children, and Type IIa the members of Type II plus unmarried or widowed siblings of the parents.

The former households are simple and the latter complex, but unfortunately their frequencies are not shown separately. Together they number 63. Nevertheless, it is significant that the complex households form at least 42.9 per cent of the households in a neighbourhood in a metropolitan city. And among them there are as many as seven in which two or more married cousins live together during or after the lifetime of their parents and grandparents (Types IV and V).

Kapoor describes at some length how the large and complex household fissions into two or more separate households and how they continue to live in the same house or neighbourhood and to be bound by a number of inter-household relationships.

KARANDIKAR, S. V. *Hindu Exogamy* (Bombay: D. B. Taraporewala, 1929).

KARVE, IRAWATI. "Kinship Terminology and Kinship Usages in Rgveda and Atharvaveda," *Annals of Bhandarkar Oriental Research Institute,* XX (1938–1939a), 109–144; "The Kinship Usages and the Family Organization in Rgveda and Atharvaveda," *Annals of Bhandarkar Oriental Research Institute,* XX (1938–1939b), 213–234; "Kinship Terminology and Kinship Usages of the Maratha Country," *Bulletin of Deccan College Research Institute,* I (1940), 327–389, and II (1941), 9–33; "Kinship Terms and the Family Organization as Found in the Critical Edition of the Mahabharata," *Bulletin of Deccan College Research Institute,* V (1943–1944), 61–148; *Kinship Organization in India* (Poona: Deccan College, 1953).

"Kinship Terminology and Kinship Usages of the Maratha Country" is one of the first few writings on Indian kinship by professional sociologists based on ethnographic data. Although it is not concerned specifically with the family it contains some useful description of interpersonal relations in the joint family.

In *Kinship Organization in India* Karve uses classical literature and empirical material in a single compass, and only a small portion of it is concerned with the family and household. At the outset Karve describes the composition of the joint family as follows: "There are three or four generations of males related to a male ego as grandfather and his brothers, father and his brothers, [ego's] brothers and cousins, sons and nephews, and wives of all these male relatives plus the ego's own unmarried sisters and daughters" (p. 11). It appears as though Karve has followed the usual three-or-four-generation formula, but she does not include the generation of the common ancestor (the great-grandfather) in the number of generations, and does not mention unmarried males at all. This means her formula of the genealogical depth of the joint family is wider than the usual formula. She lists for the joint family of her formula all the functional characteristics generally mentioned in the description of the joint family of the maximum depth (p. 10). She further states, "When such a family splits and there is partition it almost never splits into as many units as there are individual families but into smaller joint families made up of (i) a man, his wife, children, and sons' sons and daughters, or (ii) a man, his sons and daughters and a couple of younger brothers" (p. 12). According to her method of counting generations, joint families of both these types would be two-generation units, whereas according to others they would be three-generation units.

It is quite clear that according to Karve's theory there would be virtually no elementary family in any part of premodern India, a conclusion which is fantastic. On the other hand, she does not tell us in which sections of Indian society are to be found the kind of households with the genealogical depth which she ascribes to them. The only probable cases are those of the families of Pandavas and Kauravas of the *Mahabharata* fame. About one of them she first states, "It was a great joint family" (p. 66), and "People of four generations (sometimes more) lived in the same locality" (p. 67). The word "locality" here is ambiguous. She then gives expression to her doubt: "It is not certain who of these lived under one roof and shared food cooked at one hearth. In the case of ruling houses there were possibly separate establishments for the important

219

members." This shows that she regards the royal households as atypical. Nevertheless, she goes on to conjecture that "in the case of poorer people all the members lived under one roof." She does not produce any evidence whatever in support of this statement. Karve's observations regarding the royal lineages can at best provide support to the prevalence of joint families that enjoy property together and worship together but stay separately.

Karve also mentions that "in one city or a village there may be even ten or twelve houses, each sheltering a joint family, all together acknowledging common descent and capable of showing relationship through one line" (p. 11). This is obviously a lineage, but as Dumont and Pocock (1957, pp. 48–50) have shown, she uses the term "family" for many different kinds of kinship groups, including lineage and clan.

Karve's book is full of insightful observations about interpersonal relations between members of the joint family, but they all suffer from lack of specification of the size and composition of the joint family.

KHERA, P. D. *The Family in the Indian Census,* unpublished M.Litt. dissertation in the University of Delhi, 1969.

A useful guide to the census material on the family.

KOLENDA, PAULINE M. "Regional Differences in Indian Family Structure," *in* Robert I. Crane (ed.) *Regions and Regionalism in South Asian Studies: An Exploratory Study* (Monograph 5, Duke University Program in Comparative Studies of Southern Asia, 1967), pp. 147–228; "Region, Caste and Family Structure: A Comparative Study of the Indian 'Joint' Family," *in* Milton Singer and Bernard S. Cohn (eds.), *Structure and Change in Indian Society* (New York: Wenner-Gren Foundation for Anthropological Research, 1968), pp. 339–396.

The second paper was written prior to the first. It is the first systematic attempt to compare the modern studies on the Indian family (=household) to arrive at general formulations. The coverage of studies is fairly comprehensive — twenty-six studies carried out since 1949 and including quantitative data on the frequency of families of various types. The internal examination of each study and the comparison are executed with considerable care, caution, and humility. The result is formidable.

Kolenda has asked three main questions: (1) Do Indians typically live in joint families? (2) Are there caste differences in the distribution of family types, with the high castes having higher proportions of joint families than the middle and lower castes? (3) Are joint families more characteristic of land-owning castes than of landless castes?

Kolenda is aware of the necessity to study the family cycle; in fact, she is ahead of many others in recognizing a number of different family cycles (pp. 349–350). However, she is concerned only with typology and frequencies of households of various types, not with the family cycle, nor also with the family change (pp. 340–342).

Kolenda has pointed out, just as I have, how the multiplicity of definitions of family types is a major obstacle in the comparison of studies on the Indian family. "It is not an exaggeration to say that no two used the same set of definitions of family types" (p. 344). Kolenda has, therefore, devised her own typology (pp. 346–348). It includes twelve types: (1) nuclear, (2) supplemented nuclear, (3) subnuclear, (4) single-person, (5) supplemented subnuclear, (6) collateral joint, (7) supplemented collateral joint, (8) lineal joint, (9) supplemented lineal joint, (10) lineal-collateral joint, (11) supplemented lineal-collateral joint, (12) others. These types are based on certain basic terms with distinctive connotations. (1) The nuclear family means "a couple with or without unmarried children." (2) A subnuclear family is composed of either of the parents and unmarried children, or siblings. (3) A family is joint if it includes two or more related couples irrespective of whether these are father-son, mother-son, father-daughter, mother-daughter, brother-brother, brother-sister, or sister-sister relationships. (4) In a lineal joint family the married couples

221

are related by a lineal link, in a collateral joint family by a sibling link, and in a lineal-collateral joint family by lineal and collateral links. (5) The unmarried, widowed, or divorced relatives who are not children of any of the married couples in the family *supplements* the family, whether it is a joint, nuclear, or subnuclear family (see types 2, 5, 7, 9, 10, and 11). (6) "Other" is a residual category.

It is necessary to note certain peculiarities of this typology. (1) The inclusion of a couple without children in the category "nuclear family" means a deviation from its standard anthropological definition. Kolenda has done this in order to make the Indian family comparable with the family in the U.S.A. (p. 346). Such an ethnocentric definition is not likely to help develop anthropological comparisons. (2) A wide variety of households have been lumped together in the category "joint family," so much so that it includes the patrilineal and the matrilineal joint families also. This is not likely to help the analysis of the family as part of the wider kinship system. (3) While in one way the category "joint family" is very wide, in another way it is very narrow. The supplemented nuclear and supplemented subnuclear families, which would be considered joint by others, are not considered joint here. (4) This typology is not devised to help the anaylsis of the developmental process.

Kolenda has devoted a great deal of attention to the translation of other scholars' types into her types and to the recomputation of frequencies accordingly. She has not published all the steps in the translation process, because of the bulk of the total set. However, she frequently admits that there may be awkwardness, inadequacy, incorrectness, and distortion in the translations.

Kolenda finds that only twelve of the twenty-six studies provide full or almost full data to translate the types and recompute the frequencies to a full or almost full extent. In three of the twelve cases, she had access to unpublished field data — her own and that of two other scholars — and one study is an unpublished dissertation. Thus in the published literature on the Indian family she finds only eight studies providing satisfactory data on types and frequencies of households.

It is not possible to discuss here how my examination of the various studies agrees with or differs from Kolenda's. She has examined the studies with great care indeed. However, I should be less than honest if I do not point out that there are differences. I would give only two illustrations from among the eight fuller studies. I have shown how in Madan's study of a Kashmiri village (1965), emigrants from the village are included among members of the village households, leading to inflation of the number of complex households in the village. In Gough's study of a Tamil village (1956), on the other hand, emigrants from the village are not included among members of the village households, although some of them are only temporary migrants. Kolenda has not taken this complication into account in her translation of types and recomputation of figures in the two studies. There are differences in the examination of many other studies also.

There is another general tendency in Kolenda's paper: although she is aware of the inadequacies of a number of studies, she ignores them in her comparisons. I would provide just one illustration. She notes that in Kulkarni's study of Gokak *taluka*, the sample excludes (1) single-person households, subnuclear families, and most types of supplemented joint families, and (2) twenty-six small castes, with probably a high proportion of nuclear families. As a result, the sample is biased in favour of the joint family (pp. 350–352). Nevertheless, Kolenda goes on citing Kulkarni's study as showing the highest incidence of joint families in the country (pp. 366, 371, 376–377, 390). I may add that she has not noticed another bias in favour of the joint family in Kulkarni's study, namely, exclusion of 25 of the 103 villages with less than a thousand population each.

In spite of the limitations of the data, Kolenda has arrived at significant results. I assess first the conclusions regarding her three main questions (p. 390). (1) The joint family is somewhat more characteristic of higher "twice-born" castes and the least characteristic of the Untouchable castes. This conclusion supports my finding that there is greater emphasis on the principle of the residual unity of patrikin and their wives among more Sanskritized castes. Kolenda's qualification of this conclusion, that the Brahmans do not show a high emphasis, seems to be based on inadequate data. (2) The evidence on relationship between family and landownership is slight, but the available evidence shows no relationship. This conclusion agrees with the doubts I have expressed in Chapter 9 about the possibility of finding any relationship between the two. (3) Kolenda estimates typical ranges for four categories of families on the basis of eleven studies providing fuller data. The ranges are: 10 to 19 per cent subnuclear and single-person households; 30 to 39 per cent nuclear families; 20 to 29 per cent supplemented nuclear families; and 20 to 29 per cent joint families. Although these estimates are based on a small number of studies, small and diverse samples, and incomplete data, this is a worthwhile exercise and needs to be pursued further. The related conclusion, that while the majority of families are nuclear, the majority of people live in joint and supplemented nuclear families, is based on scanty evidence. However, the essential idea, first put forward by I. P. Desai (1955), that we should take into account not merely the proportions of various types of households but also the proportions of population living in them, is unexceptionable.

In the course of Kolenda's research three other hypotheses emerged (p. 391). (1) There appear to be regional differences in proportions of joint families. This hypothesis is worth testing, but the data available for different regions is uneven and mainly microcosmic, apart from having other inadequacies. (2) "There appear to be definite differences in the customary time of break-up of the joint family in various places in India, and the differences in the mores of break-up correlate with the proportions of joint families. Those with earlier break — when a married son establishes his own household separate from his father's within a few months or years after his marriage — correlate with low proportions of joint families; those with medium break-up — when married sons break up at or shortly after the death of the father — with medium proportions of joint family; and with slow break-up — where married sons continue to live together for long periods after their father's death, even until their own sons are grown and married, so that families headed by first cousins occur — with high proportions of joint families." This hypothesis does not need any empirical verification. It is inherent in the developmental process along the path set by the principle of residential unity of patrikin and their wives. If the developmental process goes to the extent of co-residence of married brothers long after the death of their father, it implies that there would be little deviation from the norm of co-residence of married sons during their father's lifetime, and therefore there will be larger proportion of joint families. Similarly, if all households of parents and married sons break up soon after the father's death, there would be hardly any household composed of married brothers, and therefore, less proportion of joint households. And so on.

The hypothesis in the preceding paper regarding the relationship between the timing of break-up of joint family and proportions of joint family is the starting point of Kolenda's next paper. She asks why are there differences in the timing of break-up in different parts of India, and tries to answer on the basis of comparison of six studies. This is the first and the only comparative study of the relation between the household and the system of kinship and marriage in India. It raises many new issues, only a few of which I shall touch upon here.

Kolenda assumes that "a nuclear family's departure from the joint family dwelling ... is prompted by the demands of the wife. ... On the whole, women find joint family living oppressive and wish a separate place of their own." Kolenda then asks under what conditions would a wife succeed in convincing her husband to set up a separate household. The answer is: "She presumably would succeed when she had in her control important means of rewarding or punishing her husband for his compliance or non-compliance to her wishes" (p. 173). Kolenda frequently talks of these means as constituting the wife's "bargaining power." The most important means are the practice of legal divorce initiated by the wife, the custom of remarriage of divorced woman, the custom of bride-price (implying high cost of obtaining a new wife), and strong economic and social support to a couple from the wife's natal family or lineage. Kolenda finds all these factors existing in the communities with early break-up of the joint family. The contrary factors — prohibition of legal divorce by the wife, prohibition of remarriage of divorced woman, the custom of dowry, and strong economic and social support to a couple from the husband's natal family or lineage — are found in the communities with late break-up of the joint family.

The co-existence of certain factors with a certain timing of break-up of the joint family, which Kolenda has painstakingly tried to establish, is true most probably of many castes and communities. However, it is a different thing to consider these factors as "the key to the explanation" (p. 172) of the timing of break-up. For example, in the extreme case of the early break-up considered by Kolenda, namely, the Pramalai Kallar, twenty-four of the twenty-six households in the sample are nuclear, subnuclear, single-person, and "other." Only one of the remaining two is joint and the other supplemented nuclear, and in both of them it seems the married son and his wife have just been married and are waiting to set up separate homes. In such a situation, it is more correct to say that the cultural ideal of the joint family does not exist, or that the neolocal rule prevails, rather than say that the joint family breaks up because of the threat of divorce. Even where the cultural ideal of the joint family prevails, it is necessary to ask: Which sort of joint family? For example, as Kolenda herself states, "the collateral joint family may not even be a sub-cultural ideal" (p. 166).

The influence of the various factors on the time of break-up should be examined for the various phases of the developmental process. For example, in what phase would the wife demand divorce? Would she demand it after the birth of a child, particularly a son? if her husband is the only son of his parents? if only the husband's father is living with them? And so on.

It is true that in certain situations the son's wife may find the joint-family living oppressive, but we should not assume that all women in all situations find it oppressive and wish a separate place of their own. Kolenda seems to neglect the positive side of joint-family life. So many observers of Indian family life have pointed out how the joint family provides a number of services to its members, including women. Many young women look after their old parents-in-law dutifully and even cheerfully. A daughter-in-law in course of time aspires to become a mother-in-law and preside over a household including her sons and daughters-in-law.

KULKARNI, M. G. "Family Patterns in Gokak Taluka," *Sociological Bulletin*, IX (1960), 60–81.

Kulkarni has taken his primary data from the 1951 National Register of Citizens of 3 towns and 103 villages in Gokak *taluka,* Belgaum district, Mysore State. There are a total of 34,496 households in the *taluka,* of which Kulkarni has selected 22,527 for his study (Table III). He has excluded 35 of the 103 villages because they have less than a thousand population each, and 28 of the 40 caste and religious groups because they are minor (p. 60). The twelve selected groups include nine Hindu castes, Jains, Muslims, and Christians. One of the nine castes is actually a group of four different castes, namely, Brahman, Lingayat, Maratha, and Panchal. Kulkarni does not state why he has put such diverse castes in one group. Finally, he has excluded four of the eight zones into which he divided the *taluka.* Thus, 22,527 households he has taken for analysis are not representative either of the *taluka* or of the four zones he has selected. I suspect that those sections of the *taluka* population have been excluded which have a weaker emphasis on the joint family.

Of 22,527 households, 1,649 (about 7 per cent) are single-member units. Kulkarni considers them to be quite different from multi-member households, so much so that he uses the term "family" only for the latter (p. 65). He presents caste and zone figures of single-member *versus* multi-member households but ignores single-member households in his analysis of the size of the family. He classifies 20,878 multi-member households in the same way as in the 1951 Census of India, except that he puts only two-member and three-member households in a single category, while the census puts these as well as single-member households in one category. Although the basic unit of his data is the household, he assumes throughout his analysis that single-member households are not a part of the system of households. This vitiates his conclusions regarding the size of the household.

Kulkarni has selected 1,064 out of 20,878 multi-member families (about 5 per cent) in such a way that they include all the twelve caste and religious groups in their proper proportions. He issued a questionnaire to heads of these families to elicit information about their kinship composition and their jointness and separation (pp. 70–81). On the basis of this information he has classified them as "joint" and "separate." He does not explain the method of classification in sufficient detail, but it is clear that it is based both on the internal composition of the household and on inter-household relations. For example, if a household composed of a complete or an incomplete nuclear family is *joint* in property *with* some other households, the former is considered a joint family (pp. 70–71). This is the reason why Kulkarni finds that "in all the zones the number of nuclear families is greater than the number of separated families. It is clear therefore that not all the nuclear families are separated families" (p. 80). On account of this method of classification, in every zone there are more than 70 per cent joint families, and in one zone there are as many as 91.3 per cent joint families. These figures prove only that households may be separate residentially but usually they are joint *with* other households in other respects.

Kulkarni has classified his sample families also into fourteen types on the basis of only the internal composition of the household. The households composed of the complete nuclear family form from 31.7 to 38.8 per cent of the households in the four zones, and the rest are joint-family households of various types. It should be noted, however, that the single-member households are excluded from the sample, there is no clarification where the households composed of the other types of the nuclear family are included, and as was stated earlier, the entire initial sample is biased in favour of the joint family.

LAMBERT, RICHARD D. *Workers, Factories, and Social Change in India* (Princeton: Princeton University Press, 1963).

This study of factory workers in Poona shows just the opposite of one of the presumed consequences of industrialization: the growth of the small nuclear family. The relatively high income of the factory worker draws added dependents and thus larger families (=households) (p. 56). The average size of the household among the factory workers is 5.2, compared with 4.5 for the general Poona population. The proportion of uni-member households is 5.4 per cent in the former, compared with 7.2 per cent in the latter. The mean number of earners per household is greater in the factories. There are 2.6 dependents per earner in the factory work force and 2.5 in the general population (pp. 39–40).

LEACH, E. R. *Political Systems of Highland Burma* (London: G. Bell and Sons, 1964).

MADAN, T. N. "The Hindu Joint Family," *Man*, LXII (1962a), 88–89; "The Joint Family: A Terminological Clarification," *International Journal of Comparative Sociology*, III (1962b), 7–16; *Family and Kinship: A Study of the Pandits of Rural Kashmir* (Bombay: Asia Publishing House, 1965).

Madan's first paper is an abbreviation of the second. In the second, although he surveys briefly the ways in which the term joint family is used in general works on the family and in works on the family in societies other than Indian, the paper is concerned mainly with the Indian family. After an examination of the meanings of "joint family" given by Srinivas, Mandelbaum, Karve, Bailey, Mayne, and Kane, Madan concludes: "The major reason for confusion concerning the connotation of the term joint family arises from the failure on the part of the concerned scholars to recognize that there is no necessary connexion between the existence of a familial group larger than the nuclear family and the existence of coparcenary rights and obligations among its members. Joint rights may exist between father and an only son in a nuclear family" (pp. 12–13). This is a valid criticism and agrees with what I have said in the chapter "The Indian Family in Law and Jurisprudence." However, the solution suggested by Madan is problematic, namely, that the term "joint family" should not be used as a synonym of "extended family," and that the ownership of joint-property rights should be its sole referent. I have discussed this suggestion in Chapter 9.

Madan defines "extended family" as "a large family, unilocal or dispersed, which has grown large in size and genealogically ramified" (p. 14). On the one hand, the criterion of size in the definition is not necessary, and on the other, there is no reference to the limits on extension or genealogical ramification of nuclear family. Moreover, while Madan suggests a definite referent for "joint family," he does not suggest any referent for "extended family." He advocates, however, the distinction between household and family, and points out that the members of an extended family may live in a single household or be divided into two or more households. This is true but it does not provide any idea of the referents of the categories "extended family" and "family." The only idea we get is that "extended family" is a genealogical model defined in comparison with "nuclear family." If "joint family" is also defined in the same way, as it is by most other scholars, "extended family" is not different from, and faces the same problems as, this "joint family."

On the composition of households, Madan says that they "may consist of segments of extended families, and may be nuclear families, or themselves extended in composition" (p. 14). What exactly the phrase "segments of extended families" denotes is not clear. The extended-family households are classified into two types, "patrilineal extended" and "fraternal extended." The former consists of "a man, his wife and unmarried daughters (if any), and an *only* son, his wife and children," and the latter consists of "a man, his wife, unmarried daughters (if any), and *two or more* sons, their wives and children, or alternatively, of two or more brothers, their wives and children." Madan states that there is higher probability of partition in the latter than in the former, and the two belong to two different phases of a developmental cycle. According to the same considerations, however, the household of parents and two or more married sons and the household of two or more married brothers should not be placed in one type; there is a higher probability of partition in the latter than in the former, and the two belong to two different phases of the developmental cycle. It is not clear why they should be placed in one type and also why a household of parents and two or more married sons should be considered only *fraternal* extended and not *both patrilineal and fraternal* extended. Finally, the distinction between a household including one married son and a household including two or more married sons is important, but the two types do not deal with several other possible compositions, such as a household composed of a widow mother and one married son.

I have published (1968b) a lengthy review article on Madan's *Family and Kinship: A Study of the Pandits of Rural Kashmir* and shall therefore deal only with its most relevant parts here.

A notable feature of this book is the rejection of the joint family as the usual central concern of the study of the Indian family, a feature shared strikingly by my analysis of the village data in Part I. Madan has organized his data within a general framework that follows the one provided by Fortes and his associates in *The Developmental Cycle in Domestic Groups*

231

(Goody (ed.), 1958). Its influence is observable, above all, in the distinction between household and family and in the importance given to the analysis of the household: five of the eleven chapters in the book are devoted to it and substantial portions of some of the other six also deal with it. This makes Madan's book an important contribution to the study of the Indian household.

Madan first describes what he calls the general form of the developmental cycle of the household (pp. 55–56). He shows how the maximum extent to which a household usually develops is the co-residence of two or more married brothers after the death of their parents, and how the household fissions usually during this phase. He distinguishes between the process of development of the household of a couple having no son, the household of a couple having only one son, and the household of a couple having two or more sons. After describing these three courses of development constituting the general form, Madan adds, "Several other interesting but unusual courses of development also are possible" (p. 65), but he does not describe them. It seems to me that he has withheld something significant. These "unusual courses of development" would be an indication of the non-cyclical nature of the developmental process of households. The detailed description of the developmental process of the Keshavanand household (pp. 59–62) also does not reveal a cycle.

Utrassu-Umanagri has 552 Pandits divided into 87 households. The average size of the household is 6, appreciably higher than 4.91, the all-India average for villages according to the 1951 census. The percentage of the "large" and "very large" households (taken together) is also higher. These frequencies regarding the numerical composition of the household are consistent with the frequencies regarding the kinship composition.

Madan has classified the households into eight major types and several sub-types within each major type according to kinship composition (pp. 65–70). The first major type is constituted of three single-member households, and the second, of six two-member households. The remaining 78 households are classified into six types mainly on the basis of the dichotomy of nuclear and extended family and the number of generations. Although there are a number of limitations of this typology, I shall point out only the more obvious of them here. Madan himself does not seem to attach much importance to his types, as he hardly uses them for analytical purposes. As a good ethnographer, however, he has defined most of the sub-types in sufficient detail so that any one who does not want to use his major types can reclassify the households.

Madan presents figures for nuclear- and extended-family households in Utrassu-Umanagri and five other villages in Table V (p. 72). He states on the basis of these figures that the "number of households which are nuclear families never exceeds the number of households which are extended families in various phases of growth" (pp. 71–72). The figures for the nuclear-family households, however, are only for the complete nuclear families. The figures of Utrassu-Umanagri, for example, do not include the three one-member and the six two-member households. If they are taken into account, the proportion of the extended-family households to the total number of households would be reduced to some extent.

Furthermore, while classifying the households into nuclear and extended, Madan has excluded the members recruited by the mode of what he calls "incorporation." (The other modes of recruitment to the household are birth, adoption, and marriage.) Madan does not define "incorporation"; he only describes the four cases of incorporation and then states that birth, adoption, and marriage are "the usual and traditionally recognized modes of recruitment" (pp. 140–142). In two out of the four cases of incorporation, the incorporated member is Ego's wife's child by her former husband, now dead; in the third case, Ego's father's sister's son's son; and in the fourth case, Ego's wife's deceased sister's son. It appears that an incorporated member is simply one who is not recruited by birth, adoption, or marriage. I wonder if "incorporation" is an apt word for dcsignating the mode of recruitment of such a member. What is noteworthy is that he or she is not taken into account in the classification of households into nuclear and extended. Madan has also excluded from his classification two childless widows who have come back to reside in their natal homes (see pp. 68–69, 124). They are not considered to be cases of incorporation either.

The data on migration presented in Chapter 7 also raise a definitional problem. Of a total of 192 adult males in the village 92 (48 per cent) are "individual earners," deriving income from salary and wages. 23 of them are resident in the village, while 69 are "absent from home for *most of the year*" (p. 151, italics mine). Madan does not mention how many of these 69 men are married, and how many of the married men have taken their wives and children away with them. It is mentioned on p. 153 that over a dozen have left their wives and children in the village. From this as well as from the information that 73 Pandits of the village are government employees and 24 of them are posted outside Kashmir (pp. 145, 148), it seems that a large number of the individual earners have gone to work in towns in and outside of Kashmir and have taken their wives and children with them. Such an individual earner and his wife and children would constitute a distinct household unit in the town; it cannot be considered as *concurrently* forming part of a household in the village. Madan has, however, considered such emigrant households part of the village households. This would inflate the number of large and extended-family households in the village, and consequently give a false perspective of the relative importance of the extended family in the village.

If the limitations of Madan's categories are disregarded, there are 35 simple and 52 complex households in Utrassu-Umanagri. Of the 52 complex households about sixteen are composed of two or more married brothers or their wives, or both (with or without the brothers' parents and some other members). Of the remaining 36 households, as many as 25 are each composed of either or both of the parents and one married son and his wife (with or without unmarried children) ; there is one case of *gari pyath* (=*ghar-jamai*) ; seven households are each composed of one married man and his wife (with or without one married son and other unmarried children) and his one or more unmarried brothers; and the composition of three households is very similar to that of the last-mentioned seven. The full-fledged extended-family households thus constitute only about 18 per cent of the total number of households in the village.

It seems to me that the inclusion of emigrants as members of the village households has considerably inflated the number of extended-family households and, among them, of the households composed of two or more married brothers. The importance of the extended-family households in the village is considerably less than what the Pandits, and sometimes even Madan, tend to ascribe to it. Nevertheless, it is definitely more than that in many castes elsewhere in India. This seems to me to be due to the fact that the Pandits are a Brahman caste with a high degree of Sanskritization.

Madan gives a detailed description of the *kotamb,* usually a group of two or more patrilineally related households. He himself states, and his description supports the statement, that *kotamb* is a flexible term (pp. 181–182, n. 1). "Family," the English equivalent of *kotamb* used by Madan, is equally, if not more, flexible and therefore of very limited use as a category in comparative studies.

MAINE, SIR HENRY SUMNER. *Ancient Law* (first published, 1861; edition used, London: Oxford University Press, 1959) ; *Village Communities in the East and West* (first published, 1871; edition used, London: John Murray, 1876) ; *Lectures on the Early History of Institutions* (London: John Murray, 1875).

MANDELBAUM, DAVID G. "The Family in India," *Southwestern Journal of Anthropology,* IV (1948), 123–139; reprinted *in* R. Anshen (ed.), *The Family: Its Function and Destiny* (New York: Harper and Brothers, 1949).

This is an attempt "to depict Indian family organization in

general terms" on the basis of available literature. The major
part of the paper, however, is devoted to "the model of the
orthodox, scriptural joint family" (p. 123). This family is
defined as a household group having three types of composition:
"All the men are related by blood as (i) a man and his sons
and grandsons, or (ii) a set of brothers, their sons and grandsons. The women of the household are their wives, unmarried
daughters, and perhaps the widow of a deceased kinsman. ...
(iii) There are even now households in which four generations
are to be found living together under one roof" (p. 123). It is
clear that Mandelbaum has followed here the three-or-four-
generation formula of Indologists. At the end of the paper he
states, following O'Malley, that the large joint family of former
times has been generally replaced by small joint families, of
fewer members and short duration (p. 137), but he does not
define the composition of these families. He also describes all
the functional characteristics usually associated with the orthodox, scriptural joint family. The major, and most valuable,
part of the paper is the description of interpersonal relations
in the joint family, although it covers only a few of its members.

MAYER, ADRIAN C. *Caste and Kinship in Central India* (London:
Routledge & Kegan Paul, 1960).

This book on a Malwa village has a brief section on the household. He considers the joint family a corporate property group
of patrikin, not necessarily a discrete living unit, and refers to
cases where brothers share the land and farm together, yet reside
separately and divide the crops (p. 182). He classifies households into *simple* and *joint*. A household where only one man
resides is simple; a household where more men than one reside
and pool their income and expenditure is joint (pp. 180–181).
The conventional distinction between elementary and joint
family (or my distinction between simple and complex household) would not apply, therefore, to Mayer's distinction
between simple and joint household. For example, the households composed of a widowed mother and her son and his wife
(with or without children) are simple households according to

236

Mayer's definition, joint families according to the conventional definition, and complex households according to my definition. Furthermore, Mayer's two types are meant to describe "the household organization of men above eighteen years. Women play a part in household activities and policy, but households are distinguished externally by the males therein, and these have at least outwardly the controlling say in the household. In the proportion between different kinds of households, then, only males have been taken" (pp. 180–181, n.). This bias toward adult men in the definition of the two types of households means the exclusion of the households composed of one or more women, or of one or more women and minor men, from the study of household life. Mayer states he has excluded them "for simplicity's sake" (p. 181, n.).

Mayer presents numerical data on households in tables 3, 4, and 5. Table 4 shows the classification of the latter into three types according to relationships between men. Table 3 shows "ten most important types of household composition" (including two of the three types mentioned in Table 5), the number of households of each type, and their total population. According to Tables 4 and 5 there are 139 simple and 46 joint households, but Table 3 of "most important" types covers only 105 simple households (see types 1, 2, 9, and 10) and 25 joint households (see types 3 to 8). This means, out of 185 households with one or more adult men, only 130 are "most important." The remaining 55 households are not "most important" even though they contain one or more adult men. In addition there are 11 households which do not contain any adult male and, as mentioned above, have been excluded for the sake of simplicity. Thus 66 out of a total of 196 households (about 33.67 per cent) are considered unimportant, and details about their composition have not been provided. Nevertheless, it is quite clear from the available data that in this Malwa village simple households (of my definition) preponderate over complex ones, and among the latter the households composed of parents and one married son preponderate over

237

those composed of parents and two or more married sons. There seem to be only four households composed of two or more married brothers living together after their parents' death.

Concerning family relationships outside the household, Mayer refers to "the unilineal descent group of up to three generations ascending from the men of about thirty years now in Ramkheri" (p. 169). Usually it is called *kutumb,* but this word has other meanings also. It is "as flexible as its English translation" (p. 167). It "has extremely debatable limits and there appears to be no constant criterion of membership" (p. 171). This seems to be the reason why Mayer uses the term "extended family" not only for the unilineal descent group mentioned above but also for a group "whose members recognize agnatic ties in some circumstances and uterine links in others" (p. 170).

MAYNE, JOHN D. *A Treatise on Hindu Law and Usage,* 7th ed. (Madras: Higginbotham & Co., 1906).

MERCHANT, K. T. *Changing Views on Marriage and the Family: Hindu Youth* (Madras: B. G. Paul & Co., 1935).

This reports the results of a questionnaire administered to 484 young men and women in Bombay, Poona, and six large towns in Gujarat. Most of these youths came from the higher castes and the middle classes and had received higher education. The book is more concerned with marriage than with family. Households are classified into "separate families" and "joint families." The term "separate family" is not defined, but "joint family" is: "A person staying with married brothers, uncles, aunts, cousins, and a father or grandfather staying with a married son or grandson is considered to be living in a joint family system" (p. 35). This definition lacks precision: the terms uncles, aunts, cousins, grandfather, and grandson are considered imprecise for describing kinship relationships in modern anthropology, and there is no reference to several important relatives such as daughters, sisters, mothers, and brothers' children and to the possibility of a father having more than one married son. On the whole, however, the definition implies the three-or-more-generation formula.

Of 484 youths, 445 gave information about the composition of their households, and of these 445, as many as 277 or about 62 per cent lived in joint families. On the basis of this evidence Merchant concludes that the joint family is fast disintegrating (pp. 35–39). This conclusion is unjustified for a variety of reasons, which I shall not go into here. I shall only point out that it is based on the Indological assumption that in ancient India all Hindus lived in joint-family households, an assumption for which there is no empirical evidence of any kind. For the youths' views on the family, Merchant asked them only one question: "What are your views on the joint family system?" (p. 290), which is too general to evoke any sociologically significant answers.

MINTURN, LEIGH, and HITCHCOCK, JOHN T. "The Rajputs of Khalapur," in Beatrice B. Whiting (ed.), Six Cultures: Studies of Child Rearing (New York and London: John Wiley and Sons, 1963), pp. 203–361.

MORRISON, WILLIAM A. "Family Patterns in Badlapur: An Analysis of a Changing Institution in a Maharashtrian Village," Sociological Bulletin, VIII (1959), 45–67.

Morrison's aim is "to determine ... if the family structure in Badlapur has changed in ways which are predictable, that is, from the Joint Family Type to the Nuclear Family Type" (p. 49). The term "family" is used in the sense of "household," and the village households are classified into three types, Joint, Quasi-Joint, and Nuclear (pp. 51–53). The unit with which the types are constructed is the conjugal family, defined as "the relationship of the marital pair" (excluding children). The Nuclear Family is a family "with or without unmarried children and with or without one widowed parent." Morrison's "nuclear family" thus includes not only the usual complete nuclear family but also one type of incomplete nuclear family and several types of non-nuclear family. The Joint Family consists of "several conjugal families, related by consanguinous ties, existing in a multi-generational relationship," and the Quasi-Joint Family consists of "two nuclear units, with or without grandchildren." The formulation of both types is vague. Only an illustration makes them somewhat clear: a family composed of parents and one married son is Quasi-Joint while a family composed of parents and two married sons is Joint. A family composed of only one parent and one married son is neither Joint nor Quasi-Joint but Nuclear.

Out of 641 families in Badlapur, 37 (5.8 per cent) are Joint, 52 (8.1 per cent) are Quasi-Joint, and 552 (86.1 per cent) are Nuclear (pp. 52–53). The unusually high percentage of Nuclear Families is obviously a result of Morrison's peculiar definition of nuclear family.

Morrison uses the same typology in his attempt to relate the family with traditionalism, individualism, caste, occupation, and education in the village, and each of his correlations is vitiated by his typology, not to mention other misconceptions.

MUKHERJEE, RAM KRISHNA. "A Note on the Classification of Family Structures," *Regional Seminar on Techniques of Social Research: Proceedings and Papers* (Calcutta: UNESCO Research Centre, 1959, pp. 133–143; "On the Classification of Family Structures," *in* T. N. Madan and Gopala Sarana (ed.), *Indian Anthropology: Essays in Memory of D. N. Majumdar* (Bombay: Asia Publishing House, 1962), pp. 352–398; *The Sociologist and Social Change in India Today* (New Delhi: Prentice-Hall of India, 1965).

The Sociological Research Unit of the Indian Statistical Institute has carried out several surveys, some wholly and some partly concerned with the family. Mukherjee, the Director of the Unit, has used the data of a survey conducted in Bengal in 1946 in "A Note on the Classification of Family Structures." It is a summary of a paper presented at a seminar, and therefore presents difficulties in fully understanding and evaluating its significance. It is nevertheless a notable contribution in several respects.

Mukherjee considers kinship relations in a family (=household) as having five attributes, namely, sex, affinity, bifurcation, generation, and laterality. His aim is to suggest a method to classify families on the basis of the combination of two attributes, generation and laterality. He takes into account the variations of the two attributes and applies mathematical formulae to find how many different types of families are possible according to the variations. He claims that the seven mathematical formulae he has evolved may be used to appreciate the possible and available structures in a particular society as well as to make inter-society comparisons (p. 138), but he does not explain exactly how this could be done. He presents two tables to compare the possible and available structures in West Bengal, but does not explain how they are useful in understanding the family system of that region.

It seems (particularly from paragraphs 3 and 4 on pp. 133–134) that Mukherjee found the conventional classifications of Indian families on the basis of generation alone unsatisfactory, and this led him to add the attribute of laterality in the method of classification. His note demonstrates admirably not only how many different types of families are possible within a generation span but also how the definition of the family in terms of the number of generations can have several interpretations. This is the most significant contribution made in this first attempt to use mathematics in the study of the Indian family. Otherwise, a method of classification based on only two selected attributes of kinship relations is not likely to be useful in the study of the Indian family.

In the paper "On the Classification of Family Structures" Mukherjee's aim is to evolve a scheme of classification which is based on what he calls the dimension of kinship composition, and which is "comprehensive, . . . taking into account (or, at least, by keeping room for taking into account) all possible variations in intra-family relations" (p. 352). The paper is much more significant, however, for the study of the family in India than for a comparative study of the family. It frequently draws not only upon well-known facts about the family in India but also upon the data of a sample survey of 4,262 households in West Bengal conducted by the Sociological Research Unit under Mukherjee's direction (see notes at the end of the paper).

Mukherjee uses the term "family structure" mostly in the sense of genealogical structure, and calls activities or functions associated with genealogical structures "para-familial attributes." He uses the term "cohort" for a husband-wife couple.

Mukherjee has divided his scheme of classification into several "orders of classification." The first order consists of eleven types: (1) "male" non-familial unit, (2) "female" non-familial unit, (3) nascent family/conjugal unit, (4) elementary family, (5) joint family, (6) "male" family complex, (7) "female" family complex, (8) nascent/conjugal family complex, (9) elementary family complex, (10) joint family complex, (11) kindred (pp. 376–377).

The elementary family (type 4) is a unit of one cohort and unmarried children. Types 1, 2, and 3 are incomplete elementary families. Mukherjee not only distinguishes but also discusses the distinction between these four types. He advances two main reasons for recognizing "nascent family/conjugal unit" as a separate type. (1) It may be a cohort-unit "which had produced or adopted children but they are not to be taken into account as components of the kin-group in question as they may have set up "family-units" of their own, or are dead, or have removed themselves in any other way from the kin-group under reference" (p. 357). Such a cohort-unit is called *conjugal unit*. (2) "If a unit is composed of a cohort only, it does not indicate merely an inter-sex grouping provided with the privileges and rights of conjugal relations. It also indicates the *de jure* acceptance by the cohort of obligations and duties in regard to 'setting up a family,' viz., their potential responsibility towards children, own or adopted. A full-fledged family with children has not yet been established but its potentaility is there" (p. 357). Such a cohort-unit is labelled *nascent family*.

Types 1 and 2, that is, "male" non-familial unit and "female" non-familial unit, are one-member units. Mukherjee states that they deserve recognition as separate types "from the negative aspect of kinship composition of a unit ... under certain circumstances," for example, "when the terms of reference to the family as a societal unit, viz., the para-familial attributes employed for its identification, allow the occurrence of one-member units in society along with the presence of family-units which must contain more than one person" (p. 359). Mukherjee has in mind here the para-familial attributes of co-residence and commensality, that is, the attributes of household. He continues, "In such a context as above, the complementary societal unit represented by an individual without any kin or affine (as for example, a servant in a 'family,' the unrelated boarders of a mess, etc.) may also have to be brought under examination ... so as to indicate the peculiar position of such individuals in society in the light of its familial organization and operation of the family as a societal institution. Therefore ... such units should be included in an order of classification within the dimension of kinship composition, and may be labelled as *non-familial units* in order to differentiate them qualitatively from the family-units" (p. 360).

Mukherjee advances a similar argument for distinguishing non-familial units on the basis of sex: "It would have a bearing upon their non-familial existence because the relevant position of males is not the same in many societies and/or in different social strata" (p. 360).

Mukherjee states on p. 357, "Where the conjugal relation is cut short and the parental relation is impaired by half, the unit should neither be rejected as beyond the sphere of family structure classification nor be equated to a childless couple or to a couple with children as classified according to *possible* (and not existing) intra-family relations in a unit." This is not a very clear statement, but it appears to me that it refers to units composed of either of two parents and child(ren). This is the only reference to such units I have been able to find in the paper, and it is a rather negative statement, but it does indicate that Mukherjee considers them a separate type. I do not understand, however, why they have no place in the types of the first order of classification and why there is no discussion of their importance. There is also no reference whatever to the unit constituted of two or more siblings (without parents).

Despite the failure to recognize these two types, this paper is the first on the Indian family to discuss the importance of distinction between the complete elementary family and three types of the incomplete elementary family. The label "non-familial" is not apt, but this is a minor matter.

Mukherjee contrasts the non-familial with the familial units, and divides the latter into extended and non-extended. The non-extended family includes elementary family and nascent family/conjugal unit. It is noteworthy that although the distinction between elementary family, nascent family/conjugal unit, and non-familial unit applies to units with the para-familial attributes of residence and commensality (i.e., household units), it is meant to apply not only to these units but also to family structures with all other attributes and even to those without any of these attributes.

In the classification of extended families, however, Mukherjee uses mainly the attribute of what he calls "the societal norms of locality," that is, "customary norms ... in terms of which either the bridegroom or the bride or both should move to the residence of kins [sic] or affines of these persons or they should form a new residence of their own" (p. 365). Mukherjee grants that there can be many types of locality norms, but following Murdock he takes into account only eight major types: Neo-local, Patrilocal, Matrilocal, Avunculocal, Matri-patrilocal, Bilocal, Alternating, and Natolocal (*taravad*) (p. 368). Each norm indicates which kin or affine of a person can be what Mukherjee calls "legitimate member or constituent" of his family-unit.

The Bilocal or Alternating norm is taken to connote "a situation in which *any* kin or affine of a person can be a legitimate member of his/her family-unit (p. 369). The extended family formed under either of these two norms is called *kindred* (type 11).

Regarding the other six norms, Mukherjee thinks that with respect to each of them the legitimate members of a family-unit can be specifically denoted. He provides formulae defining the legitimate kinship constituents of the family-unit under all the six norms. Under the Neolocal norm, strictly speaking, there is no possibility of an extended family being formed of legitimate constituents. Under the remaining five norms, when an extended family is formed of legitimate constituents, it is called *joint family* (type 5).

In the case of each norm, however, it is common to find family-units which contain Ego's "extra" kin or affine with or without legitimate constituents. Mukherjee calls families with such mixed constituents "family complexes," the legitimate constituents "stock," and the extra kin or affine "adhesions." "Stock" and "adhesions" are equivalent to what I have called "core" and "accretions" respectively in my analysis of the households showing reversal of the principle of the residential unity of patrikin and their wives (Chapter 3). A stock may be a "male" familial unit, a "female" familial unit, a nascent family/ conjugal unit, an elementary family, or a joint family, and therefore there are five types of family complexes, based on the nature of the stock, in the first order of classification (see types 6 to 10).

I have so far dealt with the way in which Mukherjee evolves the first order of classification. He goes on to evolve four more orders of classification, but they all deal with further classification of the five family complexes. If we take the entire discussion of the family complexes, it occupies 25 out of 45 pages of the text of the paper (pp. 372–396). This paper is thus the only writing so far to discuss this aspect of the Indian family system.

While Mukherjee devotes a great deal of attention to the

problems of (1) distinction between the complete elementary family and various types of incomplete elementary family, and (2) the family complexes, he does not even broach the problem of distinction between various types of "joint family." It is difficult to understand why he neglects this problem when he wants to evolve a *comprehensive* scheme of classification. It is also noteworthy that only the first four types in the first order of classification are meant for the classification of family structures with any or all para-familial attributes, while all the other types are meant for the classification of family structures with only residence as a para-familial attribute. This limitation also shows that Mukherjee's scheme of classification is not really comprehensive.

The major part of *The Sociologist and Social Change in India Today* is devoted to the findings of several projects carried out by the Sociological Research Unit under Mukherjee's direction. The findings refer mainly to changes in three major structures in Indian society, namely village, caste, and family. For the family (=household), Mukherjee uses the same terminology as developed in the preceding papers and examines his data mainly in the context of the usual presumption that the joint-family organization is contrary to the urban way of life but not to the rural (p. 25; see also p. 64). His main contention is that his data do not support this presumption. On the contrary, the emphasis on the joint-family organization increases progressively as one passes from villages through small towns to large cities (see pp. 25–31, 50–56), or from non-industrial through partly industrial to highly industrial towns (see p. 68). Mukherjee also finds that the upper castes, who usually belong also to the upper economic classes, place a greater emphasis on the joint-family organization than the lower castes and lower economic classes (see pp. 44, 117–118). All this lends support to the correlation I have tried to establish between household, caste, and rural-urban community.

MURDOCK, GEORGE PETER. *Social Structure* (New York: Macmillan, 1949).

The nuclear family is defined here as consisting "typically of a married man and woman with their offspring, *although in individual cases one or more additional persons may reside with them*" (p. 1, italics mine). According to this definition the nuclear family as a household unit may include persons who really do not belong to it. Murdock does not specify the additional persons.

MURPHY, GARDNER. *In the Minds of Men* (New York: Basic Books, 1953).

NICHOLAS, RALPH W. "Economics of Family Types in Two West Bengal Villages," *The Economic Weekly*, XIII (1961), 1057–1060.

Nicholas distinguishes between joint family and extended family, considering the former a unit of "joint property arrangements between two or more nuclear families," and the latter a unit of "co-residence or the use of certain kinds of family kinship terms [sic] outside the nuclear family" (p. 1057). Nicholas does not explain what he means by "the use of family kinship terms" in the definition of "extended family." In any case there is no other statement about the extended family in the paper. His main concern is with the joint family. He analyses it in terms of the two conventional types, one in which property is held jointly between the father and his married sons, and the other in which it is held jointly between brothers whose father is dead. However, he frequently refers to the joint family as a co-residential and commensal unit congruent with the property-holding unit, and describes the tensions between parents and sons, between brothers, and between their wives in the household group (p. 1059). He does not tell us anything about the well-known situation in which two or more separate households have joint-property arrangements, except the cursory reference to a case in which married brothers with separate households had restored joint-property relations. It is not clear whether such instances are exceptional in these West Bengal villages. On the other hand, Nicholas mentions "the case of 56 nuclear families in which two or more brothers have divided their property, though they continue to live under the same roof, a condition which is known in the society as 'separate pots' " (p. 1059). It would be worth knowing if this situation is similar to that found by Derrett among some South Indian castes (1962, p. 45) and by me among some Banias in Gujarat. In both of these the brothers live in a single household, though account-books show them separate in property, income, and expenditure.

NIMKOFF, M. F., and GORE, M. S. "Social Bases of the Hindu Joint Family," *Sociology and Social Research,* XLIV (1959), 27–36.

Nimkoff and Gore begin their article with the usual distinction between nuclear and joint family: the former is composed of husband, wife, and children, and the latter has only two types, one composed of parents and married sons, and the other, of married brothers (p. 27). They then raise two problems. The first refers to the spread of the joint family, and here they make the usual assumption that joint fmailies are more common in villages than in towns (p. 28). It is a "surprise" for them that the data collected by T. K. Majumdar in Kanpur and K. M. Kapadia in South Gujarat show greater prevalence of the joint family in towns than in villages. They go on to suppose that the lesser prevalence of joint families in villages may be due to the impact of increasing urbanization and industrialization on the traditional rural patterns; they do not pause to ask why the same impact does not weaken the joint family in towns themselves. Finally, they assert that joint families were more common in the past than they are now, which is only a re-assertion of the assumption that they are more common in villages than in towns.

The second problem raised by the authors refers to the definition of joint family (p. 29). Here they simply note that the problem arises out of the situation that families may be structurally and residentially nuclear but functionally joint. Their definition is only a repetition of the usual one of the multi-functional joint family, though in a different garb:

" 'Joint Family' implies that several conjugal units of the family
have certain *values in common*. These include a domicile, a
kitchen, a dining room, property, a treasury, and worship"
(italics mine). They consider these common values to be the
bases of the joint family, and devote the rest of the paper
(pp. 29–36) to an inquiry into "factors supporting the common
values in the traditional social system." They discuss the role
of the following factors one by one: economy, caste, polity,
religion, and education. They then conclude that "all the parts
[of the traditional social system] are essentially consistent with
the joint family and tend to support it," but "the contributions
of the several factors are not equal" (p. 34). "While all the
institutions ... support the joint family, the indispensable
basis for the joint family is agriculture and a household
economy emphasizing the accumulation of property on a family
basis" (p. 36). This does not explain the fact the authors have
themselves noted, namely, the strength of the joint family
among shopkeepers and owners of business (p. 31). It is also
difficult to accept the implication that there were no joint
families among artisans and craftsmen in traditional India. The
authors' statements that "farming is a non-individualizing
occupation" and "the work on the land fosters the sense of
jointness in the family" (p. 29) do not take into account the
existence of a vast mass of tenants and landless labourers in agriculture. It is also not clear whether their conclusion applies
to the joint family as the household unit or as the property
unit. Similar lack of clarity also prevails in the all too brief
discussion of the factors of caste, polity, religion, and education.

NOTES AND QUERIES ON ANTHROPOLOGY. Prepared by a Com-
mittee of the Royal Anthropological Institute, 6th ed. (London:
Routledge and Kegan Paul, 1957).

O'MALLEY, L. S. S. *India's Social Heritage* (Oxford: Clarendon
Press, 1934); *Popular Hinduism* (Cambridge: Cambridge University Press, 1935); "Family and Religion," *in* L. S. S. O'Malley
(ed.), *Modern India and the West*. (London: Oxford University Press, 1941).

249

ORENSTEIN, HENRY. "The Recent History of the Extended Family in India," *Social Problems,* VIII (1961), 341–350.

Orenstein examines here the common belief that industrialization and Westernization weaken the Indian joint-household organization. These two processes became effective in India during the latter half of the nineteenth century. Orenstein, therefore, tries to see if the census data which became available from this period onward help us to examine the above belief. These data up to 1951 show that (1) the average size of the household not only does not decrease, it increases slightly in almost all the states in the country; (2) the rate of infant mortality as compared with general mortality decreases, implying a larger number of adults in the population, and therefore per household, in recent times than in the past; and (3) the number of married and widowed males per household increases. All these indicate that the proportion of joint households has not only not declined but has on the contrary increased, though slightly, during the last hundred years. The census data thus do not support the hypothetical relation between the small nuclear family and industrialization and Westernization.

PAKRASI, KANTI. "A Study of Some Aspects of Household Types and Family Organization in Rural Bengal, 1946–1947," *Eastern Anthropologist,* XV (1962), 55–63.

Pakrasi presents data of a survey conducted in Bengal in 1946 by the Sociological Research Unit of the Indian Statistical Unit under the direction of Ram Krishna Mukherjee. The survey provided data about 16,000 households selected from a number of villages, both the villages and the households being selected at random. Unfortunately a portion of the total schedules were "misplaced" and not available for analysis; Pakrasi presents an analysis of only 6,061 households, with an awareness that it provides "a general and impressionistic idea of the family structures of rural Bengal" (p. 55).

The households are classified according to the typology shown in Table 26. It can be seen that Pakrasi has used the terms "kin," "extended," and "non-extended" in his own way.

Table 26

Household Types in Pakrasi's Paper

Non-extended Household		Extended Household	
A. Incomplete		**Incomplete and Complete**	
1·0	Single member	5·0	Collateral
1·1	Single member + kin	5·0·1	Collateral + kin
2·0	Married couple (without children)	6·0	Lineal
2·1	Married couple + kin	6·0·1	Lineal + kin
3·0	Nuclear–I (widowed parent + 1 child)		
3·0·1	Nuclear + kin		
3·1	Nuclear–I (widowed parent + 1 + children)		
3·1·1	Nuclear + kin		
B. Complete			
4·0	Nuclear–II (parents + 1 child)		
4·0·1	Nuclear + kin		
4·1	Nuclear–II (parents + 1 + children)		
4·1·1	Nuclear + kin		

Source : This table is reproduced from Pakrasi's tables 1 and 2 (pp. 61-62), except that " kins " is replaced by " kin " as plural.

Note : " Kin " is defined as the male Ego's all married and/or widowed female agnates, and affines related only through them, and all individuals, male or female, with whom genealogical relationship can be traced through some female who has married into the family (p 56).

"Kin" is only what I have called "accretions" due to reversal of the principle of the residential unity of patrikin and their wives (Chapter 3). "Non-extended" is not conterminous with "nuclear": it includes Type 1.1: single member + kin, Type 2.1: married couple + kin, and Types 3.0.1, 3.1.1, 4.0.1, 4.1.1: nuclear + kin. Pakrasi does not explain why he has attributed special meanings to these terms. In fact, he does not say a word about the rationale of the typology, or about the significance of the various types for an understanding of the family system in rural Bengal. Nevertheless, the category "non-extended" includes a sufficient number of clearly defined types to permit us to regroup all the types into the categories "simple" and "complex": types 1.0, 2.0, 3.1, 4.0, and 4.1 are simple, and the rest complex.

Pakrasi presents frequencies of households of the various types for West Bengal and East Bengal (i.e., East Pakistan) separately. (The survey was conducted before, but the data were analysed after the partition.) He also compares the frequencies for the two areas (pp. 57–60) but does not make any observations on the nature of the household pattern as revealed by the figures. Nevertheless, if the frequencies are computed according to the categories "simple" and "complex," simple households constitute 43.77 per cent and 46.32 per cent in West and East Bengal samples respectively. Such low percentages of simple households do not seem to reflect the actual pattern of households. It seems the frequencies are substantially affected by the peculiar nature of the sample: as already noted, both the villages and the households were selected at random, and nearly 10,000 of the 16,000 schedules were misplaced.

This paper is significant for being the first to distinguish (though not discuss) three types of incomplete nuclear family from the complete nuclear family. It is difficult to understand, however, the sociological significance of the distinction between the nuclear families with one child and the nuclear families with more than one child. This paper is also the first to distinguish households with "kin" from households without "kin" *all along the typology*. The category "extended," however, has received very little attention compared to the category "non-extended."

POCOCK, DAVID F. "The Movement of Castes," *Man*, LV (1955), 71–72; "Inclusion and Exclusion: A Process in the Caste System of Gujarat," *Southwestern Journal of Anthropology*, XIII (1957), 19–31.

PRABHU, P. N. (alias VALAVALKAR PANDHARINATH H.). *Hindu Social Institutions* (Bombay: Longmans Green & Co., 1940); *Hindu Social Organisation*, second edition of the above (Bombay: Popular Book Depot, 1954).

RADCLIFFE-BROWN, A. R. "Introduction," *in* A. R. Radcliffe-Brown and Daryll Forde (eds.), *African Systems of Kinship and Marriage* (London: Oxford University Press, 1950), pp. 1–85; *Structure and Function in Primitive Society* (London: Cohen & West, 1952).

RANGASWAMI AIYANGAR, K. V. "Hindu Law in Gujarat," *Journal of Gujarat Research Society*, VIII (1946), 63–73.

RAO, M. S. A. "Occupational Diversification and Joint Household Organization," *Contributions to Indian Sociology*, New Series, II (1968), 98–111.
This paper shows, with evidence from the peasant caste of Ahirs in a village near Delhi, that the joint-household organization in villages is not incompatible with cash income and diverse occupations accompanying economic development, industrialization, and urbanization. In fact the diverse economic pursuits tend to become complementary in maintaining joint households, and their complementary character may be sustained by kinship obligations. Lineally joint households show a greater association with occupational diversification than the fraternally joint ones, which shows how kinship obligations of brothers become weaker after the father's death.

RAY, AJIT "A Brahmin Village of the Sasana Type in the District of Puri, Orissa," *Man in India*, 36 (1956) 7–15.
The village described here includes 928 Brahmins divided in 166 households. 27 per cent of the households are "extended," 40 per cent "simple," 26 per cent "intermediate," and 7 per cent "independent." These categories are not defined, but the "independent" are single-member households, and the "simple" seem to be complete and incomplete nuclear families, and the "extended" and "intermediate" to be complex households.

Thus, the simple and the complex households would form 47 and 53 per cent respectively.

The author states, "one third of the total Brahmin population have left the village for different places for purposes of service. Most of them are, however, temporary emigrants and come home during festive occasions" (p. 9). It seems these emigrants are included as members of the village households. This as well as the high degree of Sanskritization of the Brahmins seem to be the reasons for the higher percentage of complex households.

Ross, AILEEN D. "An Approach," in "Symposium on Caste and Joint Family," Sociological Bulletin, IV (1955), 85–96; "Education and Family Change," Sociological Bulletin, VIII (1959), 39–44; The Hindu Family in its Urban Setting (Toronto: Oxford University Press, 1961).

In the first paper Ross provides an idea of her approach to the research project she had just started. In the second, she presents the preliminary results of one aspect of her project. The final report, The Hindu Family in Its Urban Setting, is the longest book to come out of research on the Indian family. The project consisted mainly of interviews of a sample of 157 individuals in Bangalore for thirty-one months by a team of six interviewers under Ross's guidance. The interviewees belonged to higher castes and to middle and upper classes; 84 were men and 73 were women; their ages ranged from 24 to 39; 76 were unmarried. Most of the interviewees themselves as well as the other adult members in their families were either highly educated or undergoing higher education; the interviewees themselves, or their family members, or both, were employed in modern jobs; and 129 of them had grown up either in Bangalore or in other towns and cities. The sample thus represented a section of Hindu society which had been under the full impact of industrialization, urbanization, and Westernization.

Ross has presented very little numerical data in the book, and she states about her data, "The sample is not homogeneous, and the tables of statistics throughout the study should be looked on more as summations of the interview material rather than as valid statistical generalisations" (p. 300). The book is largely a documentation of interview material — there are in all 174 long quotations from interview records, and many more brief quotations. The material is arranged to describe the traditional form of the joint family (chap. 1), to show how large joint families are breaking down into smaller units (chap. 2), and to present a detailed analysis of the effect of this change in the fields of rights and duties (chap. 3), power and authority (chap. 4), sentiments (chap. 5), occupation (chap. 6), education (chap. 7), and marriage and friendship (chap. 8). Ross modestly claims her book to be only an exploratory study (p. 300): "the main conclusions will appear more in the form of hypotheses for future study than verified statements" (p. 280); and "the detailed findings of this research only apply to the actual sample" (p. 300). However, she also claims that her book attempts "to develop a sounder theoretical framework within which the many dimensions of family change can be studied" (p. ix), and this demands close examination.

Ross considers the family as a structure including several substructures: (1) biological substructure of age, sex, and kinship, (2) ecological substructure of household groups, (3) substructure of rights and duties, (4) substructure of authority, and (5) substructure of sentiments (pp. 30–31). She does not explain the basis on which these substructures are distinguished from one another. It is also not clear why there is no separate treatment of the substructures of age, sex, and kinship while there are four chapters for the remaining four substructures. Kinship appears inevitably, however, in every chapter, and everywhere its treatment is unsatisfactory, for Ross is unaware of developments in anthropological studies of kinship. For example, she regards not only the anthropological definitions of the family but also the phenomenon of kinship itself as biological and physical (pp. 29–30). She mentions as facts the outdated theories of "patrilineal Aryans" and "matrilineal

Dravidians," and believes that her "interviews revealed some traces of the matrilineal system, such as the strong influence of, and affection towards, the maternal uncle, and cross-cousin marriages" (p. 13; see also pp. 38, 281). She suggests that "much family strain in the past, and present, is due to the inconsistencies of behaviour caused by the mixture of the two systems" (p. 14), although she also comments on family solidarity resulting from cross-cousin marriage (p. 38).

Although Ross regards households as forming a substructure of the family, she frequently uses the terms "household" and "family" interchangeably. She distinguishes four types of family which are in fact four types of household: the large joint family (Type A), the small joint family (Type B), the nuclear family (Type C), and the nuclear family with dependents (Type D) (pp. 33–37). She says that her typology is based on three criteria: the number of generations, the presence or absence of married couples, and the number of dependents. The large joint family is composed of three or more generations, and the nuclear family, of two generations; the generation span of the other two types is not mentioned. This suggests that the large and the small joint family have the same generation span, and size is the only criterion of distinction between them. Ross states that the small joint family is composed of (a) parents, married sons, and other unmarried children, or (b) two brothers, and their wives and children. Among families of the former type the most typical is the family including both the parents and one married son, but Ross does not state whether a family of parents and two or more married sons is a small or a large joint family. She seems to regard a family having more than two married couples (irrespective of the nature of relationship between them) and some dependents as a large joint family.

The nuclear family (Type C) is composed of one or both parents with children. The nuclear family with dependents (Type D) is composed of a man, his wife, and their children, plus one or more dependents, such as the man's grandfather or grandmother (not both), uncle, niece, widowed sister, and

unmarried younger brother or sister. Ross is aware of the difficulty of defining a "dependent." A widowed sister, for example,
may not earn but may do household work and save the expenses of a servant. Therefore, Ross considers a person a
dependent when he or she has no authority or responsibility in
family matters. This definition, however, evades certain
important problems. First, if it is accepted, even the children
in a nuclear family should be considered dependents. It is also
not clear whether Ross considers a man's widowed father or
mother a dependent. Second, what about dependents living in
large and small joint families? Is there a distinction between
joint families with and without dependents? Third, generally
there is an obligation to support certain relatives, and definite
patterns of behaviour exist between the dependent and the
supporter and members of his family. Economic dependence
is only a part, frequently an insignificant part, of this pattern
of behaviour. Fourth, is the nuclear family with dependents
a kind of joint family or not? If it is a joint family, then of
what type? Ross herself says, "A brother who lived with ego
and his wife and contributed to the family income would be a
true member of that household and it would be classified as
a joint family" (p. 36). But this joint family will not fit into
Ross's own definition of either the small or the large joint
family.

Ross collected information about the composition of the
interviewees' households for two periods of time: first, when
they were growing up, and second, at the time of the interview. Table XIII shows the classification of the households for
the first period according to Ross's typology. There is no such
table for the second period, but there is a series of statements
on pp. 36–37 regarding the shifts from one type of family to
another between the two periods, and these statements can be
easily used to prepare a table for the second period. A comparison shows that while in the first period there are 19 households
of Type A, 44 of Type B, 77 of Type C, and 17 of Type D, in
the second period there are 8 households of Type A, 48 of

Type B, 68 of Type C, and 33 of Type D. There is thus a decrease in the number of large joint families as well as of nuclear families, and an increase in the number of small joint families and of nuclear families with dependents. Ross does not use these figures in the analysis of her interview data, probably because, as she says, her sample is not homogeneous. However, apart from the figures themselves, it is significant that she recognizes the diversity of family forms in the past as well as in the present. She also states, "Describing family composition at two points of time in ego's life does not, however, give a full idea of the number of family forms that ego may actually live in during his lifetime. ... The typical middle and upper-middle class urban Hindu moves through a series of forms during his lifetime" (p. 37).

Ross warns us, both in the "Introduction" and in the "Summary and Conclusions," that it is not the purpose of her study to try to prove or disprove the familiar thesis that the large joint family in India is giving way to the small nuclear family typical of middle-class, urban, Western societies. She does not have the necessary numerical data to tackle this problem. Her purpose is rather "to study the strains and problems which arise when families do, in fact, change from one form to the other" (p. x), and "to analyse factors which are tending to break up the large joint family, and to seek out the main ways in which these changes are affecting family roles" (p. 280). The problem is thus narrowed down to suit the interview data. But, this narrow formulation assumes a very simple process of change: when the large joint families change under the impact of industrialization and urbanization they inevitably become small nuclear families. Ross completely neglects here her own four types as well as the classification of the sample households according to the types. Moreover, she does not in fact restrict herself to the narrow problem. She asserts repeatedly that the traditional Hindu family was always the large joint family and that it will change only into the small nuclear family. The discussion of all aspects of family change — rights and duties, power and authority, sentiments and emotions, education, position of men versus women, marriage patterns, and so forth — is carried on within the framework of the dichotomy of the large joint family of traditional India and the small nuclear family of modern industrial society. Along with this go a number of facile notions about the nature of other aspects of society and their relation to the family in the past.

The analytical framework of Ross's book is thus unsatisfactory. Her data, however, are rich, and refer to a section of the society about whose family system there is no other source of information at the present time.

SARMA, JYOTIRMOYEE. "Formal and Informal Relations in the Hindu Joint Household of Bengal," *Man in India*, XXXI (1951), 51–71; "The Nuclearization of Joint Family Households in West Bengal," *Man in India*, XLIV (1964), 193–206.

In the first paper, Sarma uses the term "joint household" instead of "joint family" and states clearly that she is not concerned with the historical and legal aspects of the Hindu family (p. 51). She defines the composition of the joint household in terms of the usual three-or-four-generation formula. Her statement "three generations of persons in the male line with their wives and children" (p. 51) is imprecise, for children of the third-generation males would obviously constitute the fourth generation. She considers the four-generation household a rare occurrence because usually the first generation is deceased before the fourth generation makes its appearance. The sons may remain together, but this is also a rare occurrence. The entire paper is devoted to a description, within the ideal joint household, of interpersonal relations as expressed in kinship terms and in joking relationships. The second paper is concerned with the process of separation of the joint household into several nuclear family households (p. 193). The main aim is to show that every joint household is subject to nuclearization or a history of growth and decline (p. 198). The first part provides a generalized description of the stages in which the various kinds of property and income and expenditure of a joint household (of the ideal conception) are divided (pp. 193–198). Particular attention is given here to the problems of a joint household owning and living in a brick house. The author then briefly presents data collected in one rural and one urban survey.

In the rural survey (pp. 198–201), 593 families (=households) were taken from four villages of Burdwan District for investigation. They formed about 80 per cent of the total number of families; we are not told why and how the remaining households were excluded. The families are first classified into nuclear and joint. The former includes not only complete nuclear families and incomplete ones of some types, but also some families consisting of minor brothers or sisters living with one married brother, that is, actually non-nuclear families. Joint families are classified into three types: (1) joint families with parents: they have one or more married sons living with one or both parents; (2) joint families with brothers: they consist of two or more married brothers; (3) joint families with others: they include "persons not normally found in patrilineal families, such as mother's or wife's relations." It is not clear whether this type covers even those families in which "others" live with joint families of types (1) and (2). The percentage of nuclear families in the four villages varies from 53.80 to 63.56, which leads Sarma to doubt the usual assumption that joint families are universal in villages. Not only that, but the percentage of joint families with brothers is also much smaller than that of joint families with parents in each village.

In the urban survey (pp. 202–205), Sarma took only 201 families (=households) from two localities in Calcutta: 101 from the Lake area, a predominantly modern, rich, and high caste locality, and 100 from Shyambazar, a predominantly traditional, poor, and lower caste locality. Sarma clarifies that her sample is small and unrepresentative, but she does not say anything about the method of sampling. Her typology for the urban families is different from that for the rural ones, but the reason for this difference is not stated. There are five types:

(1) single persons; (2) nuclear; (3) nuclear variant, which includes families with widowed mother and minor dependents (i.e., incomplete nuclear families), and families with widowed mother and one married son (i.e., non-nuclear families); (4) joint, which includes "joint families with parents" and "joint families with brothers" of the rural typology; (5) joint variant, which is equivalent of "joint families with others" of the rural typology. Joint families of all the types form 37 per cent of the Shyambazar sample, and 42 per cent of the Lake area sample, which leads Sarma to doubt the usual idea that nuclear families, are universal in cities, and more particularly the idea that they are more prevalent in newer and modern residential areas than in older and traditional ones (p. 205). It is noteworthy that the percentages of joint families would be even higher if she had considered families with widowed mother and one married son as joint families and not "nuclear variant."

Sarma concludes: "Joint families grow naturally ... and they also disrupt naturally" (p. 205).

Sarma also tries to find out if there is any correlation between family types and caste status, and between family types and occupation in the rural survey, and finally between family types and ownership of property in the urban survey. Even if we ignore the point that her data are insufficient, the categories into which she classifies castes, occupations, and property are very broad (in fact the categories are not explained at all) and the discussion of the data is cursory. She concludes from the rural survey that "the family types are more influenced by occupation than by caste status" (p. 201), and from the urban survey, that the family types are influenced by property (p. 204). This leads her to make a general conclusion that "joint families grow naturally whenever there are sufficient means to keep the members together," but she at once adds, "provided that there is a normal amount of amity between them" (p. 205). This is such a big qualification that it makes the conclusion circular.

Sen, Lalit Kumar, "Family in Four Indian Villages," *Man in India*, 45 (1965), 1–16.

Sen studied the same four villages as those studied by Sarma (1959). They have a total of 594 families (=households). 56 per cent of them are "nuclear," 38 per cent "extended," and 6 per cent "other." The last seem to be complex households. It is not clear whether the "nuclear" category includes incomplete nuclear families also. Nevertheless, Sen rightly concludes that the predominance of the nuclear families is contrary to the common notion that the extended family is the predominant family type in peasant societies.

Sen cross-tabulates the frequencies of the three types of households with caste, occupation, education, landownership, ownership of productive assets, income, outside contacts, and movie attendance. It is difficult to assess this analysis due to lack of details about the categories used in tabulation.

SENGUPTA, SUNIL. "Family Organization in West Bengal: Its Nature and Dynamics," *The Economic Weekly,* X (1958), 384–389.

Sengupta presents here an analysis of families (=households) in three villages in three different districts in West Bengal. He defines the nuclear family as a unit of parents and children. He does not state whether he includes the households composed of incomplete nuclear families in his definition of the nuclear family, but I shall assume that he does so while presenting his figures. He distinguishes two types of joint families: (1) "vertical," composed of parents, one or more married sons, and unmarried children, and (2) "horizontal," composed of two or more married brothers. He poses the problem of classifying the families which fall between the nuclear and the joint. He does not solve the problem, and he seems to regard all such families as "inherent" in the joint family system. He also distinguishes two types of nuclear families: (1) "broken within this generation," that is, residing separately during the lifetime of the male head's parents and brothers, and (2) "neutral," in which case though the male head's father is dead, he has also no son or brother of marriageable age and therefore the question of his living separately from his father or brother is irrelevant (pp. 384–385).

Sengupta presents useful figures about the composition of the households in the three villages. He presents figures of nuclear and joint households and the total number of households in each village. He also shows how many of the nuclear households are "neutral" and how many are "broken within this generation" (p. 386). He leaves out certain households, and I presume they are the problematic households mentioned earlier as falling between nuclear and joint family. I shall consider them complex households. Accordingly, the complex households would form 24.4 to 28.6 per cent of the total number of households in the three villages. It is significant that even though Bengal is known, on account of its *Dayabhaga* school of family law, to be a region with a strong emphasis on the joint-family system, these three villages in the region have much less emphasis on the norm of joint residence than the villages in central Gujarat.

As in the rest of India, so also in these Bengal villages, married brothers tend to separate from one another after the death of the father. Sengupta finds a difference between the higher and the lower castes with regard to the tendency on the part of sons to establish separate households during the lifetime of their father. The tendency is greater among the lower castes who also belong to the lower classes (pp. 385–386).

SHAH, A. M. "Social Change in a Multi-Caste Village," *in* A. Aiyappan and L. K. Bala Ratnam (eds.), *Society in India* (Madras: Book Centre, 1956), pp. 161–180; "Social Anthropology and the Study of Historical Societies," *The Economic Weekly*, XI (1959), 953–962; "Basic Terms and Concepts in the Study of Family in India," *Indian Economic and Social History Review*, I (1964), 1–36; "Changes in the Indian Family: an Examination of some Assumptions," *Economic and Political Weekly*, III (1968a), 127–134; "Family and Kinship among the Pandits of Rural Kashmir: A Review," *Eastern Anthropologist*, XXI (1968b), 305–317.

SHAH, A. M. and SHROFF, R. G. "The Vahivancha Barots of
Gujarat: A Caste of Genealogists and Mythographers," *Journal of
American Folklore,* LXXI (1958), 246–278; also *in* Milton
Singer (ed.), *Traditional India: Structure and Change* (Phila-
delphia: American Folklore Society, 1959), pp. 40–70.

SHAH, A. M., SHROFF, R. G., and SHAH, A. R. "Early Nineteenth
Century Village Records in Gujarat," *in* Tapan Rayachaudhuri
(ed.), *Contributions to Indian Economic History* — II (Calcutta: Firma K. L. Mukhopadhyaya, 1963), pp. 89–100; also
in *Journal of Gujarat Research Society,* XXV (1963), 126–134.

SHAHANI, SAVITRI. "The Joint Family: a Case Study," *The
Economic Weekly,* XIII (1961), 1823–1828.

This paper is based on data collected through a questionnaire issued to high school students in Baroda, and almost
throughout the paper the Ego in the description of genealogical
relationships is a teenage student. This is a somewhat novel use
of the term "Ego," which in anthropological convention usually
refers to an adult man or woman.

Shahani regards the joint family as primarily a household
group wider than the elementary family, except that a household consisting of the student's parents and siblings (i.e., an
elementary family) plus the mother's relatives or a widowed
sister with her children, is not regarded as a joint family
(p. 1823). She considers two major types of joint families: one,
joint in student's own generation, and the other, joint in
student's father's generation. In the first, the family is composed
either of the student and his married brothers, or of these
brothers and their father. In the second, the family is composed
of the student's father, mother, and unmarried siblings, plus
father's parents, father's brothers and their children, or any one
of these.

In the second type, there are sub-types. (Shahani herself does
not call them sub-types.) First, there are families composed of
the student, his parents and siblings, and one or both of the
aged grandparents or an unmarried father's brother. Shahani

calls such families "incomplete or atrophied joint families," because "the inclusion of an aged grandparent or of an unmarried uncle is actually like giving shelter to a social dependent and not real jointness" (p. 1827). There are only a few families belonging to the second sub-type. Each is composed of Ego's paternal grandparent(s), his father, mother, and father's married brothers, and his own married brothers (pp. 1827–1828), that is, there are married men in both father's and Ego's generation. The inclusion of grandparents is considered insignificant because they are social dependents. Shahani rightly regards these households as showing a higher degree of joint-family development — of course, within the context of her data — but it is not clear why she considers these families joint only in the father's generation.

In between the above two sub-types there is a third sub-type in which the household is composed either of the student, his parents, and father's married brothers, or of all these and one or both of the grandparents (p. 1827). It is noteworthy that there is an emphasis on jointness among married brothers, while the inclusion of their aged parents is considered insignificant because these are social dependents.

All the families joint in the student's own generation, that is, composed of the student and his married brothers or of these brothers and their father, are considered *real* joint families because there is jointness among married brothers (pp. 1823, 1827). It is noteworthy that a family of this type is called "joint in the student's own generation" even though it includes the brothers' father (i.e., the student's own father). I do not understand why the father's existence in the family is considered so insignificant, and also why the mother is not mentioned. There is also no reference to families composed of the student and *one* married brother. And finally, how should we classify a family composed of the student, his parents, *and* one married brother — as joint in the student's or in his father's generation?

We may conclude that, according to Shahani, the unity among married brothers is the only test of real jointness. It is difficult to understand why the married brothers' father should always be considered a social dependent. Why should it be assumed that all fathers stop earning by the time sons begin to earn? Even when they stop earning, do sons treat them as social dependents? and do fathers lose all their authority in the household? Similar questions can be asked about the position of the mother during the lifetime of her husband as well as during her widowhood. And finally, are children not social dependents? What about the student himself?

SINGER, MILTON. "The Indian Joint Family in Modern Industry," *in* Milton Singer and Bernard S. Cohn (eds.), *Structure and Change in Indian Society* (New York: Wenner-Gren Foundation for Anthropological Research, 1968), pp. 423–452.

Singer presents here preliminary results of his study of family histories of nineteen industrial leaders in Madras city. It is concerned mainly with the ways in which the nineteen families have functionally adapted their preindustrial family structures to industry, rather than with the relative frequency of occurrence of joint families versus nuclear families in industry. Although certain changes have occurred in the industrial families, Singer's findings do not support the familiar hypothesis that participation in modern industry results in the breakdown of the joint-family system. In fact, as Singer states, for every item of evidence indicating change there is a complementary item of evidence indicating continuity and persistence (p. 437). He puts forward a number of new fascinating hypotheses to analyse this situation.

Although Singer refers to the household organization here and there — he points, in particular, to the fact that seven out of nineteen industrialists maintain joint households — he is concerned more with joint-family relationships in their entirety.

SRINIVAS, M. N. *Marriage and Family in Mysore* (Bombay: New Book Co., 1942); *Religion and Society among the Coorgs of South India* (Oxford: Clarendon Press, 1952a); "A Joint Family Dispute in a Mysore Village," *Journal of M. S. University of*

Baroda, I (1952b), 7–31; *Caste in Modern India and Other Essays* (Bombay: Asia Publishing House, 1962); "Social Structure," in *The Gazetteer of India: Indian Union* — I (New Delhi: Publication Division, Government of India, 1965), pp. 501–577; *Social Change in Modern India* (Berkeley and Los Angeles: University of California Press, 1966).

Marriage and Family in Mysore is one of the first few works on the Indian family based on ethnographic material. It is even now valuable for its description of marriage rites and customs and of interpersonal relations between some members of the joint family in the setting of cross-cousin marriage, particularly the description of relations between mother-in-law and daughter-in-law and between a woman and her husband's sister (pp. 185–202). Srinivas refers to the dichotomy of joint and individual family generally to pronounce on their merits and demerits (p. 202). However, he neither defines the terms nor does he consider their numerical incidence.

Throughout *Religion and Society among the Coorgs of South India* Srinivas refers to the *okka* of the Coorgs as joint family, but his actual description of the *okka* applies not only to the co-residential, commensal, property-owning, and ritual group consisting of "two or three generations of agnatically-related males, their wives, and their children" (p. 50) but also to a wider group which is "divided into segments, one or two in-habiting the ancestral house and the rest scattered all over Coorg, and occasionally, all over India" (p. 49). The definition of the composition of the *okka* as an exogamous group is also perhaps the definition of the composition of this wider group: "A man may not marry the daughter of his father's brother (classificatory). The father's first, second, and third cousins are his 'brothers', and a daughter of any one of these relatives is avoided for marriage" (pp. 144–145). This means a group consisting of six generations of agnatically related males, including the Ego's and the common ancestor's generations. I doubt if the large, co-residential and commensal *okkas* mentioned as existing in the past (pp. 49, 50) were such six-generation groups.

Srinivas has not made a distinction between joint family and lineage in this book, but in his recent essay in *The Gazetteer of India* he has considered the *okka* as lineage (p. 552). It seems the Kodagi word *okka* is used in the same way as the Sanskrit word *kutumb* to refer both to household and lineage.

There is no information in the Coorg book about the types of family composition included under the two-or-three-generation formula. The subject of description and generalization, however, is the ideal type.

In the important but less known paper "A Joint Family Dispute in a Mysore Village" Srinivas distinguishes the joint family from the "brotherhood" or lineage. He takes the joint family as a multi-functional group and defines its composition in general terms: "It consists of the descendants in the male line, of a common ancestor, and their wives, sons, married as well as unmarried, and unmarried daughters" (p. 9). This statement does not refer to the generation depth, but it is clear from the general discussion of joint family in the paper (pp. 8–9, 29–31) that Srinivas has in view the joint family in which the male members are either (1) father, his two or more married sons, one or more unmarried sons, and unmarried grandson, or (2) two or more married brothers, one or more unmarried brothers, and brothers' unmarried sons. Some categories of relatives who do not fall within the scope of these joint families or of the elementary family are classed along with the latter: "Where the elementary family is the nuclear kin-group, it frequently includes besides a man, his wife and children, an elderly parent or widowed sister of the man, or a relative of the wife" (p. 8). This is an illustration of an inconsistent application of the dichotomy of elementary and joint family.

The most important aspect of the paper, however, is that Srinivas is not bound by these types. What he provides is not, as in many writings by others, a stereotype description of interpersonal relations between father and son, between mother-in-law and daughter-in-law, between brothers, and between their wives, but a graphic description of the process of partition of a joint-family household composed of a widowed mother, her three married sons and their wives and children, one married son, and a deceased son's son. He shows what happens to a joint family when two or more married brothers live with their widowed mother after their father's death and when the brothers have the responsibility of looking after an unmarried younger brother and a deceased brother's minor son.

The last few sentences of the paper are noteworthy: "It is only where the joint family has vast lands, or huge commercial interests, or a great sense of family tradition, or *when it is spread over a wide area,* that it continues to remain joint even after the brothers have become heads of elementary families. The management of the huge properties require the cooperation of a number of people and this gives new opportunities for the joint family. The joint family also aids, if not necessitates, the expansion of family commerce: *tensions between brothers or cousins diminish considerably if they do not share the same house"* (p. 31). I have italicised certain phrases to show that "joint family" is used here for a group of brothers or cousins who live in separate households but manage property and occupational activities jointly. Actually, Srinivas seems to suggest that joint property and production units are more frequently found when brothers or cousins live in separate households, because they thus avoid the tensions of daily life in a joint household.

STEED, GITEL P. "Notes on an Approach to a Study of Personality Formation in a Hindu Village in Gujarat," *in* McKim Marriott (ed.), *Village India* (Chicago: University of Chicago Press, 1955), pp. 102–144.

STENNING, DERRICK J. "Household Viability among the Pastoral Fulani," *in* Goody (ed.), 1958, pp. 92–119.

VALAVALKAR, PANDHARINATH H., 1940. See Prabhu, P. N., 1940.

Glossary

bhāi:	brother
bhābhi:	brother's wife (sister or younger brother speaking)
bhatriji:	brother's daughter
bhatrijo:	brother's son
chulo:	hearth; household
dérāṇi:	husband's younger brother's wife
dharma:	that which is right or moral; totality of one's duty according to one's station in life
diyer:	husband's younger brother
diyervaṭu:	widow's remarriage with deceased husband's younger brother
foi:	father's sister
ghar:	house; household
ghar-jamai:	son-in-law residing permanently in parents-in-law's home
jajamāni:	relatively permanent relationship between patron and client, usually involving payment in kind for the goods and services provided by the client
jéṭh:	husband's elder brother
jéṭhaṇi:	husband's elder brother's wife
kākā:	father's brother
kāki:	father's brother's wife
kanyādān:	ritual gift of bride

karma:	net balance of good and bad deeds in previous births; fate
kartā:	manager of the Hindu joint family (in Hindu Law)
māyā:	illusion
naṇand:	husband's sister
paṇḍit:	traditional Hindu priest and scholar
puṇya:	spiritual merit
sāsu:	mother-in-law
shāhukār:	money-lender; creditworthy; respectable
shrāddha:	a ritual in propitiation of dead ancestors
vahu:	daughter-in-law
varṇa:	one of the fourfold divisions of the Hindu society enunciated in classical Hindu texts and tradition, namely Brahman, Kshatriya, Vaishya, and Shudra

Index